Practical social work

Published in conjunction with
the British Association of Social Workers
Series Editor: Jo Campling

B A S W

Social work is at an important stage in its development. The profession is facing fresh challenges to work flexibly in fast-changing social and organisational environments. New requirements for training are also demanding a more critical and reflective, as well as more highly skilled, approach to practice.

The British Association of Social Workers has always been conscious of its role in setting guidelines for practice and in seeking to raise professional standards. The concept of the *Practical Social Work* series was conceived to fulfil a genuine professional need for a carefully planned, coherent series of texts that would stimulate and inform debate, thereby contributing to the development of practitioners' skills and professionalism.

Newly relaunched, the series continues to address the needs of all those who are looking to deepen and refresh their understanding and skills. It is designed for students and busy professionals alike. Each book marries practice issues and challenges with the latest theory and research in a compact and applied format. The authors represent a wide variety of experience both as educators and practitioners. Taken together, the books set a standard in their clarity, relevance and rigour.

A list of new and best-selling titles in this series follows overleaf. A comprehensive list of titles available in the series, and further details about individual books, can be found online at :
www.palgrave.com/socialworkpolicy/basw

Series standing order **ISBN 0–333–80313–2**

You can receive future titles in this series as they are published by placing a standing order. Please contact your bookseller or, in the case of difficulty, contact us at the address below with your name and address, the title of the series and the ISBN quoted above.

Customer Services Department, Macmillan Distribution Ltd, Houndmills, Basingstoke, Hampshire RG21 6XS, England

Practical social work series

New and best-selling titles

Robert Adams *Social Work and Empowerment (3rd edition)*

Sarah Banks *Ethics and Values in Social Work (3rd edition)* **new!**

James G. Barber *Social Work with Addictions (2nd edition)*

Suzy Braye and Michael Preston-Shoot *Practising Social Work Law (2nd edition)*

Veronica Coulshed and Joan Orme *Social Work Practice (4th edition)* **new!**

Veronica Coulshed and Audrey Mullender with David N. Jones and Neil Thompson
   Management in Social Work (3rd edition) **new!**

Lena Dominelli *Anti-Racist Social Work (2nd edition)*

Celia Doyle *Working with Abused Children (3rd edition)* **new!**

Tony Jeffs and Mark Smith (editors) *Youth Work*

Joyce Lishman *Communication in Social Work*

Paula Nicolson and Rowan Bayne and Jenny Owen *Applied Psychology for Social
   Workers (3rd edition)* **new!**

Judith Phillips, Mo Ray and Mary Marshall *Social Work with Older People
   (4th edition)* **new!**

Michael Oliver and Bob Sapey *Social Work with Disabled People (3rd edition)* **new!**

Michael Preston-Shoot *Effective Groupwork*

Steven Shardlow and Mark Doel *Practice Learning and Teaching*

Neil Thompson *Anti-Discriminatory Practice (4th edition)* **new!**

Derek Tilbury *Working with Mental Illness (2nd edition)*

Alan Twelvetrees *Community Work (3rd edition)*

veronica coulshed
and
joan orme

social work practice

an introduction

fourth edition

palgrave
macmillan

First edition 1988
Second edition 1991
Third edition 1998
Fourth edition 2006

Published by
PALGRAVE MACMILLAN
Houndmills, Basingstoke, Hampshire RG21 6XS and
175 Fifth Avenue, New York, N.Y. 10010
Companies and representatives throughout the world

PALGRAVE MACMILLAN is the global academic imprint of the Palgrave Macmillan division of St. Martin's Press, LLC and of Palgrave Macmillan Ltd.
Macmillan® is a registered trademark in the United States, United Kingdom and other countries. Palgrave is a registered trademark in the European Union and other countries.

ISBN–13: 978–1–4039–2155–0
ISBN–10: 1–4039–2155–5

This book is printed on paper suitable for recycling and made from fully managed and sustained forest sources.

A catalogue record for this book is available from the British Library.

10   9   8   7   6   5   4   3   2   1
15   14   13   12   11   10   09   08   07   06

Printed in China

This text is dedicated to
Dennis West (1936–2004)
who at one point in his life
thought about becoming
a social worker

Contents

Figures

Acknowledgements

This book would not have been possible without the foresight of Veronica Coulshed. The aim of the original version, to introduce students and practitioners to a range of social work interventions and the theories that underpin them, has proved to be timeless. It remains central to social work education and training, despite the many reforms and reorganisation since the first edition.

However the contribution that students and practitioners have made to the development of the ideas and practice discussed in this fourth edition is incalculable. I have benefited from feedback from, and discussion with, colleagues worldwide, but particularly at the universities of Southampton, Glasgow and Strathclyde. Also my experiences of teaching students, and engaging with them and their practice teachers in dialogue about the ideas and how they transfer into practice, have contributed immensely to the content and format of this edition. However any interpretation of these ideas, and any errors or misrepresentation, remain my own.

As ever I feel honoured and humbled to have been asked to take responsibility for this project and remain indebted to John Coulshed, Jo Campling and Catherine Gray for their confidence and support. My thanks and love go to Geoff, Emily and Tim who provide enthusiasm and encouragement whatever the project.

Joan Orme

Introduction

Since its inception social work has faced major threats from governments of the left and right. Despite these threats it has survived, and some would argue that at the beginning of the twenty-first century it is in a stronger position than it has ever been. The introduction of an undergraduate degree as the qualifying level for social workers in the UK is due recognition that social work requires not only practitioners who have skills in human relationships, but that those skills have to be underpinned by theory and knowledge about the complexity of those relationships. Registration for the profession of social work, accompanied by a code of practice, reflects the importance of the roles and tasks that social workers perform. It also recognises that service users and carers deserve high-quality practitioners who not only have skills informed by theory, but are also committed to core values.

Writing a textbook for beginning social workers in this context is therefore both exciting and challenging. This is particularly so when it is the fourth edition of a well-used and well-respected text. The aim of this edition is to draw on the best of what has gone before, but to ensure that students and practitioners are equipped for what is to come. It is the anticipation of the future that is particularly problematic. Ironically, despite the strengths identified above, changes in the organisation of Children's Services in England, the review of the Social Work (Scotland) Act and emphasis throughout the UK on joint working with health services mean that, for some commentators, there is the possibility that social work might disappear.

In my view that is unlikely. The tasks that social workers perform, the understanding they bring to those tasks and the nature of the relationships they build with people in need remain vital whatever the arrangements for delivering services. What gives me the confidence to say this is the growing body of research and knowledge in social work that is testimony to work that social workers do.

Additionally there is developing a global movement to celebrate social work. The international definition of social work agreed in 2000 by the International Federation of Social Workers and the International Association of Schools of Social Work affirms a shared understanding of social work:

> The social work profession promotes change, problem solving in human relationships and the empowerment and liberation of people to enhance well being.

It recognises that the holistic focus of social work is universal, but the priorities of social work practice will vary from country to country and from time to time depending on cultural, historical and socio-economic conditions.

The local conditions in the UK framed the requirements for the social work degree. In launching the degree in England the Minister for Health, Jacqui Smith, stated that it must prepare social workers for the complex and demanding role that will be required of them. She went on to say:

> The new award will require social workers to demonstrate their practical application of skills and knowledge and their ability to deliver a service that creates opportunities for service users.
> (DoH, 2003, p. ii)

In some ways it does not matter where that service is being provided. Whether it is in a social services office, a community school, a local health centre or a not for profit organisation, what is important is that the skills, knowledge and values of social work are recognised and incorporated into the delivery of high-quality services for those in need.

The challenge then for anyone writing about social work theory and practice is to frame it in ways that make sense to those who are going to be involved in practice and using theory. There are many ways of organising such writing. Traditionally social work has been described in what has been called the 'holy trinity' of work with individuals, communities and groups. Another way of organising writing about social work is to think about it in terms of the contexts where social work is delivered, or the user groups who might benefit from services, for example, children and older people.

A third way of thinking about social work is to identify what social workers do – for example they undertake assessment, they make relationships, they intervene to provide services.

A fourth way would be to link the text directly to the requirements for the new degree. These incorporate both the Quality Assurance Agency (QAA) Subject Benchmark statement for Social Work and the National Occupational Standards. In England these are not analysed, while in Scotland they have been developed into a comprehensive framework, the Standards in Social Work Education (SiSWE).

The aim of this text therefore is to ensure that students have an introduction to specific theory relating to what in the QAA Benchmark statement are described as social work theory and the nature of social work practice. In providing this introduction it is anticipated that students will be able to begin to fulfil the six key roles in the National Occupational Standards.

To achieve this, this edition has been extended and reorganised to address the different ways of thinking about social work practice.

Part 1: Social work processes

A discussion of the need for a theoretical base and the inter-relationship of theory and practice are the subject of Chapter 1. Ironically some of theoretical developments discussed, particularly those associated with postmodernism, might describe texts such as this as being counter-intuitive. The process of describing (and some might argue prescribing) theories for practice runs counter to postmodern critiques of 'grand' theories. However, as Chapter 2 demonstrates, social work has much in common with post-modernism in its capacity to recognise multiple perspectives and different discourses. It was very early in my social work career when dealing with family and marital situations that I realised that those in a situation very rarely shared a common perspective about what was going on. It is not that there is no such thing as truth, more that there is a multiplicity of truths. Such a position is vital for social workers undertaking assessment.

Assessment is core to all social work practice and it is for this reason that this edition has devoted a separate and significant chapter to it. It also shares a particular place in writing about social work with other topics such as 'communication' and 'advocacy'. The significance of these is recognised in that they are identified as Key Roles in the National Occupational Standards. These topics have therefore been brought together in this section on the foundations for intervention because, it is argued, they combine theoretical approaches with skills that inform all social work interventions.

Chapter 3 in this section deals with interestingly different challenges that arise from changes in delivery of services. The development of the user movement is a logical progression from the values of social work that supported the development of advocacy and empowerment. Agencies that provide social work services may now be organised and run by people who are in receipt of social work services. This could be seen to undermine the notion of a separate and trained profession. However, there is no reason why service users cannot be educated and trained in the necessary knowledge and skills to undertake the complex tasks of social work. These tasks depend upon effective communication, the subject of Chapter 4 in the section on 'processes'.

Part 2: Methods of intervention

This part describes some of the key strategies for intervening in the lives of those who come to the notice of social work services. It recognises changing perspectives and changing contexts for established methods of intervention and reflects the commentary on the international definition of social work which states that:

> Social work utilises a variety of skills techniques and activities consistent with its holistic focus on persons and their environment.
> (IFSW/IASSW, 2000)

Chapter 5 begins with a discussion of counselling in recognition that the principles of counselling are basic to much social work intervention. Developments in social work practice such as narrative work are also documented in Chapter 5. The significance of loss and change in social work and the relevance of crisis theory are discussed in Chapter 6. Chapters 7 and 8 explore the development of task-centred practice and behavioural approaches in contemporary social work, discussing how these methods develop and differ from other methods in this section.

Part 3: Contexts of intervention

The final part is much more explicit about the contexts in which social work is practised. Recognising that much of what is discussed in Section 2 can be applied to work with families, groups and communities, Chapters 9, 11 and 12 explore how policy developments impact on the contexts for social work and shape the way skills and methods of intervention are utilised. A new chapter on working with adults (Chapter 10) discusses the lasting changes that have been brought about in social work practice by care management and community care, which was the focus of the third edition. It also discusses important new developments in arrangements for practice, and the skills needed to work with these.

It is apparent that there is no separate chapter or section on anti-discrimination or on feminist theories for social work. This is not because these are not important: in fact the opposite view is held – that they are central and should permeate the thinking of students and practitioners in all they do (see Orme, 2002). Therefore when it is appropriate specific and separate discussion appears in the text; otherwise the whole text is designed for practitioners working with people from diverse backgrounds and with different experiences and perspectives.

Writing the fourth edition of a text that that has become a classic is a daunting prospect. The challenge is to retain all that was good about the earlier editions but to ensure that the resultant volume is pertinent for current and future generations of social work students and practitioners. In many ways I have been assisted by the timelessness of the approach adopted by Veronica Coulshed in the very first edition; her commitment to drawing on a wealth of theory, but grounding this in practice. Such an approach is consistent with the imperatives of the social work degree where the emphasis is on practice and the practical relevance of theory.

That said, it is impossible for any one text to cover in detail all that is required for such a demanding, but rewarding, profession as social work. This text is an introduction, a grounding in the ideas. While it is not intended to be a 'how to do it' text, a skills manual, a further innovation has been the inclusion of suggestions for further reading at the end of each chapter and exercises to help readers think about what is involved in putting the ideas and theories into practice. It is hoped that this will encourage and excite students and beginning practitioners to want to learn and discover more.

Joan Orme

1 | Theory for practice

Introduction

For social work there is a continuing tension between practice and theory. This tension exists both *within* social work and *about* social work. At times students and practitioners have protested that it was necessary to forget theory once in practice. The argument has been that theory is abstract, inaccessible, and that it reduces spontaneity in helping people. Using theory implied distance and objectivity which contrasted with feelings and the living reality of social work encounters. As such it was seen to be a stumbling-block to developing individual style, and the most that could be hoped for was that students would admit that they might subconsciously be using theory that they had absorbed during their education and training.

Other discussions that have taken place, mainly among academics, are that social work has suffered because it has been seen to be theory-less or atheoretical. The suggestion is that because social work is about practice then it is neither a profession nor an academic discipline, it is merely the appliance of other social sciences (Orme, 2000a). While this might be seen, in more ways than one, to be an academic debate it is important because social work's uneasy relationship with theory has made it vulnerable in many ways. Policy-makers could argue that anyone can do social work, or that social work was not necessary. Or they could introduce policies and practices, such as care management, that sought to displace social work to the extent that they rename it social care. In universities the fact that social work did not develop, or was not seen to be developing, theory meant that its legitimacy was being challenged. Social work did not have a place in universities. For those who deny the need for theory, education and/or training for social work practice this is not a problem. For social work as a whole and those for whom social work exists, client/service users, it constitutes a threat to the quality of services provided.

In a text about social work practice it is vital that we consider the role of theory. This is not because theory should prescribe how social work must be practised, but because the use of theory is the hallmark of a good practitioner. This introductory chapter will explore what is meant by theory, and how social workers apply theory in practice. To do this is not merely a justification for the text; it is a contribution to the defence of social work as an activity.

Why practice needs theory

Over time students have become less antagonistic to theoretical ideas, naming and trying to integrate what can at first glance appear to be a smorgasbord of apparently contradictory explanations of behaviour. Education about theories that might underpin decision-making, or that might inform what action to take, is enjoying resurgence in the form of the social work degree but this has not been without a struggle.

The competence-based approach to education and training introduced in the 1980s (CCETSW, 1989a), reflected assumptions that social work is a set of functions, and that practitioners need to be trained merely to perform these functions. This was reinforced by legislation and policy initiatives that were accompanied by sets of 'guidelines', attempting to set limits on social work activity. The consequence of this prescriptive account of social work intervention was that the emphasis was on tasks, and task performance, not on workers' abilities to analyse and process information drawn from their skilled interactions with individuals, families or groups. Such an approach was unethical, failing to provide users of social work with appropriate interventions, and as such it is incompetent. As Howe (2000) argues, practitioners who develop and offer coherent applications of what is going on in their practice keep their professional bearing and sustain their commitment. Service users deserve professional and committed practitioners.

More importantly if such a mechanistic approach is adopted, there is no understanding that the information gleaned during social work interventions might be interpreted in many different ways, depending on which theoretical approach is used. Nor is there any expectation that students and practitioners will review their intervention in the light of the growing amount of practice-based research available in social work. The competence-based approach (see Ford and Hayes, 1996, for a discussion of this approach) requires certainties; that if you are dealing with A, you can intervene with B and that will secure an acceptable outcome C. In the history of social work such assumptions were associated with a scientific approach when social workers, in their quest for a professional identity, looked to medicine.

In a climate of increased managerialism, workers are scrutinised on performance indicators that include the number of service users or problems dealt with, the time taken to respond to a referral (or to prepare a report) or other calculations of throughput and output. The 'management' outcome is often that the required form has been completed. The quality of the intervention, what has occurred or might occur between the worker and the service user while the form is being completed, was not covered in national standards for probation practice, competences for care management or definitions of 'best value'.

The dilemma for social workers is that there are tasks to be performed and skills to be utilised, but prescriptions of 'the what' and 'the how' cannot be constructed in a vacuum. Social workers, to be truly effective, need to be constantly asking 'why?' It is in this quest for understandings about, for example, why situations arise, why people react in certain ways and why particular interventions might be utilised, that theory informs practice. However, this might suggest that there is a certainty about what theories should be taught, that theory for social work practice is uncontentious. What follows in this chapter is a discussion of what constitutes theory and the contribution of theory to 'ethical and effective' practice.

The use of that phrase brings us back to the developing relationship between theory, practice, education and training. A change of government in the late 1990s and concerted efforts by academics and practitioners led to a reclaiming of the place and function of social work. The incoming Labour government initially attempted to dismiss the need for social workers. However repeated child abuse tragedies, concerns about mental health users and other social problems led to a re-think and a decision to 'modernise' social work. In the process this offered a chance to increase qualifying levels in social work. In the development of the degree some important tensions emerged. The announcement that an undergraduate degree was to be the minimum qualification was accompanied by a statement from the Minister for Health, Jacqui Smith, that this was to be a 'practical degree', that services users needed social workers to do practical tasks to resolve their problems, not think about why the problems had arisen. Others felt that undergraduate study of both practice and theory would prepare workers for the complexity of the social work task (Orme, 2001a).

Theory, practice and research

The developments in social work education and training were accompanied by increasing attention to the relationship between research and practice. That a research base for social work is necessary is indisputable. Initiatives such as Making Research Count and Research into Practice focus on ways of encouraging social workers to utilise research findings to inform their practice. These initiatives were supported by the setting up of the Social Care Institute for Excellence (Scie) with a remit to ensure 'knowledge transfer', that is, to gather research findings, evaluate them and disseminate them to the social care workforce.

This infrastructure was to support an evidence-based approach to practice, described in criminal justice as the 'what works' approach (McGuire, 1995). However the terms 'evidence-based' and 'what works' have been contentious. Debates about the nature of the research, appropriate methodologies, ethical issues and the impact of research are central to social work, both in academia and in practice. Parton (2000) suggests that crucial to discussions about an evidence base for social work is an understanding of whether evidence of good practice refers to the way problems can be solved, or the effectiveness of the organisation. For example, the development of the 'what works' agenda has influenced service delivery in the criminal justice field. Chapter 8 describes how research evidence that demonstrated that accredited groupwork programmes based on behavioural approaches were effective ways of working with offenders led to their proliferation in the criminal justice services. However notions of 'effectiveness' were part of a managerialist agenda that required requisite numbers of offenders to be processed, and prescribed methods of intervention (Chapman and Hough, 1998; Home Office, 1999) irrespective of the quality of the intervention or the appropriateness for the individual offenders.

Such developments could be seen to fulfil fears that emphasis on theory curtails the spontaneity and freedom of practitioners. But approaches to research that merely describe findings and assume that these are the answer to practice dilemmas are not good research, and do not constitute theory. This does not mean that practitioners can adopt an 'anything goes' approach. In research, as in practice, workers have to be reflexive. That is, they do not accept information uncritically and they must be able to test out ideas in the light of practice experience. This has been crucial in the development of good research-informed practice. It has also contributed to approaches to research that involve practitioners and service users in research, acknowledging that the best way to understand situations is to ascertain the views of those in the situation. While such approaches are desirable they are not straightforward, not least because they challenge the power of both the practitioner and the researcher (Orme, 2000b). More importantly they recognise an important strand of theory building – theory from social work.

What is theory?

Educationalists have debated at length competing positions regarding social reality and the production of knowledge, in other words, theory (for discussion see Rojek, 1986; Howe, 1987). Put more simply theory is a framework for understanding a clustering of ideas that attempt to explain reality in a self-conscious way (Stepney and Ford, 2000, p. viii). This self-conscious explanation involves 'making sense' of what is going on by observing, describing, explaining, predicting and intervening (Howe, 2000, p. 81). It is also this imperative to explain that distinguishes a theory, which seeks to explain *why*; from a model, which seeks to describe *how* factors interact; or a method which involves formal written accounts of how to do the job (Stepney and Ford, 2000). Hence in many of the following chapters descriptions are given of how to undertake a particular social work intervention, but these are accompanied by different theoretical perspectives on why this model has been developed and which theoretical perspectives explain why it is effective.

However, as has already been stated, this does not mean that there is only one explanation or perspective. Academics and practitioners with particular theoretical perspectives will observe, describe, explain, predict and intervene in different ways. This is referred to on a number of occasions throughout this book when critiques of particular approaches are provided to help practitioners reflect both on what is being proposed, and on their own particular position in relation to those proposals. While for some this lack of certainty might seem unhelpful, Howe suggests that it should be embraced positively: 'Rather than bemoan the number and range of theories the practitioner needs to acknowledge that diversity reflects the subtlety and complexity of the human condition' (Howe, 2000, p. 83).

Also there is no need to assume that because there are different perspectives, these are necessarily contradictory rather than complementary. The 'gladiatorial paradigm', that is, the notion that social work theories compete and cannot be integrated since they offer opposing interpretations of social reality, ignores the commonalities and interdependence of explanations of how human beings shape, and are shaped by, their internal and external worlds. Moreover it ignores ambiguity, uncertainty and doubt which are features of the complexity of social work practice (Parton, 2000).

Either/or arguments, such as insisting that counsellors must be either Rogerian or behaviourist, or that social workers are either radical or traditional in their approach, fail to see the underlying continuities that hold together such apparently diverse positions. Most theories have elements in common as well as elements in opposition. The eclectic practitioner, who claims to take the 'best' from different theories, actually holds a consistent view of people and their situations (Howe, 1992: Payne, 1998). Purists might attack this seemingly undisciplined and incoherent way of working; yet this is the way in which practice is generally conducted, not least because it reflects the complexity of situations in which social workers intervene. However such debates do highlight the range of theoretical perspectives upon which social work draws, and demonstrate that social work is certainly not atheoretical.

Theory for practice

Since there are competing explanations for the situations social workers meet, it is not surprising that there is little agreement about the nature of theory that is required to intervene in those situations. Siporin (1975), for example, believed that social workers needed foundation knowledge (personality theory, social theory and social policy theory) that would contribute to an understanding of the person in society. Jones (1996) on the other hand criticised social work academics' selectivity in identifying and privileging certain theories or, in his words, 'seeing (theory) as a resource to be plundered and pillaged' (Jones, 1996, p. 203).

Another way of framing theory is offered by Pilalis's (1986) six meanings of 'theory' which reflect visions that are carried amongst student groups. Some regarded theory as general rules or laws testable against observable evidence. Others, similarly influenced by the physical sciences, took it to mean a probability, a hypothesis or a speculative explanation subject to research. The third and fourth meanings, specific to the human sciences, involved a system of principles which help us to understand events more clearly or to capture, for practical purposes, underlying ideological and value bases of say psychological, sociological or political ideas. Finally, popular uses of the word 'theory' are encapsulated in the fifth and sixth examples. That is the way in which it is distinguished from practice ('this is theory rather than practice') and the dismissive, 'that is all very well in theory' which sees knowledge as idealistic, and representing unattainable goals.

A more common way to classify theory is to distinguish between 'levels' of theory. So called 'grand theories' included Freudian or Marxist explanations of what motivates human nature, giving seemingly all-inclusive accounts. On the other hand, 'mid-range theories' are not so comprehensive, they address particular phenomena such as loss, attachment, delinquency and so on and try to explain their causes and consequences. Such explanations can be offered within Marxian or Freudian understandings of the world (see Howe, 1987 for examples). Finally, micro theories describe and explain particular practices.

These classifications, also known as the deductive approach (Howe, 2000), can be described as theories *for* social work. That is, the relevant social sciences are applied to practice. However practice is more than a 'rational–technical' activity (Parton, 2000) of applying knowledge from other disciplines to help decide what to do. An inductive or constructive approach, that is, building theory from practice and observation is just as, if not more, important.

In developing a particular approach to practice, a constructive approach, Parton and O'Byrne argue that there has been a failure to articulate and develop concepts and theories for practice. By this they mean 'a range of insights and concepts which had previously been derived from detailed analysis of what goes on between social worker and service user' (2000, p. 7). However, these are, in fact, theories *from* practice. Before considering what that means, we need to recognise that there has also been a development of theories *of* practice.

Theories of practice

Theories of social work include understandings of, for example, what it is and who is it for, but also contribute to models of how to do social work. Often this theory is developed inductively when workers build up theory from observations of their practice and observation. An example of this is task-centred practice, where a whole new approach to practice was developed after existing practices were observed and new ones introduced and assessed (see Chapter 7).

However other developments are not so overt. Theory that is implicit (Evans, 1976), alternatively called practice theory or practice wisdom, makes assumptions about what social workers do and how they make sense of their experiences. This explains in an organised way how social workers may usefully act, using their knowledge of the social world. England (1986) argues that a social worker's 'practice knowledge' involves a unique understanding of the people who constitute the clients, 'the general processes of perception and the creation of meanings which determine the individual's capacity to cope' (England, 1986, p. 34). However, in espousing a commonsense approach, England is being neither atheoretical nor anti-theoretical, but argues that 'defined' knowledge is not enough on its own. Professional learning has to be accompanied by, or mediated through, 'personal' knowledge that will inform intuitive knowledge and intuitive behaviour (England, 1986, p. 35). This position is reinforced by Parton (2000). His definition of social work as a practical moral activity involves social workers drawing upon tacit knowledge to inform and make sense of their interventions.

Significant in the development of an evidence base for social work is the work of Scie in trying to elucidate this tacit knowledge. By producing practice overviews and practice guides, resource guides, knowledge reviews, reports and positions papers (all available on the Scie website: www.scie.org.uk), Scie promotes good practice by reviewing knowledge to find out what works best and sharing this knowledge with all kinds of people involved in social work.

Theories from practice

Knowledge gained from theory exists to inform social workers' understanding, not to dominate it. As England argues, theory is not an end in itself, 'Abstract knowledge in social work, whilst it remains abstract knowledge, is utterly useless' (England, 1986, p. 35). If effective strategies and techniques are recorded and developed, then knowledge is created and can be used to direct others to what is common and regularly occurring in human experience. Some codification of activity enables social workers to evaluate their practice. When social workers evaluate their efforts, be they services to individuals or whole programmes of care, they begin to engage in theory building. Much social work theory derives from someone's experience that has been written down and shared with others. This can be described as theory from practice. However this does not mean that it is unassailable. What it does mean is that everyone's perspective is valuable, and importantly this recognises the perspectives of users and carers in the development of theory.

Postmodernism

As social work searches for a theory base, the notion of theoretical coherence is being challenged by postmodernism (Howe, 1994; Fook, 2002). Postmodernism focuses on how and why we seek for explanations or underlying causes, rather than what those causes might be. Hence postmodern notions of practice theories for social work would be 'a kaleidoscope of ideas, research findings, argument, practice wisdom, values and critical speculation, whose coherence would lie in relationships between the different parts, and between them and the reader's experience' (Tuson, 1996, p. 70).

But as Stepney and Ford point out, while academics might usefully debate theoretical dilemmas such as whether truth exists, practitioners can only afford such luxuries if they bring about tangible benefits and lead to positive outcomes (Stepney and Ford, 2000, p. 21). But accepting that there are many influences on the construction of social work theory, and ultimately practice, can be enormously helpful to practitioners. That there is no one timeless, all-embracing theory for social work, and that social work evolves and reforms according to local and cultural conditions of all social life (Howe, 1994) creates the potential to build theory from practice. More importantly, doing so calls into question who defines relevant theory, or which theories are privileged at any one time.

Social work theory should never become an end in itself, it can be generative offering new insights and perspectives (Parton, 2000). It therefore has to be both interactive and reflexive, and will change in response to practice constructions (Payne, 1991).

Reflexive practice

The notion of reflexive practice has contributed to the synthesis of postmodern critiques and theory building in social work. This synthesis has contributed to the development of emancipatory or transformational theory (Payne, 1998). As Fook (2002) explains, part of the resistance to theory is that there has been an inexorable link between knowledge and power. Postmodernism questions the supremacy of professional knowledge and thus significantly undermines the professions' claim to dominance (Fook, 2002, p. 37).

This might seem ironic in that so far this chapter has argued for developing a theory base as part of the recognition of something called 'social work'. But this depends on a particular use of knowledge by professionals. Schon (1987) argues that technical knowledge helps professionals only to a limited extent. Reflecting on the different contributions to any social work interaction involves identifying the limits of existing theories and developing new ones. Hence a reflexive stance requires practitioners to 'reflect in action' and demonstrate or construct accounts of what they have done, in what order and the outcomes; the values, strategies and assumptions that make up 'theories' in action (Schon, 1987). It is this that holds the potential for change (Fook, 2002), not only in professionals' perceptions of the situation that they are dealing with, but also in theories that inform the situation, the theories *for* and *of* practice.

However a truly reflexive stance, a one that develops theory from practice, has to recognise that explanations of what is happening in social work interactions are not the sole prerogative of practitioners. Any understanding has to incorporate the contribution to knowledge from users and carers. Postmodernism questions assumptions about 'legitimate' knowledge. Often legitimacy is granted because of the way things are known, who knows them and how knowledge is conveyed to others (Fook, 2002). Writers such as Foucault (1980) have highlighted that some knowledges (that is what people know about their experiences) are classed as inauthentic, not valid and not taken into account. In the past the knowledge, experience and views of service users have been treated as inauthentic or subsidiary. This contributed to the oppression of service users by the processes and practices of social work. Practice informed by user and carer perspectives is emancipatory and reflects the anti-oppressive value base of social work.

The potential of critical reflection is not that it overthrows or throws out all other understandings of theory, but that it challenges assumptions that only certain theories are valid. It does not mean that only one form of knowledge, that is, either professional knowledge or service user knowledge, is valid; it accepts that both have a contribution to make to understanding situations, and therefore constructing theory about them. This is crucial in the process of undertaking social work assessments, as we shall see in the next chapter.

Praxis

Critical reflection also helps to bring together theory and practice in a way that is meaningful to practitioners. The educationalist/ community worker Freire (1972) calls the ability to think and do 'praxis', a Marxist term that has been explored further by feminist scholarship (Stanley and Wise, 1990). The notion of praxis encourages people to perceive, interpret, criticise and transform the world around them. In social work a lot of time is spent in giving tangible, immediate, practical help, but this does not invalidate attempts to look beyond the obvious to ensure that experiences of inequality and oppression are revealed and challenged. Underpinning praxis is the notion that it is not enough to study the world; the aim is to change it. Hence we have come full circle in exploring the relationship between theory and practice.

Conclusion

Professional social work practice requires that workers deploy a wide-ranging repertoire of skills, underpinned by a value base that respects others. This will enable them to respond to the diversity of experiences and reactions that are encountered when working with fellow human beings. Skills and values are only meaningful if they are informed by theories. However as we have seen in this chapter theory building and theory application require a complex interaction between knowledge and process, challenging notions of who produces knowledge, how it is used and what are the implications for practice.

In this context the aim of this text is to provide not a recipe book, a manual of how to do social work, but an array of approaches which themselves arise out of, and are constructed by, the attempts of others to describe practice. It is important for practitioners to be able to utilise the knowledge generated and to understand that each intervention in which they are involved will add to their knowledge and understanding, and help to contribute to their own theoretical approach. In this way, and in many others, this text should be considered as a beginning, and not an end in itself.

---

putting it into practice

1. Identify a piece of your own practice. This might be a case or just one interview. While you are thinking about it list all the 'assumptions' that you made when dealing with the situation: about the people involved; what was going on; what might happen; what you might do to help those in the situation and so on.
2. When you have made the list try to organise it into themes around the kind of theory that has informed your thinking. This might be theory about human development, theory about oppression and discrimination or it might be theory associated with a particular way of intervening.

3. You might not always be able to identify specific theories – so ask yourself: 'Where did that idea come from?' and see if that helps you link with any of the ideas in this chapter about the relationship between theory and practice.
4. Finally, think about what you have learned from the situation that you have been reflecting on – Do your particular experiences help you understand more? Do they change they way you think about things? Do they challenge what you have read or learned?

This is the beginning of developing theory from your own practice – so now try to write down the one most important thing you have learned about intervening in this situation. You might then want to go to the Scie website to see if you can find out if anyone else has written about or researched this aspect of practice.

Further reading

Stepney, Paul (2000) 'The theory to practice debate revisited.' In P. Stepney and D. Ford (eds) *Social Work Models, Methods and Theories*. Lyme Regis: Russell House. A brief chapter that uses diagrams to help clarify the relationship of theory to practice.

Parton, Nigel and O'Byrne, Patrick (2000) *Constructive Social Work: towards a new practice*. Basingstoke: Palgrave. An important book that develops new approaches to social work practice based on social theory.

Trevithick, P. (2005) 'The knowledge base of social work.' In *Social Work Skills: a practice handbook*. Maidenhead: Open University Press. Explores different ways to think about practice.

Social Care Institute for Excellence website: http://www.scie.org.uk/ This is a rich source of information. It includes knowledge reviews, practice guidance and the electronic library for social care – a gateway to even more resources such as research findings.

part **1** | **Social work processes**

2 | Social work processes: assessment

Introduction

The process of assessment is core to social work practice. Increasingly, as the organisation and delivery of social work services change and develop in response to political and economic reforms the assessment process is the one part of service delivery that depends on the skills, knowledge and values of those who have been educated and trained as social workers. This is not to say that an assessment, or the process of assessment, is unique to social work, but the use that is made of social workers' judgements puts them in significant positions. These judgements are not always made in isolation. The development of multi-professional working requires comprehensive assessment to which a number of workers contribute. However what is vital is that the social work contribution is recognised and seen as an essential part of any assessment.

Assessments, multi-professional or otherwise, take place in a number of contexts and are prepared for a variety of purposes. They occur at the point that a service user first makes contact with an agency, and are used to decide whether services can be offered, what level of service is to be offered, and who should be involved in offering services. Initial assessments might take place as part of a duty officer system, but often lead to more comprehensive assessments required by legislation such as the National Health Services and Community Care Act (1990) or the Carers Recognition (Services) Act (1995). However assessments are also required at other points in service delivery: for example an assessment should be undertaken when decisions are made to withdraw services or terminate contact. Assessments may also be requested by other agencies at any point during a worker's contact with a service user. For example the criminal courts, children's panels in Scotland, mental health tribunals and child protection panels can request reports, which constitute assessments.

Increasing emphasis on assessment has led to developments in theories of, and guidance about, what an assessment is and how it should be conducted. In some areas of social work this has been associated with increasing prescription of what should be considered in an assessment and how this should be recorded. For example, pro formas for assessments have been developed in both community care and childcare, some of which have also been incorporated into computer based information systems. Other developments have been in the area of risk assessment. This chapter, as an introduction to the section on social work processes, will consider different perspectives on assessment in social work. In doing so it will discuss the contribution of theory to these perspectives. It will also describe and discuss developments in assessment schedules and the implications for social work practice of multi-professional working.

Assessment theories

Assessment is not a single event, it is an ongoing process, in which the client or service user participates, the purpose of which is to assist the social worker to understand people in relation to their environment. Assessment is also a basis for planning what needs to be done to maintain, improve or bring about change in the person, the environment or both. Assessments are undertaken in counselling and therapy, but what is unique to social work is that workers are involved in assessments that are public. Social work assessments involve making judgements so that decision-making can be better informed (Parton and O'Byrne, 2000, p. 134).

It has been argued that although assessment is a core process in social work it has been inadequately theorised. To quote the Chief Inspector of Social Services in England, 'the core social work skill of assessment as an analytical and evaluative tool is being lost or undervalued' (SSI, 1999). Ford and Ford (2000) find it ironic that such a statement was made at a time when assessment schedules were burgeoning. The Inspector's conclusion was that weaknesses in assessment had implications for social work training. It is therefore significant that as part of the initiative to identify an evidence base for social work practice, a literature review undertaken for the

Social Care Institute for Excellence identified that little work has been undertaken to evaluate how prepared social workers are to undertake this vital task (Crisp *et al.*, 2003).

What follows is an attempt to synthesis some of the work that has been undertaken on assessment.

Assessment as CORE

Over time social work literature has explored both the purposes and processes of undertaking assessment. An overview of this literature indicates that, at a simple level, assessment is core to social work and involves CORE skills. These are:

- Communication
- Observation
- Reflection
- Evaluation.

The skills of communication and observation are basic to all social work interactions, and are dealt with in detail in Chapter 4 on 'communication'. At this point however it is important to highlight that communication and observation skills do not just operate when social workers meet with service users. All information gathering is part of the process of communication. In assessment, workers receive written and verbal information from colleagues and others which is key to understanding the situation that has to be assessed. Many factors will impinge on a worker's understanding or making sense of situations in which he or she becomes involved. Observation of patterns of behaviour as well as body language are crucial to getting a sense of what is happening for this particular person at this particular time. For example, if an older person is being referred for community care services it is important to note: who is making the referral – is it a family member, a neighbour or someone in the health or care services? What actions have been taken prior to the referral? Does the older person know about the referral? Answers to these questions give important information about the context.

In some ways the purpose of communication and observation in assessment is clear. It is to gather information. However there is sometimes confusion in understandings of evaluation and reflection. Some people use the terms 'assessment' and 'evaluation' interchangeably. There may be an evaluative component to an assessment (for example, measuring if a service user, or a whole care programme, is achieving goals), but in general assessments are more akin to an exploratory study that forms the basis for decision-making and action. It is for this reason that reflection is important. Reflection involves reviewing the different perspectives accessed during the process of gathering information and being alert to the ways that these perspectives are themselves informed by the role and function of the people involved. Also reflection requires that these perspectives be reviewed in the light of theory and research evidence.

The notion of evaluation within the CORE skills is an exploration of the effectiveness of the process of assessment, including the contribution the service user and worker have made. Importantly, in this context, reflection and evaluation are designed to ensure that the assessment has drawn on as much information as possible (including social work theory and research findings). The evaluation must also be alert to the potential within the assessment process for stereotyping individuals and their problems, unfair discrimination in the allocation of services, and the operation of power in the relationship between workers and service users.

This basic analysis of assessment, however, can be interpreted and extended depending on the theoretical approach that informs the process of assessment. There are two major distinctive approaches to assessment – positivist and constructivist.

Positivist assessment

In positivist assessment the skills involved in undertaking and producing an assessment vary depending on who undertakes it, but in general a good assessment depends on administrative talent coupled with skills in human relations. This assumes that the person undertaking the assessment is someone who has the ability to organise, systematise and rationalise the knowledge gathered, together with a gift for communication and sensitivity in taking in the uniqueness of each person's situation. 'Hard' knowledge (that is, facts) is pertinent; the worker's thoughts and feelings and clarified intuition are acknowledged but are secondary. Documentation issued by bodies such as the Social Services Inspectorate (DoH, 2000a) provides guidelines on assessment, and such schedules are often used as essential everyday handbooks. However the emphasis in such assessment is on finding causes or reasons for the problem or situation – the worker is expected to be positive about his/her assessment. The judgement-making in this approach requires a high level of certainty, and it requires comparison against an assumed norm (for example, of behaviour or attitude). It leads to the production of a profile on someone, the completion of a schedule, pro forma or a report for the court. Because of this the work undertaken to produce the document is often referred to as 'doing' or 'making' an assessment.

Early writings on social work assessment suggested that assessments could be formed around 4Ps (Perlman, 1957), each of which stimulates a set of questions:

- Problems   What are the problems being presented?
- People   Who are the people involved?
- Place   Where is the situation happening?
             Which agencies are involved?
- Process   What is happening here?
             What is the social worker's role?

The work undertaken however involves continuously collecting and synthesising available data, which includes thoughts and feelings, in order to formulate plans. It is on this basis of understanding people and circumstances that we reach initial appraisals. These appraisals used to be called 'diagnostic formulations' (Coulshed, 1991), which included requirements to:

- Describe
- Explain
- Predict
- Evaluate
- Prescribe.

This formulation reflects how early writing on social work drew on a medical model. The assumption was that individual and social problems could be diagnosed and that social work could find a formula or 'magic bullet' that could be prescribed to 'solve' or 'cure' these problems. Those writing about social work in this way (for example, Sainsbury, 1970) made an important contribution to the development of social work theory. However this early writing on assessment in social work also urged caution. The inexperienced worker was encouraged to learn the art as well as the science of carrying out this task. It was the development of the notion of the 'art' of assessment that has led to a constructive approach to both social work and assessment (Parton and O'Byrne, 2000).

Constructivist assessment

The constructivist approach is based on constructionism, which argues that people construct their own social realities (see Berger and Luckman, 1967). The implication of this is that those undertaking assessment in social work should be careful not to offer false certainties. Social workers making assessments may be cast in the role of expert witness. However as controversies in both health and forensic processes have highlighted, expert witnesses are *interpreting* evidence, there are no absolute certainties. What is important is how the data on which assumptions are being made has been collected and whose version of events and situations is being privileged. Assessment is not just an event; it is a process. Parton and O'Byrne (2000) in drawing on constructionist and narrative approaches have argued for *constructive* social work. By this they highlight the theoretical and metaphorical usage of the word – they describe practice that is about building and/or putting together. This approach is particularly relevant to the process of assessment which involves constructing an account of a social situation and those involved in it for a particular purpose.

Writing that draws on the contribution of postmodernism, including constructionism, to social work has encouraged workers not to see problems as absolute, but to recognise that there might be more than one cause, and more than one solution (Pease and Fook, 1999; Milner and O'Byrne, 2002; Fook, 2002). Importantly the social construction of social problems recognises that sometimes individuals and groups are seen to be problematic by others because they do not conform to norms of behaviour. However these 'norms' are often reflective of dominant cultures (for example, Anglo-centric or Judaeo-Christian expectations of behaviour, dress and diet). It is therefore not the person who has the problem, but he or she is made to be a problem.

A constructivist approach makes reflection more central to the assessment process. As has been said, reflection is about a reconsideration or re-evaluation of the information, thoughts, feelings and understandings that have been amassed during the assessment process. As Milner and O'Byrne comment, assessment has sometimes been seen to be a search for the 'truth', but in fact what is often revealed is that there are many truths or understandings of situations (Milner and O'Byrne, 2002, p. 58). It is important that social workers recognise this, but are not frozen into inactivity by the complexities and dilemmas that this may create. Fook (2002), drawing attention to the role of the worker in the assessment process, argues that critical reflection assists individual workers to understand what perceptions they bring to assessments and how these might influence interpretations of a situation. It is impossible to eradicate fully the way that each individual reacts to information and observations. What is vital is that there are opportunities for these to be made transparent. This involves the worker acknowledging both his/her own biases and prejudices and the theoretical models he/she is using to interpret the information.

The constructivist approach requires that students and practitioners are conscious of the different theoretical approaches they may be applying in their assessment. Different approaches have been seen to influence models of assessment.

Assessment models

The skill in undertaking and recording an assessment lies in the ability to collect enough of the right kind of information, and this can only be done in the right kind of environment. Frequently learners attempt to find out everything in a 'scatter-gun' method: they hope to find out something worthwhile by asking more and more questions, resulting in confusion from information overload. It is as well to remember that it is not possible to know all there is to know about people or systems – assessments are always continuous and dynamic and, in this sense, never complete. As was discussed at the beginning of the chapter, assessments are never 'true' inasmuch as they tend to be filtered through the assessor's perspective, despite attempts at exactness and comprehensiveness and careful reflection. Also, as will be discussed later in the chapter, reflection will provide checks and balances on possible discriminatory or negative stereotyping that may occur within the process.

Once that has been said, an analysis of approaches to assessment and research into the assessment process reveals certain models.

These can be classified either by the purpose of the assessment, that is, initial assessment, needs-led assessment, risk assessment, or they can be classified by the way that they are carried out. This chapter will look at both these classifications, and in the first instance will look at how assessments are conducted.

Questioning model

Perhaps the most fundamental approach to assessment is reflected in what has been called the questioning model. Communication theories accept that dialogue between workers and service users is based on questioning, but urge the use of open rather than closed questions (see Chapter 4). Such approaches are said to facilitate the social worker in gathering as much information as possible. Questions are important to facilitate communication, but it is the nature of the questions and the way the answers are utilised that is significant.

The classic questioning model reflects what Milner and O'Byrne (2002) call the reductionist approach to assessment associated with psychosocial casework. In this model problems, and solutions, are seen to rest in the individual, and the social work task is to identify the problem and find the appropriate resources or solutions. One limitation of this model is the assumption that there is a truth that can be gleaned by interrogation, along the lines of a police inter-view. Another limitation of the model is that social workers are seen as the experts who interrogate each aspect of the system and come to a final decision on the basis of their expertise and the knowledge gained. Such approaches have been deemed to be oppressive and disempowering (Smale et al., 1993).

However the questioning model does not have to be employed in such a negative way. It is not necessarily the questioning that is disempowering, but how it is undertaken and what is done with the information. Systematic methods of gaining information can ensure that as many perspectives as possible are acquired to ensure that all sources of help, and as many resources as possible, can be brought to bear. These methods are sometimes known as 'triangulation', when information from different sources is compared and used to build up a picture. It is imperative that while seeking other opinions hearsay or gossip is not relied on when assessments serve the purpose of planning and intervening in someone's life. Also, questions are asked not to trick people or to 'catch them out' in the mode of an interrogation. They are asked in ways that try to help understand what is influencing the particular presentation of the information. This is particularly important to help avoid stereotyping or labelling people as deviant because they do not conform to one individual's perception of 'normality'.

Procedural models

Procedural models have been associated with the development of assessment schedules that have been produced as a result of guidance related to legislation (for instance the 'Orange Book' associated with the Department of Health's Protecting Children Initiative and the guidance on assessment associated with the NHS and Community Care Act). Other assessment schedules have come about as a result of research on, for example, assessment of children (Ward, 2000). The aim of such assessments is to improve practice and address theoretical and practical shortcomings, and to ensure that there is a consistent approach to identifying need and responding to it.

A procedural model means that workers undertake assessment according to a set of systems developed to ensure consistency and comprehensive data collection. Such systems are often rigid and typified by large numbers of forms to be completed. In some areas of practice data is inputted into computer programmes to facilitate the process of documenting all the information required. For social workers working in community care the accumulation of information can be paramount, and that information can be gleaned from a number of sources. Research has also shown that in the case of community care assessments, models are often a one-way process constructed to meet the worker's and the agency's needs (Richards, 2000). As such they can be undertaken without any positive impact on the person being assessed.

Procedural models were developed in childcare in the late 1980s and were often associated with assessment of risk. Guidance for such assessment (DoH, 1988), referred to as the Orange Book, gave background rationale, including policy and legislation, for particular actions, providing detail on who to see and the kinds of questions to ask in order to glean the information necessary to establish whether a child is at risk. The list of topics to be covered and guidance on questions provided a wealth of information for beginning social workers. However, while a 'how to do it' manual might produce technically correct social workers, it does not encourage them to reflect on what they are doing, and why. Such an approach does not equip workers to react to complex situations. There is no easy formula for predicting, synthesising or understanding the wealth of human experience.

Once that has been said, to collect data systematically and to record it as a basis for decision-making with individuals and families is essential, and has been associated with the 'evidence-based approach' to social work. Also Richards (2000) found that in working with older people, some assessors valued the clarity of using an assessment form and the ease with which it could be completed. The problem is that once forms are in place they can dominate the exchanges. Richards found that workers focused on the information for the form rather than conducting:

> a wide ranging enquiry, which might uncover unanticipated problems and enable the older person to think through the situation more productively or accept help more easily.
> (Richards, 2000, p. 42)

In 2001 the Orange Book was replaced in England by the *Framework for Assessment of Children in Need and their Families* (1999). The Framework was accompanied by the *Family Pack of Questionnaires and Scales* (Cox and Bentovim, 2000), which included seven questionnaires or scales to complete and score. This constituted attempts to screen children and families (by using scoring techniques), but critics (Garrett, 2003) have warned that this might lead to inappropriate labelling. Garrett also raises questions about how the various 'instruments' and 'tools' that go together to make the Framework might be used and deployed. For example, he speculates that in future managers will want to know about particular 'scores'. He also suggests that scores or assessments derived from the questionnaires will be required by child protection case conferences, and that judges and magistrates will 'seek from social workers "certainties" which "hard" data provides' (Garrett, 2003, p. 455).

Forms, schedules and computer programs may contribute to the collection and storage of data, but Garrett's critique highlights that it is the use of the data and information that is crucial. Data is collected for different purposes and can be stored in different places. For example, a financial assessment might indicate than an older person has very few resources, while another pro forma assessing health issues might indicate he/she is depressed because he/she has few social contacts. It is only when the two pieces of information are brought together that it becomes obvious that the older person is not able to go out or join social activities because of his/her lack of resources. There is therefore nowhere for a picture of the whole person to be presented. In such situations the procedural approach is not a helpful process for the potential service user, but an imposition. More worryingly, assessment processes that privilege agency agendas and marginalise the thoughts of service users may lead to inappropriate intervention based on inadequate understanding (Richards, 2000).

Just as importantly, information about the individual is collected that does not obviously relate to the problem or issue that has brought him/her to the attention of social services. Even with the checks and balances of the Data Protection Act to prevent the misuse of information, it is the process of gathering information that becomes counter-productive. Workers become obsessed with gathering data rather than focusing on the person who requires a service, and who may be distressed or angered by having to reveal so much about him or herself.

Exchange model

Smale *et al.* (1993), in critiquing other assessment models, provide an alternative, the exchange model of assessment, where users and carers, as experts in their own needs, are empowered by being involved in the assessment. This model involves more than merely sharing assessments with users. While emphasising that the worker has expertise in the *process* of problem solving, the model recognises that the people in need and those involved with them will always know more about their problems. The aim is to involve all the major parties in arriving at a compromise for meeting care needs. Rather than simply making an assessment, the worker manages the process; he/she 'negotiates to get agreement about who should do what for whom' (Smale *et al.*, 1993, p. 16). The focus is very much on the social situation, rather than the individual, and recognises that people come to social services for help because other support systems may have broken down or are not available. It is argued that everyone in the social network should be involved in the assessment, as each person will have his or her own perception of the problem. The project sees assessment and care management as a continuous process, which should be undertaken in a way that empowers people. In summary, the main tasks of assessment in the exchange model are to:

● facilitate full participation in the processes of decision-making
● make a 'holistic' assessment of the social situation, and not just of the referred individual
● help create and maintain the flexible set of human relationships that make up a 'package of care'
● facilitate negotiations within personal networks about conflicts of choices and needs
● create sufficient trust for full participation and open negotiations to actually take place, and
● change the approach to all these broad tasks as the situation itself changes over time.
(Smale *et al.*, 1993, p. 45)

However, as Richards found in her research into the assessment of elders, what is significant is the way the assessment is conducted. For people to participate effectively they need the opportunity to think through their situation as well as have intelligible information (Richards, 2000, p. 45). This suggests that they are not always expert – but that they should at least be equal participants in the process of considering relevant information. Richards (2000) concludes that effective exchange in the assessment process requires careful attention to narrative. It also requires making the necessary adjustments to ensure that those with sensory and other impairments are able to understand and be understood.

Such approaches however do not necessarily simplify life for social workers. As Richards points out, giving older people (and indeed anyone) the space to talk might well reveal problems that are not necessarily resolvable (2000, p. 47). For example, when faced with illness (either their own or that of their partner), older people often have to face the inevitability of death. It is because of this that assessment should be seen as not only a process but also an intervention in itself, an opportunity for people to articulate their pain and their difficulties. Often insensitive and abrupt assessments governed by schedules will unwittingly precipitate this pain. It is the responsibility of the worker to be alert and responsive to this.

Narrative assessment

Building on the exchange model, those who support narrative approaches suggest that exchange is not enough, as it denies that workers have professional responsibilities. What is required is critical reflection that involves constructing a narrative jointly between the worker and the service user (Fook, 2002). Workers are acknowledged to have some expertise – in thinking about solution development and building solutions with people (Parton and O'Byrne, 2000) – but they are not the only experts in the situation. Service users do have 'agency', that is, they are not just passive recipients of the assessment, they have responsibility for making decisions and for being involved in the sense-making activities of assessment. This does not mean there will be agreement: 'the emphasis is on mutual exchange, not necessarily mutual agreement' (Fook, 2002, p. 121).

Significantly, in developing a narrative approach Parton and O'Byrne (2000) do not totally dismiss the need for questions. They have constructed what they call 'scale sheets' for different situations. These sheets, used properly, enable the worker to develop a reflective story because they can facilitate various answers that are more than just a 'yes' or 'no'. Such questions are open questions, and tend to use 'What ...?' to develop the reflective story rather than a 'cause and effect' analysis. The scale sheets then become the focus for analysis as part of the process of assessment. The narrative is relevant to communication, observation, reflection and evaluation (CORE) because it is through narrative that the worker can understand the service user's perspective of the problem. By engaging with the person, negotiating perceptions and acknowledging difference reflected in the sheets, the worker can 'invite the service user to help the worker see life as they see it' (Parton and O'Byrne, 2000, p. 142). To do this workers engage in conversations, and these conversations are informed, but not driven, by theory. The conversations are part of the narrative.

Fook also argues for conversations, suggesting that questions can be avoided by an invitation to the service user to 'tell me about your experiences' (Fook, 2002, p. 125). This leads to engagement in a conversation rather than an interview or an interrogation. This is because, although the assessment has to deal with the immediate situation, other perspectives can be revealed which will be important even when these are contradictory. It also acknowledges that just by being involved in the situation social workers can change that situation. Finally, by revealing and reflecting on situations the perspectives of both the worker and the service user may change.

Ultimately it is the responsibility of the worker to construct a professional narrative that functions to assist the service user in different contexts. As was said at the outset, in social work these contexts are often very formal settings such as courts, child protection conferences or case reviews in hospitals or residential settings. It is for this reason that Parton suggests that a move to assessment that does not offer false certainty will require wider support – especially from those who ultimately have to make decisions. However it is argued that it is better to have honest accounts of struggles with judgement and understanding than to search for false certainty (Parton and O'Byrne, 2000, p. 135).

In the box below is an example of a situation not uncommon in social work. Another agency raises concerns and expects the social worker to 'find out' what is going on and to identify the causes of what is seen as a problem – and to alleviate the problems. It illustrates that if mishandled the assessment might not necessarily 'find out' the issues, and this could have serious consequences for all concerned.

Case example

A local school alerted the local social work team because a seven-year-old boy, Jack, was not attending school, and when he did attend he looked dirty and ill fed. When the school tried to contact the family it had had little response. The case was allocated to a student social worker and was initially seen as a problem of 'school refusal'.

The student contacted the family in advance and arranged to visit. When the student arrived, Jack's mother, Mrs Adams was welcoming and, in response to questions, denied that there were any problems, stating that at times Jack was a little slow in the mornings, dressed in a hurry and missed his breakfast. The children were not at home at the time of the visit and the student arranged another visit, to which Mrs Adams agreed.

On the second visit Mrs Adams was much more wary of the student social worker. All the family (Mrs Adams, Jack and his younger sister) were in the same room and the television was on, making it difficult to hold a conversation. When the student asked if the television could be turned down, Mrs Adams became angry and abusive to the student. The student waited while Mrs Adams expressed her anger and eventually became calmer, but in doing so she also became very upset.

It emerged from the conversation that Mrs Adams' partner had left her some months before and that she was in extreme debt. There was no heating or water in the house because she had not been able to pay bills or arrange for repairs. She was also in arrears with her rent. She described symptoms of extreme depression, not being able to get up in the mornings and at times feeling suicidal.

The student was able to discuss with Mrs Adams her need to have appropriate medical support, while at the same time arranging practical support to ensure that the minimum needs of the family were met in terms of water and heating.

While she did this Mrs Adams was able to talk about the possible impact of the various pressures on the children, and she was prepared to cooperate while the student undertook separate interviews with the children to ensure their safety and well-being.

The student was aware that had she taken the initial situation at face value she would have missed the many problems that Mrs Adams was experiencing, and that Mrs Adams and the children might have experienced further and more chronic problems. At the same time she was aware that she had not fully explained the purpose for her initial visits. Mrs Adams had become hostile because she saw the student as a 'spy' and had real concerns that, if the student social worker became aware of the conditions in which they were living, the children would be removed.

While this illustrates the many dimensions to situations in which social work is involved, it also highlights that often social workers do have to make judgements. In this case it was about the level of potential harm to the children. While allowing Mrs Adams to talk about her experiences the student also had to manage the complex issue of assessing risk to both the children and Mrs Adams.

Risk assessment

Social workers frequently have to deal with risk. Obvious examples are, as in the above case, where there are concerns about the safety of children. The assessment here is not just the potential risk of harm to the children, but also an assessment of the propensity of adults to commit an act of harm. Such risk assessments echo the judgements required of criminal justice social workers when writing reports for the court and having to make predictions about whether someone will reoffend.

Other situations of immediate risk are in community care with adults. For example, older people are brought to the attention of workers because they appear to be neglecting themselves. Workers have to assess whether such neglect constitutes a danger. In mental health the immediacy of risk assessment is apparent in situations where social workers have to make decisions about whether a person should be sectioned on the basis that his or her behaviour constitutes a threat of harm to him or herself or to others.

These examples illustrate the complexity of the social work role in risk assessment. The fact that decisions have to be made seems to require a degree of certainty that is not consistent with the dialogic, constructivist approach to social work. However if such an approach is not taken then false conclusions might be reached. What is sometimes frightening for social workers is the consequence of reaching the wrong conclusion, of making the wrong decision. These concerns are not driven by selfishness or self-protection, although that would not be surprising in the light of the treatment of social workers in the wake of various child abuse enquiries. Social workers take seriously their responsibilities to individuals, be that the child who may be abused, the older person who might die of hypothermia or the person suffering mental ill health who might lose his/her liberty. They also recognise their responsibilities to members of the public who might suffer harm or loss as a result of decisions made on social work assessments and recommendations. This reflects the balance between promoting the rights of service users while recognising agency responsibilities.

Hence it is apparent that assessing risk causes social work a number of dilemmas. These dilemmas are compounded because risk decisions are made in a context where philosophies and policies on risk minimisation and normalisation are in conflict. On the one hand people have to be protected, but on the other they should be allowed to live their lives as they choose, as long as this does not negatively affect others. This constitutes service users' right to self-determination, or the promotion of their choice while needing to reduce risk to the service user and others. These inherent tensions in risk assessment have led to policies on risk assessment and management but without accompanying practical guidance (Kemshall and Pritchard, 1996, p. 1). Workers are required to assess risk, but are not helped in this complex task.

Corby's (1996) work on risk assessment in child protection can be adopted and made relevant to many situations in which social workers have to assess risk. He suggests that there are three significant aspects of risk assessment, each associated with the point in social work intervention at which they are carried out. These are:

● preventative risk assessment
● investigative risk assessment
● continuation risk assessment.

Preventative risk assessment

Preventative risk assessment is often carried out before any intervention takes place, and may influence decisions about whether to intervene or not. Such assessments are usually predictive, and use indicative factors to inform judgement. Corby quotes Browne and Saqi (1988) as an early example of the kinds of lists of indicative factors that could be drawn on. Increasingly as the research base for social work develops, more information is becoming available to workers about both the contributory factors in social problems and the effects of intervention. Using evidence-based practice social workers are rightly expected to be familiar with studies that are relevant to their area of work, and to draw upon these as a source of knowledge and information. In terms of reflective practice mentioned earlier in this chapter, the research base is an important resource that has to be incorporated into the worker's reflections.

Having said that, discussions about evidence-based practice, or as some prefer to call it, research-informed practice, highlight that it is not unproblematic (Orme, 2000a). One concern is that the results of research will be seen as incontrovertible and will be used as predictive factors (sometimes developed in the form of scales), either to assess the likely cause or outcome, or to dictate the way in which workers intervene. There is a worry that this will detract from practice wisdom and professional autonomy. A further complication is that research is sometimes contradictory and therefore confusing (Parton, 1998). However it is clear that good professional practice requires social workers to be aware of the available evidence and be able to weigh up the implications of research findings in each situation.

There are ethical issues surrounding the use of predictive factors in preventative risk assessment. Corby points out that the use of predictive scales or schedules in child protection might mean that non-abusers are identified as potential abusers. He points out that because of bias in the 'samples' that are used to produce the results this might impact more negatively on women (as mothers) and on people in lower socio-economic groups (Corby, 1996, p. 17). He also draws attention to the fact that such assessments are often undertaken covertly – referrals are made to agencies and workers have to undertake a risk assessment to decide whether to intervene. While this might be seen to be appropriate where it saves a child's life, it is thought to be intrusive if social workers intervene in situations where there is no evidence of abuse. As has been said, risk assessment continually involves the balancing of rights and responsibilities.

Investigative risk assessment

An investigative risk assessment is often an initial assessment into a social situation that has been drawn to the attention of statutory agencies by someone who has expressed concerns. Many agencies have procedural guidelines for how to respond to such concerns. However, as many investigations into the handling of child abuse enquiries highlight, these procedures are not always followed. Even when they are followed they do not always help the workers because they are about procedures and not about processes and skills.

Producing guidelines that are useful is challenging to the notion of CORE skills for social work assessment. Often the situations to be dealt with involve *communication* between professions as well as within professions. In the case of child protection, for example, social services, health services and the police are frequently involved. Multi-agency involvement will mean that service users have to tell their stories on multiple occasions, and they will be heard differently be different professionals. Similarly, *observations* may often differ because the perspective taken by workers within the situation is influenced by their different professional backgrounds and the aims and purpose of the agency in which they work. *Reflection* is often limited because of both the timescale in which actions have to be taken and the lack of narratives about the different aspects of the situation, or the impact of interventions. In the case of Mrs Adams above, the student had time to return to the home and also had the luxury of time to stay with Mrs Adams and hear the different complexities of her situation. Finally, options open to workers will influence the outcomes so *evaluation* becomes problematic.

An illustration of how problematic investigative risk assessment can be is in cases of domestic violence. The greater awareness of the incidence of domestic violence has led to a number of police forces instituting policies and procedures for responding to calls from women who experience domestic abuse. These have been welcomed by social workers. However when situations involve children, the police referring cases do so with an expectation that social workers will treat the case as a child protection case. The evidence that children are negatively affected by situations of domestic violence is clear (see Mullender and Morley, 1994, for informative research on this), and might well lead police to feel that children should be removed from the situation immediately. Social workers are understandably concerned that a policy of removing the children might suggest that the mother is in some way to blame for the violence experienced. The knock-on effect of this may be that women will not report incidences of domestic abuse if they fear their children will be removed. Social workers prefer to deal with such situations under children in need procedures, and to find ways of working with women and their children to assure the safety of both. They do so, however, knowing that if the man remains in the situation, both women and children may be at risk.

Each situation therefore demands complex processes to ensure that the risk assessment is appropriate, and that the actions taken are effective in the short and long term. This requires information sharing between the workers in the situation. This is not just information about the particular case they are involved in, but also about agency policy and understandings of research.

Communication has to happen at a number of different levels. To assist open communication there has to be comprehensive recording of information, perspectives and opinions.

One way in which causal factors have been codified to assist workers has been in the use of checklists, personality inventories and structured interviews. However there are limitations to the usefulness of such mechanisms. Milner and O'Byrne (2002) point out that child abuse research demonstrates that it is only possible to predict 65–80 per cent of known future abuse. Corby argues that often the questions, sometimes devised for, or based on, research for other purposes, are over-intrusive and irrelevant, and risk raising resentment in those who have to answer them (Corby, 1996, p. 25). Also there are concerns that these tools merely codify situations that have been dealt with, but that in doing so they might misrepresent or enshrine past discriminatory practices. This has been the case in, for example, risk assessment of black men within the mental health services. Because of racist attitudes that have failed to acknowledge diversity in behaviour, or that have precipitated violent incidents because of the way individuals were dealt with, analysis of mental health statistics might indicate that black men suffering schizophrenia might be more likely to be violent. Enshrining this in some risk inventory only serves to institutionalise racist attitudes.

Alternatively stereotypical assumptions about male and female behaviour might serve to leave some people at risk. For example, if it is assumed that women are non-violent then workers might fail to identify situations in which elder abuse is taking place. Bruises, wounds and other symptoms might be accepted as the result of falls or clumsiness, and not investigated as possible carer abuse, where the prime carer is a woman.

These reservations highlight that workers have to approach such situations with an open mind, making no assumptions about who might be responsible for what. This is consistent with the social work value of maintaining a non-judgmental attitude. But this does not mean that all judgement is suspended. It is possible to identify someone as being responsible for harm or abuse and still respect him or her as a human being requiring help. Workers should not jump to premature conclusions, nor should they condemn a person because of their actions. The concepts of acceptance and empathy are core to social work practice, and constructivist and reflective approaches to practice facilitate narratives based on these principles. In particular, the notion of empathy as trying to understand the situation from the perspective of another person while not condoning their actions is fundamental to trying to understand why people are abusive. Only if the causes of abuse are identified will risk assessment be effective, and social workers able to protect vulnerable people.

Continuation risk assessment

This notion of empathy and of trying to identify the causes of violent and abusive behaviour (which includes neglect and all other actions or inactions that put individuals and others at risk) is also important in continuation risk assessment. These are the assessments that have to be made at regular intervals in situations in which an identifiable risk has been uncovered. Corby (1996) suggests that these assessments are often about risk reduction and not risk elimination.

In that involvement with social work agencies often carries with it stigma, discrimination, disempowerment and disadvantage, it is important that there is constant assessment of whether there is a need for social work to continue to be involved in situations. Continuation risk assessment is about balancing the risks of intervention against the risks of non-intervention. To do this it is necessary to evaluate the situation in the light of the original concerns, acknowledge changes that have occurred, and assess whether these changes influence the situation for better for worse, or make no difference at all.

Assessment of need

The National Health and Community Care Act (1990) introduced assessments that were to be needs-led rather than resource-led. However when considering the operation of power in assessment, the important question is which interpretation of need will prevail – that of the worker or the user? Also, as with risk, need cannot be assessed in a vacuum. Workers often have to assess competing needs, especially those between users and carers. In community care these competing claims were first formalised in the Carers (Services) Recognition Act 1995, which gives carers the right to assessment. However, formalising assessment of need does not necessarily resolve the dilemmas. If an older woman wants to remain in her own home, and to do so requires informal care, she might also want to be able to say who will care for her. The request that the daughter in the family does the caring might be at odds with the daughter's own plans for employment, or even the way she chooses to spend her leisure, or organise her life.

For a more theoretical discussion of human need, Doyal's chapter 'Human need and the moral right to optimal care' in *Community Care: a reader* (Bornat *et al.*, 1993) is a good starting point. Doyal argues that there are no easy resolutions to some of the conflicts around community care needs, but that a 'procedural theory of need' might facilitate communication and an acceptable compromise. Such a theory argues that 'those participating in policy formulation must include all parties in the dispute' (p. 284) and this will involve users and carers as well as workers from voluntary, statutory and independent sector agencies. The outcome of such procedures is that at the end of the assessment users should know:

● who has taken the decision on eligibility
● which needs are, or are not, eligible for assistance, and why
● which needs might be eligible for assistance from other care agencies
● when, and under what circumstances, they may request re-assessment
● the means of complaining if dissatisfied.
    (SSI, 1991, p. 54)

This reflects the philosophy that both the way information is gathered and the use to which information is put are crucial in ensuring that assessments are empowering and anti-oppressive. Power operates with the allocation of resources. In community care assessments, services have to be allocated as a result of systematic and careful deliberation of needs, not simply what services are available. This requires that people are listened to, and assessment are not just constructed according to some bureaucratic category of community care (see Orme, 2001a, for further discussion).

Assessments and oppression

Attention to issues of risk and to allocation of resources is a stark reminder of the power that social workers wield. Those working in the statutory sector have legislation to legitimise actions taken to protect others. However even workers in the non-statutory sector have power. This power may come from having access to, or knowledge of, resources. Knowledge in particular is said to imbue power, and in assessment knowledge operates in a variety of ways. In addition to knowledge of resources, knowledge of theories may lead workers to interpret behaviour and label individuals. Even when this does not lead to specific actions that might curtail the freedom of the individual (that is by recommending custody for an offender or residential care for a child or an older person), the very fact that someone might be labelled, stereotyped and pigeonholed is an abuse of power.

Hanmer and Statham (1988) were among the first to describe how the common assumptions of good parenting in childcare assessments were in fact expectations of good mothering that assume that women will devote their lives to the full-time care of their children. Bandana Ahmad (1990) highlighted that social workers tended to view black users who did not fit into assessment schedules as *problems* as opposed to *different*. As Keating (2000) points out, over time black perspectives have been important in ensuring that black people were able to claim a space for their views to be heard.

Most policy documents now make explicit reference to the need for assessments to be sensitive and alert to differences in people's background, according to their race, colour or religion. It might be argued that such statements are not necessary. If an assessment is done properly it will focus on the individual in his/her situation, and that situation will include his/her age, gender, race, religion or sexuality. As has been said with dialogic approaches, those that involve conversations with service users, priority is given to the person's perceptions of his/her own circumstances.

When assessment schedules are being devised to recognise different approaches and lifestyles, it is important that the way the information is collated, and needs constructed, also reflects the range of different approaches that can be provided for multi-cultural communities. Criticisms of assessment schedules have highlighted that they are often based on assumptions about the way that people live their lives, including diet, clothing and childcare practices, all of which are defined from the perspective of white, usually middle-class, values (Garrett, 2003).

However arguing that assessments have to respond to certain aspects of an individual's identity does not necessarily make them anti-oppressive. Focusing on one aspect of identity, and assuming that this is problematic or leads to negative experiences, can be oppressive and discriminating. For example assumptions that women are passive, are 'natural carers', leads to assumptions in community care that it will be women who undertake caring roles (Ungerson, 1987). It also means that women are often the focus of attention in cases involving children, even when there is a male partner involved (see Scourfield and Coffey, 2002). Stereotyping also has an impact on the way that services are provided for men. In community care, gendered assumptions have implications not only for who does the caring (Fisher, 1997), but also for the services that are made available for men (see Orme, 2001a, for detailed discussion of these processes). In relation to race Ahmad and Atkins (1996) have provided an important analysis of how racial stereotypes influence the provision of community care services. This evidence leads Keating (2000) to argue that rather than focusing on one aspect of a person's identity, developing an understanding of the inter-relatedness of all systems of domination and the multi-faceted role of power inherent in the processes of oppression will be more productive and empowering.

Another drawback to assessments, particularly when they are carried out by statutory agencies such as criminal justice services and personal social services departments, is that they can be used to control disadvantaged sections of the community. Stigmatising and scapegoating clients via negative assessments (see Jones, 1983) does occur. Dossiers are kept on so-called 'problem families' or those who have assertively sought assistance. The adjective 'aggressive' is applied to black clients who assert their needs for equitable services. As B. Ahmad (1990) shows, such assessments fail to take into account black realities and environments, but assume passivity attributed to those who are powerless.

User participation in assessment

One way of ensuring that assessments are non-oppressive and non-discriminatory is to ensure the participation of those who are being assessed. Constructivist models of assessment described above attempt to reduce power imbalances between worker and service user. However one criticism is that they assume a high level of knowledge by the service user, and imply that the role of the social worker is to facilitate the process of the individual undertaking her/his own assessment. For some service users this is not possible, sometimes because their illness or impairment makes it difficult for them to participate, and at others because they are in such a state of distress that they want and need support, help and knowledge from people they see as experts. Also, in assessments required by the courts, case reviews and other situations where risks and needs are being balanced, workers may have to get information that service users might not want to give.

What is important is to balance all these expectations and demands in ways that acknowledge the role of the worker, but also recognise the rights of the individual. This can be achieved by involving the user in the assessment process in ways that ensure he or she understands the purpose of the assessment, and the reasons why the information is sought. Doing this can help alleviate fears about the possible outcome of the assessment. An example of this is in cases where social workers have to investigate allegations of child neglect or abuse. Often in such situations the concern of those being 'investigated' is that children might be removed. However it is also possible, indeed probable, that in many situations families are experiencing real need with which the agencies might be able to help. As the case of Mrs Adams illustrated, reluctance to be open about difficulties means that social workers become at best concerned, and at worst suspicious, of what is being 'hidden'.

User involvement in assessment can go further than merely sharing the purpose of the assessment or giving the service user the opportunity to comment on the final assessment. To avoid becoming complacent in assessment it is important to:

● work collaboratively
● view users as competent
● help users to see themselves as 'causal agents', and
● develop people's confidence by affirming their experiences.
  (Dalrymple and Burke, 1995)

User involvement and empowerment are discussed in greater detail in the next chapter, but it is important to remember that assessments are about people and should therefore include them. As the discussion of the constructivist approach highlighted, this is not only good anti-oppressive practice, it will ultimately lead to more effective assessment.

Monitoring assessments

Another way of ensuring that assessments are non-discriminatory and non-oppressive is to have systems for monitoring assessment. Getting feedback on assessment not only improves accuracy, it also provides the basis for an honest exchange. Sharing assessments with other colleagues is a way of reducing the risk of bias or error.

There could be value in *team assessments*, as opposed to our usual practice of leaving this to one worker. The purpose of this may be to check out how personal interpretations influence the presentation of the information. Shared assessments were developed in the probation service as part of the development of anti-oppressive practice. The process of gatekeeping for pre-sentence report required that once a report had been prepared the author shared it with a colleague or a group of colleagues. This provided checks to ensure that the language, the information and the basis of the assessment did not in any way reflect oppressive or discriminatory thinking. Although increasing the time needed to complete the reporting process, this process challenged stereotyping and negative stigmatising (Orme, 1995).

All assessments contain the risks of error or bias that might be partly counteracted by cross-checking data; extra suggestions for reducing worker bias include:

1. Sharing the assessment with those who participate in it.
2. Improving self-awareness so as to monitor when you are trying to normalise, be over-optimistic or rationalise data.
3. Getting supervision to help release blocked feelings or confront denial of facts or to cope with the occasional situation where you have been manipulated.
4. Being wary of standing in awe of those who hold higher status or power and challenging their views when necessary.
5. Treating all assessments as working hypotheses that have to be substantiated with emerging knowledge; remember that they are inherently speculations derived from material and subjective sources.

Shared assessments in multi-disciplinary work engage the other and begin the process of change, giving equal value to each participant's views and precipitating a dialogue about differences of perception.

Multi-disciplinary assessment

Increasingly in social work assessments have to be carried out in conjunction with those from other agencies and professions. In community care arrangements a key responsibility to collaborate with medical, nursing and other caring agencies (DoH, 1989a) was introduced. The care manager is the person who facilitates and co-ordinates a multi-disciplinary assessment. In the case of health assessments of older people, these can take place at home, in a day or residential centre or in a hospital setting. Various professionals (for instance, health visitors, occupational therapists, physiotherapists, general practitioners, district nurses and social workers) work together in shared assessment of older people, but this does not mean shared perceptions. In the work of children and families teams, child protection investigations are frequently carried out with colleagues from the health services and/or the police, and increasingly arrangements for children's services involve the collaboration between social work and those in education.

The use of multi-disciplinary assessments has been the subject of a great deal of scrutiny in the provision of community care and has resulted in Scotland in a specific recommendation for a *Single Shared Assessment* (Scottish Executive, 2001) for working with adults and through parallel legislation in England. This is therefore discussed in greater detail in Chapter 10.

However as the Laming Report (2003) into the death of Victoria Climbié clearly identified, arrangements for joint assessments sometimes do not work because workers either do not communicate with each other, or they do not always accept or trust the judgement of those not in their own profession.

At the outset, when a referral is made by another agency, information comes either in written form, or by a phone call. The person making the referral obviously has access to some information, and has come to certain conclusions. The skill at this point is to ensure that enough appropriate information is received in order to make an accurate assessment without being influenced by the views and perspectives of a worker who is already involved, and has his or her own views, albeit from a different agency perspective.

For example, in the case of school attendance, schools are under pressure to produce league tables that include statistics on attendance rates. The priority of someone in the education system might therefore be to ensure the child either attends school, or is referred to another facility. A social work assessment might focus on the social and economic circumstances of the family, family dynamics or other factors that are influencing the behaviour. That does not mean that the assessor will ignore the failure to attend school, but that he/she will consider it in a different context, with different imperatives. It is at this point that liaison and negotiation skills are paramount, recognising the expertise, status and concerns of all involved.

Conclusion

This chapter has focused on the process of assessment as a CORE task in social work. It is core because it provides an important first contact between service users and helping agencies, it facilitates decisions about intervention, it influences the allocation of resources and it determines whether or not there are potential risks in the situation.

In discussing different theoretical approaches to assessment the chapter also describes the core skills that are required to undertake effective assessments. These include communication, observation, reflection and evaluation, all of which operate within the assessment process. While there are systems and schedules that can be adopted to ensure that assessments are comprehensive, the very act of intervening in someone's life and trying to ascertain information can be seen as oppressive. Even if the core skills are utilised effectively it must be remembered that the process of assessment involves the operation of power. This is certainly the case in situations that involve risk assessment. While assessment is fundamental to social work, social work values have to be fundamental in assessment processes.

putting it into practice

1. When you are in practice you will have access to a number of assessments written by different workers for different purposes. Choose one to consider in more detail. Try to ensure that this assessment is not just a set of forms but has some written text. Read the assessment carefully and write down:
   - what information is given
   - what assumptions are made
   - what opinions are given.
   Do not do this in a negative way – the focus is not on criticising the writer of the report but on whether you can make the distinctions.

2. Now look at the CareNAP website[1] and note all the information that is required on the different aspects of assessment. In what ways does this differ from the assessment you have analysed? Do you have any thoughts on these differences?

3. Now consider the situation described in the report you read in (1) above. With the benefit of the information that you have available and the issues discussed in this chapter write down how you would approach this assessment if you were expected to use the kind of pro forma illustrated on the website. The things to think about are both practical and procedural such as: Where will the assessment take place? How long will you allow for it? How would you prepare yourself? How would you introduce the assessment to the service user(s)? How would you ensure that the service user(s)' opinions were given? How would you assess risk? How would you ensure that the information was accurate? How would you ensure that you did no harm?

Note

1 If you are in an agency that has a particular set of pro formas you might want to think specifically about using these in this part of the exercise.

Further reading

Milner, Judith and O'Byrne, Patrick (2002) *Assessment in Social Work*. Basingstoke: Palgrave. This is one of the most comprehensive accounts of assessments in social work, looking at assessment processes in association with different methods of intervention.

Chapter 8, 'Constructive assessment'. In Parton, Nigel and O'Byrne, Patrick (2000) *Constructive Social Work: towards a new practice*. Basingstoke: Palgrave. This chapter deals in detail with the theory behind constructive assessment and how this influences the content of assessment.

http://www.ecare-scotland.gov.uk/partnerships/carenap/carenap_ home.htm This is the part of the Scottish e-care website that is devoted specifically to the development and use of online assessment schedules for single shared assessment for adults.

3 | Social work processes: advocacy, negotiation and partnership

Introduction

Over time social work has changed either in response to policy developments or as a result of practitioners and academics critically reflecting on the role and purpose of social work. The impact of the changes has been to either introduce new methods of intervention, or cause practitioners to work differently within particular methods of intervention. This chapter discusses an important set of changes that have occurred, which reflect the way the value base has impacted on the process of social work. In focusing on advocacy, negotiation and partnership it will outline how social workers have redefined the relationship with those who are the users of social work services.

This redefinition has occurred over time and is the result of a number of different influences. In 1970 Mayer and Timms first drew attention to the need to listen to the views of those who were receiving services. In the 1990s changes brought about by the National Health Services and Community Act were organisational, practical and ethical. *Caring for People* (DoH, 1989a) used the language of choice and user involvement, much of which was to operate at either the level of the individual, or as a mechanistic bureaucratic process within community care planning. Community care requires social workers acting as care managers to negotiate with agencies, organisations and individual users and carers to ensure that individual needs are identified and appropriate services made available, but also to ensure that individuals are treated with respect and are empowered within the processes.

Developments in community care occurred at the same time as the rise of the user movement and the formation of citizens' rights groups. Minimal changes brought about by community care policies involved groups of users in more active consultation and encouraging them to make demands for services. A more fundamental change to user-led and user-controlled services developed not as an outcome of the market approach to social work, but because of a shift in values. The development of a rights-based approach to social work and the recognition of service users as citizens in their own right have been influenced more by debates about social inclusion than by the rhetoric of community care (Braye and Preston-Shoot, 1995). The Disability Rights movement in particular not only challenged social workers' attitudes to those who require services, it also challenged the principles of who provides services. The implications of this are far-reaching, going beyond interventions in individual situations. Advocacy, negotiation and partnership are processes associated with empowerment. This reflects a shift in thinking in social work from an approach that reacts only in terms of providing for service users, to one that recognises that service users can themselves be service providers.

This chapter therefore considers the processes that have developed as social work has responded to these changes. It begins with a discussion of a systems approach as the underpinning theory for social work interventions. This leads to a consideration of the different skills required to meet both the policy requirements and the different perspective that a systems approach brings. These skills include advocacy and negotiation on behalf on service users, underpinned by notions of empowerment Other applications of negotiation skills are in commissioning services from other agencies to meet the identified needs of service users. These agencies can include those that are provided by organisations run by those who in the past would have been identified as 'clients'.

Systems theory

From the outset social work has been required to consider individuals in their environment (Hollis, 1964), but this has been interpreted in different ways. Often what was required was no more than being aware of the immediate economic and social situation in which people are situated, and how this impacts on their problems or the way that they perceive themselves and their problems. Systems theory however encourages workers to focus attention on different aspects of the environment. The notion of systems is basic to a number of social work interventions. In

Chapter 9 systems theory is used in work with families, where what is happening to one member in, for example, employment or school can have an impact on the whole family, and members adjust to cope with it. In community development (discussed in Chapter 11), systems theory can be used to help work with people, groups and organisations. In community care, packages of care are constructed on an individualised basis but require consideration of the involvement of family and friends as potential carers, the capacity of local volunteer groups to provide support services, and the lobby groups that advocate and negotiate for a range of approaches. These are all part of the user's network or system.

The core of systems theory comes from biology and engineering, where the body, engines and so on are seen to be either open systems – that is, influenced by factors outside themselves – or closed systems – that is, totally self-contained and impervious. Social work's adoption of systems theory has come through sociology, and is based on an understanding that social systems are open systems (Goldstein, 1973; Specht and Vickery, 1977). The significance of this is that:

- all parts of the system are connected, and what happens in one part of the system will have an effect on all other parts of the system
- the system needs to keep in a steady state (homeostasis) and will always adjust itself or adapt to try to maintain that steady state
- there is a feedback loop within the system, which provides the capacity for change.

Among the first to apply systems theory to social work were Pincus and Minahan (1973), but their approach has been developed by Goldstein (1973) and, in the UK, Specht and Vickery (1977) have written about an integrated approach. All of these writers recognise that if the analysis of social systems as open systems is accurate, then it is possible to reframe the way social workers approach their work. The focus does not have to be on bringing about change in the individual; other parts of the individual's social system can be the target for change. But the analysis is wider than this. Pincus and Minahan identified four systems within social work:

- *Change agent system* – includes social workers, their agency and the policies they work with.

- *Client system* – involves individuals and their networks including family, community and other groups with whom the change agent system might work.
- *Target system* – the part of the system with which the change agent system is working for change.
- *Action system* – people with whom the change agent system works to achieve its aims.

It is possible for the change agent system, the target system and the action system to be the same. In this way, it is not necessarily the individual who is seen as 'the problem'; it might be the way the individual interacts with different parts of his/her system, or the way that the individual is influenced by the social, or other, system. A systems approach therefore allows for an analysis that encourages workers to be more innovative in the way that they approach situations. An example from social work in community care illustrates how the focus on the person and his/her situation, as opposed to just the person, can help reframe the problem and utilise strengths and resources.

Case example

Mrs Clark is 70 years old. She has a long-term chronic condition, arthritis, but has also recently suffered a stroke which has affected her mobility even further. She lives in a council house where the bathroom is upstairs. Even though she has an active network of family and friends who provide meals and company and ensure that she is helped in and out of bed, her increasing inability to climb the stairs means that she is at risk of going into residential accommodation. She is resistant to this and is showing signs of depression – not eating and not wanting to engage with anyone.

The local social services department, in prioritising the community care budget, cannot sanction the expenditure on the work necessary to fit a downstairs toilet. The social worker tries counselling to help Mrs Clark comes to terms with residential care. However Mrs Clark's son intervenes and encourages the social worker to lobby her manager. The son also contacts their local councillor. The decision is reversed. After negotiations with the housing department the necessary alterations are made – and Mrs Clark remains in her own home and becomes much more outgoing.

This illustrates how the approach focuses on problem-solving and change. The work involves identifying the particular system, or part of a system, in relation to which the worker carries out his/her role. In this case, the focus for the work, after the son's intervention, was not on encouraging Mrs Clark to accept residential accommodation, that is, seeing her resistance as a 'problem', but on the social services department itself.

In systems theory there are phases of planned change that include problem-solving over time, and require analytic and interactional skills such as interviewing, assessment and counselling. The eight practice skills differentiated for working with systems theory are:

- assessing problems
- collecting data
- making initial contacts
- negotiating contracts
- forming action systems
- maintaining and co-ordinating action systems
- exercising influence
- terminating the change effort.

This approach, and the opportunities it gives for different approaches to assessment and intervention, do not preclude individual work; in some situations it may be that the assessment is that the individual needs some sort of support or counselling. Some have criticised the systems approach as continuing to have a narrow focus on the individual's experience of social problems, and ignoring structural causes of disadvantage. However this does not have to be so. Jack and Jack (2000) describe the application of systems in what they call ecological social work. Here consideration of macro-systems such as the cultural, political, legal and religious contexts can help understand how structural discrimination (such as ageism and racism) can impact on individuals, the problems they experience and their perception of these problems. This highlights how systems theory can ensure that an individualised approach is not the only form of intervention considered.

In community care, as the case example above shows, systems theory helps to identify different points within the care system that need to be targeted. For this to be effective, a variety of organisations and agencies need to be engaged to ensure there are a range of resources for care. This is achieved by commissioning services.

Commissioning services

Commissioning activities in community care involve ensuring that services are available so that identified needs can be met. Service commissioning is undertaken by social workers in statutory agencies from among voluntary and independent sector facilities. It requires that information is collected from individuals and collated it into sets that will identify population or area needs. Just as importantly it requires liaison skills to work with the other agencies and workers.

Service commissioning therefore involves an ability to assess and understand organisations, not only our own but also those with which we interact. Effective care management concerns the matching of choices with resources. This means that no assumptions can be made about what a person wants, but requires trying to ensure that, recognising resource constraint, needs can be met in a flexible way. For example older people may decide to live in residential homes as a positive solution to loneliness, increasing frailty or a desire for fulfilment through the use of recreational facilities. So, if such a plan is part of a designed 'package', then how does a worker go about ensuring quality care is provided? The Social Services Inspectorate teams in their report *Homes are for Living In* (DoH, 1989b) and later guidance from them and the Department of Health (1990) provide useful indicators. Residential and day-care centres for other client groups equally may have the following criteria applied when assessing for quality assurance purposes. The main features to look for are:

- *Choice* – the opportunity to select independently from a range of options; sensitivity to ethnic and religious dimensions; the environment, such as choice of furnishings, adaptations, and so on.
- *Rights* – for instance in relation to care practices such as handling one's own affairs, confidentiality, respect, consultation.
- *Independence* – including a willingness to accept a degree of calculated risk, such as being able to make meals for oneself and others.

- *Privacy* – recognising the need to be alone, to 'own' a bedroom, to have an opportunity to discuss problems in private.
- *Dignity* – which recognises one's intrinsic value and uniqueness; for example mode of address, access to bathing, sensitivity of admission procedures (see Neill, 1989).
- *Fulfilment* – whereby all aspects of daily life help in realising personal aspirations and abilities.

Each of the above sets yardsticks for measuring tangible and intangible elements in a particular form of service delivery. In the twenty-first century this approach has been supplemented by more interactive and empowering ways of involving service users in identifying and achieving quality. This includes expanding the forms of care, and the variety of services that might be available. So, for example, the website of the Care Commission in Scotland is set up as a requirement of the Regulation of Care (Scotland) Act (2001) and associated legislation which states that the Care Commission has to keep and update a list of registered care services on the Internet.

Within the context of quality assurance and regulation, social workers operating as care managers need to be aware of the processes for commissioning services, but also have the criteria in mind when working with users and carers to set up a package of care. In preparing for a stay in residential accommodation for example, users and carers need to have their expectations regarding personal care, mealtimes, diet, sleeping arrangements, smoking and use of alcohol norms, medical support, night staff support, gender of staff carrying out intimate care, frequency of bedroom cleaning, laundering facilities, and so on, clearly written down and agreed. Any quality-assured home will ensure that the individual's service expectations and plan are regularly monitored and reviewed, perhaps by a designated practitioner, who ensures that all the other care staff implement these processes with clients and relatives. Such expectations should also operate in other forms of care and support that are provided, whoever provides the service. Whether it is day care or services provided for the individual in his/her home, the benchmarks should be – do they reflect the variety and complexity of the needs of the service user? In terms of social work processes achieving this requires skills in communication and negotiation with both service users and workers, at a variety of levels, in different agencies.

Negotiating

Negotiation is a core skill used by care managers when constructing packages of care on behalf of user and carers. Appropriate levels of service from, for example, individual volunteers or independent care agencies have to be agreed, to ensure the quality of care described above. This process raises questions about whether care management can be truly empowering, because users and carers are not necessarily directly involved in the process, and can only comment on services provided or advocate for changes, if they are not appropriate. True empowerment, which might involve giving users and carers the means to negotiate their own services, is discussed later in this chapter.

Commissioning services for care management or negotiating packages of care are not the only situations in which social workers are working with parts of the system other than that traditionally called the 'client ' system. Social workers spend about one-third of their time in face-to-face client work; the rest is spent in intra-organisational and inter-organisational communications. A great deal of this effort is connected to mobilising resources. What was once identified as the 'hidden face' (Bar-On, 1990) of social work is now a core function within care management, with the expectation that services will be provided from many sources: family, friends, neighbours, volunteers from the community, voluntary and private sector organisations, as well as the statutory sector. However it is also relevant in work with children and families, and is central to the work of criminal justice social work services (formerly the probation service), where negotiations with different parts of the criminal justice system constitute a great deal of indirect activity (Orme, 1995).

The practice skills required for indirect activities include negotiation, bargaining, resolving conflicts, mediation, liaison, planning, advocacy, consultation, setting up new projects and co-ordinating resource provision. The purpose of negotiation is to influence in order to get a just outcome; thereby, negotiation can be both competitive and collaborative (Payne, 1986). Where the social worker has to fight to secure justice or combat the abuse of power, perhaps by a higher authority, then competitive tactics are in order. Where parties are negotiating towards agreement rather than to gain advantage, then collaborative elements are to the fore. In both instances, however, it is important to not lose one's temper but use anger constructively, and to not stray from the point but keep in focus each part of the bargaining process.

Much practice is about negotiation with different parts of a wider system. This might involve:

- stimulating voluntary sector community care services
- welfare rights work
- negotiating accommodation or family care for looked-after children
- persuading schools to cope with disruptive pupils
- constructing appropriate community sentences for offenders
- inducing policy-makers to fund new projects or helping to resolve staff disputes in day and residential centres.

Many of the communication skills identified in the next chapter can contribute to becoming a skilled negotiator. Publications in management and elsewhere address this subject: they ordinarily suggest the following ideas.

Negotiating for agreement relies on:

- good preparation, that is, knowing what you want to achieve, having the facts, and planning priorities
- creating a cooperative climate
- agreeing the purpose and procedures for any contact
- exploring via brief opening statements your understanding of the situation, your aims, priorities and contribution so that there is seen to be joint advantage
- listening, clarifying and summarising what the other party's opening statement seems to say
- generating creative, interdependent suggestions and then deciding which of these are realistic possibilities
- agreeing on the action necessary to achieve mutual interest.

Negotiating to get justice may involve having to fight for resources, getting the best deal for one's clients by:

- preparation as before, but being more specific about what one is bidding for and not being prepared to be exploited by power games such as giving to get something, appeals to higher authority, being deflected by numerous questions or dominated by angry outbursts or red herrings

- creating a climate of goodwill
- exploring in a probing way what is important to the other
- reaching agreements on a broad front before tackling the detail of what you are asking for
- being prepared to make compromises if this does not involve loss of integrity and equity
- remaining task-focused rather than attacking someone's personality.

Case example

This situation could be referred to agencies for many different reasons, but in fact Paula (a single parent) was referred anonymously by her neighbours, who complained that her two children were at risk, being brought up in a house that was used by drug addicts, 'dossers' and other 'down-and-outs'. Before the social worker could visit, the police became involved and insisted that the children be taken from their mother. When seen in her home, Paula did have others staying with her. They exploited her limited intelligence, refusing to move out until forced to do so by the police. In the meantime her home had been wrecked, and savage dogs had ripped up most of her furniture and other belongings. The crisis was so severe that, coupled with her lack of social skills, Paula was quite unable to discuss her situation with the social worker, despite the latter using various communication approaches to help her tell her story.

The social worker used all her powers of persuasion to make the two police officers who were at the house let her help Paula without resorting to the need to receive the children into care. She asked for their help to deal with the dogs, and later to take some of Paula's belongings to a homeless families' unit, where Paula and her children were to stay until the social worker could negotiate alternative housing with the housing department. The police and the housing department were identified as part of Paula's system where social work intervention was necessary, rather than focusing only on Paula as the source of the problem and the part of the system that had to change.

This goal of rehousing demanded the most careful preparation, especially as Paula lived in the district's worst quarter, where the poorest tenants were housed until they 'proved' to the housing department that they were 'fit enough people' to be transferred into less temporary property. Knowing it was politic, the social worker did not make the mistake of attacking council policy or of challenging the attitudes of housing personnel. She presented a clear, well thought-through plan for preventing Paula and her children needing to be kept in the homeless unit. The offer of another house, though not much of an improvement on the former, was a start from which longer-term work with Paula could begin.

The social worker had to negotiate with her own department and other agencies, as part of Paula's system was concerned at her capacity for 'good enough' parenting. Again, influencing and negotiating with integrity, listening to other points of view and not resorting to pushing people to see her point of view, together with a business-like and confident attitude, helped.

Advocacy

In the case of Paula, the social worker could be said to act as an advocate as well as a negotiator in that she was operating on Paula's behalf. However, it is apparent that in making decisions and taking risks, the social worker had views about what was in Paula's best interests, and also had to take the needs of the children into consideration. In the case of Mrs Clark above, the social worker responded to pressure from Mrs Clark's son, even though it meant challenging the decisions of her own managers. If there had been no response from the worker, Mrs Clark's son might have felt it necessary to act as advocate with the social services department and the housing department. However it should not automatically be assumed that relatives and/or friends could or should act as an advocate. Often people come to the attention of statutory services because they are without friends or relations, or are currently not in contact with them. Where a relative or friend is available he or she might not always be independent; he/she may be involved in the caring and support in some way, and therefore might have a vested interest in the outcomes of decisions.

Over the last decade advocacy has been used in more radical ways. Policy changes in both childcare and community care did not introduce advocacy, they have made the need for advocacy that much more important. Children's rights enshrined in legislation have led to the development of organisations that will advocate for children in negotiations with families and/or voluntary statutory agencies. The office of Children's Commissioner in Scotland and Wales is designed to not only to generate widespread awareness and understanding of the rights of children and young people, but also to consider and review the adequacy and effectiveness of any law, policy and practice as it relates to the rights of children and young people. In community care, working with users who are unable to express their views, for example, those with severe learning difficulties or dementia, requires advocacy skills that are sensitive to individual needs. Groups who have previously been disadvantaged in service delivery because they have not been consulted may feel reluctant to express their views, distrusting any invitation to do so. Users who are black, or from ethnic minority backgrounds, may feel that they have consistently been ignored, and see little point in participating, or feel deskilled. Kemshall and Littlechild have brought together a number of accounts of research that has deliberately prioritised what they call 'previously hidden and marginalised accounts' from users (2000, p. 235). In the context of evidence-based practice, research that involves users, or is user led, can be seen as a form of advocacy.

Types of advocacy

Advocacy is associated with a rights-based approach to meeting need and a more radical approach to social work (Braye and Preston-Shoot, 1995). Advocacy, especially self-advocacy, is user-led and arises directly out of recognition that services have traditionally disempowered users (Mullender and Ward, 1991). More positively it depends upon understandings of citizenship that recognise the rights of all to participate in definitions of need and decisions about how those needs may be met. This does not assume that all needs will be met, but it assumes that the processes of decision-making will be transparent and informed by the views of those who have the experience operating as active agents within the system (Doyal and Gough, 1991).

The most well-established form of advocacy is legal representation, where expertise, knowledge and experience combine to ensure that arguments are put in such a way as to ensure that the individual is presented appropriately to the particular system, be it court, tribunal or organisation. Other forms of advocacy have included the notion of befriending (this involves being with someone to offer support, rather than act on his/her behalf) and representation. Also, although advocacy is now seen as a central principle of care management, it is not confined to this area of social work. In the field of childcare the notion of advocacy is complicated because the representative, legal or otherwise, may be acting for one party, either parent or child, against the other, or against the social worker. Nevertheless, the emphasis on partnership in the 1989 Children Act reflects the need for all in social work practice to address the principles of advocacy. Examples of early projects on effective advocacy on the basis of partnership with children include the Dolphin Project (Buchanan, 1994). Partnership has been developed by organisations such as Barnado's and Who Cares? Scotland, which have pioneered rights-based approaches to working with children. They have provided advocacy but more importantly, have enabled children to become advocates in their own right.

In community care, the Case Management Project (CMP) was set up by the King's Fund as a special independent project along North American lines, where the case manager was seen as the advocate. This meant case managers did not merely 'broker', that is, connect people to services that addressed their needs, they negotiated and fought for services (Dant and Gearing, 1993). However, in the arrangements for community care there is a clear distinction between advocacy and care management. The social worker as care manager may intervene on behalf of the user in negotiations about the services to be provided, but also has other issues to consider. The worker may well have to make judgements about what the service user wants and what he/she as a professional thinks might be in the user's best interests, paying attention to issues of risk. An independent advocate can be involved in any part of this process. The independent advocate can accompany the user at the point of assessment, make representation when the package of care is being developed, intervene with, and on behalf of, the user with service providers to insure quality care, and can initiate reviews or attend those called by others in the process. At whatever point of the process an advocate is involved, his/her sole purpose is to represent what the user (or carer) wants, and he/she does not deviate from that.

For certain user groups, for example those with mental health problems, their situation might require intense periods of advocacy combined with an assurance that the service is available at short notice. There will be times, of course, when they are able to act as self-advocates. Older people and people with disabilities may have more sporadic contact with independent advocacy services, and may be more ready to advocate on their own behalf. However, it is important not to make assumptions about the situations in which advocacy might be effective, or the forms of advocacy that might be utilised. For example, Monach and Spriggs (1994) report that there has been a significant increase in the number of self-advocacy groups in the field of learning disabilities. This is a major advancement since the Disabled Persons Act 1986, when it was assumed that certain groups would always need someone to advocate on their behalf.

These distinctions between when, how and by whom advocacy is undertaken can be explored through understandings of citizen advocacy, self-advocacy and group advocacy.

Citizen advocacy

This works on a one-to-one basis, where volunteers act on behalf of those who require services, representing their views where needed. It is a form of lay advocacy developed in the United States to promote the rights, interests and acceptance of people with learning disabilities, but has now been extended to other groups. It specifically recognises that long-term service users were unable, or had been denied the means, to speak for themselves, and that this led to users experiencing powerlessness and devaluation. Basic to citizen advocacy is the belief that all people have value and rights, and its objective is to empower those who have been kept powerless and/or excluded (Monach and Spriggs, 1994). Its function therefore is to include the excluded, empower people, and enable them to obtain the rights of citizenship – as far as is possible.

The main component is partnership between an individual who has a disability (partner) and another who has not, but who is independent and unpaid (citizen advocate). The one-to-one relationship is important, as is the understanding that the person with the disability has been devalued, but it means that the citizen advocate works on an individualist level in terms of both the advocacy relationship, and the relationship of the user/carer to the service delivery organisations. The citizen advocate primarily performs an *instrumental role* which can focus on, for example, solving welfare benefits problems, or negotiating the care plan. There is also an *expressive role* to be fulfilled that involves meeting emotional needs, befriending, sharing family and friends and providing support.

The four key characteristics of successful citizen advocacy are:

- the individual advocate must be independent of any service provision used by the person requiring the advocacy
- a one-to-one relationship between the advocate and partner
- the relationship is a long-term and continuous one, and
- the prime commitment and loyalty of the advocate should be to his/her partner, not the advocacy organisation or the partner's family.

(Butler and Forrest, 1990)

Self-advocacy involves training and group support to help people learn skills and gain emotional strength to advocate for themselves. This may be achieved by being assisted by a citizen advocate in the initial stages. Self-advocacy is also about personal and political needs, about being involved in a range of activities, and utilising skills that ensure participation. The self-advocacy movement is associated with a reformist approach focusing on participation in all areas of service planning and delivery, as well as responding to the needs of individuals at any one time. The aim therefore is not just to improve services but also to improve the status of service users.

Self-advocacy has the important function of facilitating collective action, as well as making it easier for individuals to be assertive. There are criticisms of professionals who might display 'benign paternalism' towards users and carers. It is apparent that, if self-advocacy is to be effective, professionals need to be prepared to recognise the advocates. Just as importantly they need to make changes in their practice necessary to ensure not only that advocates have a voice, but also that they have access to the necessary information and training to make that voice effective. The barriers to such changes in professionals have been associated with professional fears: professional mistrust; fear of change; organisational constraints and legislative ambiguity (Braye and Preston-Shoot, 1995).

Group advocacy brings together people with similar interests, so that they operate as a group to represent their shared interests.

Groups can include users, carers and professionals, and advocacy is usually at the level of collective or organisation, rather than at the individual level. However, the aim is to be involved in service delivery decisions, to reframe how certain problems or groups of users are perceived, and to ensure that users and carers are involved in the decision-making shared with other forms of advocacy. Group advocacy may well be subsumed under the umbrella of campaigning organisations operating in the voluntary sector. There is growing concern that the policy initiatives to involve voluntary sector organisations in service provision may well have the effect of depoliticising them and reducing their advocacy role. As they become dependent upon contracts for service provision in order to survive, they have to be less adversarial or critical of commissioning agencies. Also, as service providers they themselves become the focus or target for advocacy. However, as we note below, there are some important advocacy projects emerging at the level of citizen and group advocacy that also involve training and supporting individuals to become advocates.

Support for advocacy

While in practice there may be limitations to all forms of advocacy, common to all are the processes and practices that have to be utilised to ensure that users at least have the opportunity to make their voices heard. Whoever acts as advocate, the necessary skills are in line with the general principles of working in partnership (Dalrymple and Burke, 1995) and include:

- retaining the flexibility to adapt the process to the wishes of the individual involved
- ensuring the user feels in control of the process and trusts the advocate only to take action that has been agreed
- empowering the individual
- supporting people to speak for themselves
- ensuring that people are able to make informed and free choices, and
- advising, assisting and supporting; not pressurising or persuading.

Organisations for advocacy have emerged over time. At a national level, disability rights groups became visible in the late 1980s, and organisations were formed in the area of mental health, such as

Survivors Speak Out, in 1986. Since the introduction of community care many local independent advocacy schemes have been developed. For example, an independent advocacy service for users of mental health services in Hampshire was set up in 1992 on the impending closure of a local mental health hospital. The project, although funded by the Department of Health and the local social services department, aimed to provide information and advice on a short-term basis on issues such as housing, tribunals, benefits, treatment and medication, access to, and quality of, social and community services. The service reflected the basic principle of the 1983 Mental Health Act that users should be treated, or cared for, in a way that promotes as far as possible their self-determination and personal responsibility, consistent with their needs and wishes. This is summed up in the acronym:

Acting on behalf of oneself or another person

Duty of independence and loyalty to Advocacy Partner

Voicing the needs, concerns, and views of the Advocacy Partner

Open to everyone

Challenging oppressive and discriminatory behaviour

Advising on rights and how to enforce them

Commitment to equality of opportunity

You can be an advocate.

(Fareham & Gosport Advocacy Project Information Leaflet, 1994)

Discussions about who provides an advocacy service make a distinction between the focus and function of advocacy. For Rees (1991), *cause* advocacy involves arguing for reform of the system, and *case* advocacy involves advocating on behalf of an individual for resources and/or services. It has been argued that it is cause advocacy that is difficult for care managers who are employed by the systems that they are expected to change. As we have seen, systems theory offers a role for social workers as change agents and illustrates the potential for identifying employing agencies as the target for change, but it is still done on behalf of individual cases. Independent advocacy services, often acting on behalf of user groups, are more likely to advocate for causes, such as resistance to closure, withdrawal of services or changes in the procedures for user involvement. These services are increasingly staffed by people who are, or have been, users of community care services,

In addition to being equipped with skills for acting as advocates themselves, social workers are increasingly expected to work in ways that put users in touch with independent advocates and to be able to work with those who are advocating on behalf of users and carers. Skills involved include:

● ensuring all involved have access to necessary information
● being available to meet with the advocate
● giving advocates a role in relation to the decision-making
● acknowledging that different user/advocate relationships will have different balances of involvement liaison and consultation, but recognise confidentiality, and respect the user.

Professionals can support advocacy projects, making skills available and accessing resources and information, but some argue that is impossible for professionals to avoid playing the dominant role and take over the services, or at least limit their power and direction (Chamberlin, 1988). Much of this assumes that the advocate will be someone other than the user and carer. The response of professionals to individual users who are advocating on their own behalf requires a shift of emphasis in the relationship, recognising the power imbalances that have traditionally existed within social work practice. The real test of effectiveness is the extent to which advocacy movements can challenge the power of professionals, not only in terms of service delivery but also in the conceptualisation of the disability, or the particular problem or user group (Monach and Spriggs, 1994). Often, the furthest that agencies will go is some tokenistic procedure for involving a 'representative' of users and carers.

User participation

The basis of advocacy is that the voices of service users are heard at both the level of individual interventions and in policy development within agencies. These developments are often referred to as user involvement or user participation. As was outlined at the beginning of the chapter a number of factors have contributed to increases in user participation. Some of these are positive, such as:

- user/self advocacy mandate
- professional mandates
- legal/policy mandates
  (Braye and Preston-Shoot, 1995)

Others are less positive, such as those that have emerged from a critique of services as centralised ossified bureaucracies that have sought to regulate users rather than empower them. However these aspects of services have to be challenged if they are to respond to the radical agenda for user involvement/participation. As Nina Biehal argues (1993), the fact that an agency has a value base that espouses user involvement will not guarantee that users will be involved in decision-making:

> Such 'mission statements' will be little more than window dressing unless accompanied by specific strategies to ensure that service users participate in decision-making.
> (Biehal, 1993, p. 445)

This means that ways have to be found not just of giving users a voice in processes defined by policy and legislation, but of engaging with organisations and social movements that are organised and managed by people who might otherwise be defined as 'users' of services. This depends on different interpretations of involvement and participation.

Consultation

The National Health Service and Community Care Act 1990 (NHS and CC Act) requires social services departments to consult with users in the care planning process. It has also been argued that the only effective and efficient way of commissioning services is by identifying what users and carers need (Orme and Glastonbury, 1993). However, most systems set up by agencies are at best consultation, and at worst public relations. Users and carers are told what is available, and asked to give their opinions. As such the mechanisms are patronising, being led totally by the needs of the service providers (Croft and Beresford, 1990; Orme, 1996). Also, the rhetoric of consumerism that arises directly out of a market approach to welfare provision assumes users and carers ('consumers'), on the basis of information given, will make choices about services. There are however factors that influence and restrict the choices that are available to users and carers of services, and structures and processes that deny some people choice (Braye and Preston-Shoot, 1995). While the principles of user consultation and participation cannot be disputed, the practices need to be carefully considered to ensure that they are truly empowering. The notion of consumerism is therefore an empty rhetoric that affords only restricted user participation and therefore limited empowerment.

For example, a requirement of care management in community care is that users have to be involved at all levels. To ensure that services are relevant and appropriate, local authority social service departments are required to consult users and carers in the community care planning process, and the assessment of each individual for a care plan adds to the sum total of information about community and group needs. Such imperatives are also present in other policy initiatives, for example the requirement for partnership in working with children.

This is not to say that consultation is totally bad and should not be used. However workers and users have to be clear about the limitations of such methods, and should not claim that they constitute full user participation. That said, there are methods that can be used to access a greater number of users and pre-users. These include postal and telephone surveys for those who are housebound, accessing people via GPs, housing departments or benefit payments, or having a link worker to work with community groups which include those other than current users of services. For example, in a research project trying to determine how users and pre-users of services for older people wanted to be consulted, one research team visited luncheon clubs and adult education classes (Avison et al., 1995). Some of the views expressed about the consultation process by users and pre-users in this project process included:

● Involve users in the issues for consultation.
● Ensure all communication is jargon free.
● Access a truly representative sample of users.
● Be clear to users how their views will be put into effect.

All of these are at one level very simple, but depending in the context and culture of organisations it may be very difficult to adhere to them. Consultation should involve full participation in decisions about the way services are to be offered. This might include the range of services available, policies on eligibility criteria and charging for services, and policies that will impact directly upon how services are delivered. If they are consulted at this level, then users will feel fully involved. While this requires changes in organisational procedures, it also requires each individual worker to uphold the principles of empowerment, otherwise the procedures become patronising rather than participatory (Orme, 2000b).

Barriers to user involvement

There are however many barriers to such levels of involvement. The first is that statutory agencies are not practised in open decision-making with the consumers of their services, and because of this workers are not used to asking the opinions of the users. The Social Work in Partnership (SWIP) project encouraged professionals to reflect on the ways that they defined needs, made assessments and decisions *on behalf of* rather than *in partnership* with users. It collaborated with managers, social workers, home care organisers and occupational therapists in two social service departments to develop a model of practice that allows greater participation by users. (For a fuller discussion of this project see *Good Intentions: partnership in social services,* Marsh and Fisher, 1992.) The principles of the project included:

- Investigation of problems must be with the explicit consent of the potential user(s) and client(s). (A client is an involuntary user.)
- User agreement and/or a clear statutory mandate are the only bases for partnership-based intervention.
- Intervention must be based upon the views of all the relevant family members and carers.
- Services must be based on negotiated agreement rather than on assumptions and/or prejudices concerning the behaviour and wishes of users.
- Users must have the greatest possible degree of choice in the services that they are offered.
  (Stevenson and Parsloe, 1993, pp. 38, 39)

The evaluation of the SWIP project highlighted difficulties. Significantly, workers were concerned about involving users when they thought the case was 'difficult', where the needs were complex or resources limited, or where there was some element of risk. Here workers had to balance their commitment to users' rights to involvement with their own sense of responsibility to exercise care, and therefore some control, to protect vulnerable users. But it has to be remembered that the assessment as to which situations are difficult and who is vulnerable is at the discretion of workers.

That said, there are situations where the users themselves do not expect to be involved in decision-making – and indeed might not want to be. This may be influenced by views of the professionalism of both workers and users, where there is an expectation that workers should know the answers. However, there are users who have not normally been consulted or involved, despite the fact that they would wish to be.

There may also be some reluctance or resistance on behalf of workers to deviate from routine approaches because they recognise that this might be time-consuming, and they have no spare capacity to respond to the extra demands. Equally user involvement and participation require resources. At a minimum payments for users and carers' expenses to attend meetings are required, but other payments might also be necessary – it should not be assumed that service users, or those representing them, are sitting at home waiting to be consulted. Compensation for lost earnings or payment for attendance sometimes makes demands on an already stretched budget.

Arguments for user participation are invariably couched as user and carer involvement. However this suggests that users and carers are a homogenous group, and ignores the possibility that there may be conflict of interests, for example, between users and carers, between different user groups and even within user groups. Differences within user groups, based on, for example, age, gender, level of (dis)ability, race, sexuality, have to be recognised and worked with positively, not seen as problems.

Procedural involvement

It may be because of difficulties of working at an individual level to facilitate user involvement that many social services have resorted to what are commonly called procedural models of consultation, which involve:

- open days
- public meetings

- documentary consultation (responding to the plan)
- surveys
- involvement of users and carer on committees
- setting up fora.
  (Hoyes and Lart, 1992)

However these procedures have their limitations. First, they require that people are both mobile and able to utilise readily accessible forms of communication. This can immediately exclude many users of community care services. Second, they require that people are aware of the particular events or processes; they need to be on the relevant mailing list, or part of a network or circulation list that means that they receive the information about the event, or the documentation that requires comment. Third, even if these two requirements are met, users do not necessarily feel assertive enough to attend a meeting, or give their views when they do. Involvement is therefore confined to a small group of people who feel confident enough to address public meetings, or engage in debate with managers and policy-makers. Also such models of involvement occur predominantly with existing users and not with potential users; this further complicates the alienation that some groups in the community might feel. For example, if black people are not accessing services because they see them as not relevant or potentially racist, how will they be able to communicate that to the organisation in order to bring about change?

Engagement

Practice guidance and research literature have explored the implications for user participation and have identified a continuum that includes:

- involvement in needs-led assessments
- consultation about care plans (for example, care planning approach in mental health, family group conferences in child and family work)
- involvement in care provision
- direct payments (Community Care (Direct Payments) Act 1996)
- advocacy
- commissioning services from user-led organisations
- user involvement in policy and planning.

These different approaches indicate that user participation operates at a number of levels:

- *individual* – how individuals are involved in having their needs met (for example assessments, contract work)
- *organisational* – agencies set up systems for groups of users (for example consultation forum, questionnaires)
- *groups* – how user groups influence policy; provide their own organisations.

At an individual level, strategies for involving users include:

- encouraging users to describe their own needs through the construction of jointly constructed problems, goals and tasks
- sharing the assessment with the user (including the written assessment) and explaining why particular services are being offered, giving users the right to refuse what is being offered
- ensuring that users have sufficient information both about the decisions made, and the services available.

This individual approach is associated with person-centred planning (PCP), which is discussed in Chapter 10. At the group level, empowering practice reflects the value base of social work, but also demands a more radical approach that includes notions of participation, citizenship and empowerment (Braye and Preston-Shoot, 1995). It is when the concept of citizenship is understood and applied that truly radical models of user involvement and participation are developed. These recognise the collective action of people who are usually defined by social care categories (Beresford, 2000), and require that social workers engage with, and commission services from, user-led and user-controlled organisations. While this is a position to be supported it is not always straightforward, as a number of research projects have demonstrated (see Kemshall and Littlechild, 2000).

The Joseph Rowntree Foundation, which has a commitment to user and carer involvement, has funded a number of projects on, and evaluations of, user involvement. One study on *Increasing User Involvement in Voluntary Organisations* provides an overview of arrangements for user involvement. Its findings include the following:

- Interpretations of user involvement could include almost any kind of engagement with the organisation.

- The study distinguished between 'management-centred user involvement' and 'user-centred user involvement'. Users really only value the latter.
- There was no single template for involvement.
- There were some common enablers of, and barriers to, change. The long and often slow process of change was usually driven by the persistent actions of leaders, both users and managers, to optimise the enablers of change and to overcome the barriers to change.
- Key enablers were a consistent commitment to user-centred user involvement, translated into practical change at many levels, and supportive leaders. People in leadership roles who were influential within existing power structures and who operated with a facilitative leadership style opened up opportunities for users to have influence themselves.
- The sustainability of progress was often fragile because it was dependent upon variables such as organisational and individual commitment, leadership style, key individuals and availability of resources.
- Much of what worked was about building strong relationships between those in decision-making roles and those seeking to have more influence.

(Robson *et al.*, 2003)

Empowerment

In the above discussions about user involvement, the notion of empowerment was mentioned repeatedly. While this concept is frequently invoked in social work practice, it is one that is extremely complex. As a conclusion to this chapter it is important to consider different understandings of empowerment. This is relevant not only to the processes of advocacy and user involvement, but to all the methods of intervention discussed in the second part of the book.

In the discussion of advocacy it was suggested that the purpose of advocacy was to give users a voice. Means and Smith (1994) discuss 'voice' as a model of user empowerment. 'Voice' involves case advocacy on behalf of those who want to remain, or have no choice about remaining, with existing providers of community care services. Those who exercise other choices, for example to leave the services, are said to be exercising their right to 'exit' services. Both 'voice' and 'exit' are approaches to user empowerment, with voice mechanisms being particularly important for potential users who need to influence services right from the outset, before becoming part of them, for example to ensure that they get access to a full assessment.

Exit mechanisms are relevant to those already in the system. To express dissatisfaction by leaving, you have to be in receipt of the service. You also have to have the means to exit. This is why for some economic power, having the capacity to control how care is provided, and by whom, is the ultimate power. The introduction of direct payment schemes provides for certain groups the financial means to arrange their own services, and, just as importantly, the power to influence the range of services available. This affords the status of active citizen through having choices about involvement, not just that of a passive consumer who chooses from a limited range of available services. However, for a variety of reasons purchasing power is not available to all users of community care services, nor is it attractive to all user groups. The demands of having to organise and negotiate the provision of care can be time-consuming and exhausting, and hence disempowering. Perhaps unsurprisingly some social workers also have difficulties with direct payments. (See Clark and Spafford, 2002 for an account of care managers' reactions to direct payments.)

For some groups (for example those who are users of mental health services against their will) exit is not an option, but they have a right to be heard, to have a voice. A clear example of this is the patients' equal opportunities committee at one of the most secure mental hospitals in England, Broadmoor. Here, women in particular were able to question policies and procedures that they experienced as oppressive. Similarly, coalitions of people with disabilities have exercised their 'voice' to great effect to ensure new legislation acknowledged their rights to services and to an enabling environment, rather than treating them according to medical criteria. Even though the Disability Discrimination Act 1995 was not as radical as was hoped, it did change the emphasis from medical models of disability to social models. Such activities can be clearly seen as cause advocacy, but are also clear examples of user empowerment.

Another means of empowering users is thought to be by conferring rights, an approach that has been at the centre of the campaign of the disability movement, and is often linked to discussions about citizenship. For some writers, citizenship as participation is clearly linked to empowerment. Coote suggests that citizenship 'entails being able to participate in society, to enjoy its fruits and fulfil one's own potential, and it follows that each individual citizen should be equally able (or "empowered") to do so' (1992, p. 4). Mullender and Ward (1991), in describing empowering groupwork, see social justice as paramount in ensuring that:

- all people have skills, understanding and ability
- people have rights to be heard, to participate, to choose, to define problems and action
- people's problems are complex and social oppression is a contributory factor
- people acting collectively are powerful
- methods of work must be non-elitist and non-oppressive.

An important statement about worker responsibility for empowerment in community care is the Joseph Rowntree Study *Community Care and Empowerment* undertaken by Olive Stevenson and Phyllida Parsloe. Here the term empowerment is used for both a process and a goal:

> Step by step the worker acts to empower the user; the user becomes more powerful. Both work together in a continuous process, the goal of which is to shift the balance of power. (Stevenson and Parsloe, 1993, p. 6)

In the discussion of a strengths model based on a project for users of mental health services, they identify that:

- The focus of the helping process is upon consumers' strengths, interests and abilities; not upon their weaknesses, deficit or pathologies.
- People with mental illness can learn, grow and change.
- The consumer is viewed as the director of the helping process.
- The consumer–care manager relationship becomes the indispensable foundation for mutual collaboration.
- Assertive outreach is the preferred mode of working with consumers.
- The community is viewed as an oasis of potential resources for consumers, rather than the obstacle. Naturally occurring

resources are considered a possibility before community or hospital mental health services.

Such frameworks provide excellent guides to the way that we must approach practice at the level of individual interventions. They seek to ensure that users and carers are viewed as partners, whether we are assessing someone for a package of care, or providing a service in a care plan that has been devised.

Theories of empowerment

However while these prescriptions for, and descriptions of, practice seem straightforward it is important to recognise that notions of empowerment are complex and contradictory. It is significant that the social work literature on empowerment (see Adams, 1996; Braye and Preston-Shoot, 1995) resists giving simplistic definitions of empowerment but concentrates on the processes. But even these processes can be paradoxical. Adams (1996, pp. 12–15) helpfully summarises some of the risks associated with empowering practice or practising empowerment. Some useful observations include:

- The practice of empowering should not involve doing people's empowering for them.
- One person's empowerment might be another person's disempowerment.
- Be aware of the danger of dilution – from empowerment to enablement.
- Be aware of the danger of addressing too many target groups and addressing none adequately.
- There is an ambiguous relationship between self-help and empowerment.

The risks reflect discussions about understandings of both power and empowerment. Dominelli (2000) for example suggests that we need to recognise both the theoretical and practical complexities of understanding how power operates. She suggests that in social work it sometimes operates because workers have power *over* service users and that this is hard to relinquish. If empowerment is seen to operate at the level of the individual then power is assumed to pass from one person to another in interpersonal relations. If it is seen to operate at the structural level, empowerment involves the transfer of power across social categories. But both of these models seem to treat power as a commodity, as some concrete and finite substance that can be passed around, quantified or apportioned. Fook (2002) suggests that power is often assumed to be situated in external structures and in constructed ways of thinking, but these can be challenged. However such challenges have to recognise what she calls the 'disempowering experience of empowerment' (Fook, 2002, p. 51). For example if empowerment is about giving power to the powerless, who defines who is powerless? Often attributing labels and categories to people is potentially dehumanising and discriminating. This can be particularly so in social work, where categories for community care make assumptions about individuals and deny them their identity (Orme, 2001a). Equally disempowering is the assumption that certain groups are disadvantaged; 'In the very act of defining disadvantage in order to empower we in fact create disadvantage and disempower' (Fook, 2002, p. 51).

In order to avoid becoming locked into such processes Fook suggests that we need to practise from a critical perspective, and this requires workers to:

● analyse and reflect on situations
● redefine and reconceptualise power relations and structures through dialogue and communication
● negotiate a changed system of power relations and structures, and
● reconstruct and reconceptualise the situation in ways that are empowering for all parties.

Hence empowering practice does not mean specific ways of intervening but involves ways of thinking about all situations in which social workers are practising.

Conclusion

This chapter has illustrated that increasingly social workers have to review the way that they work with service users – both individuals and groups. Policy initiatives included lip service to consultation with users, but the user movement has been far more influential in requiring social workers to reflect on the nature of their relationships. Commissioning services, advocacy and negotiation can involve procedural ways of responding to users' demands for involvement, but only when social workers recognise that users can both receive and provide services will user involvement become effective.

The chapter has also demonstrated that notions of user involvement are underpinned by understandings of how power operates in relationships especially when social workers have responsibility to provide services, protect users and balance competing needs. However these responsibilities do not mean that social workers cannot work in partnership with those who require their services.

---

putting it into practice

This chapter has encouraged us to think about situations with which we deal from a variety of perspectives. For the purposes of these exercises we will concentrate on the situation of Mrs Clark outlined in the chapter.

1. From the perspective of Mrs Clark: think about the situation of Mrs Clark described in this chapter. Using a systems model, write down or draw a diagram to show potential parts of Mrs Clark's 'system'. These might include Mrs Clark herself, her son, other relatives, neighbours, the local social services and housing departments and so on. Obviously without more detail you will not know precisely who or what is involved, but from your knowledge of similar cases (or from the perspective of older people that you know), think of as many possible parts of the system as possible.

2. From the perspective of being a social worker: write down the processes that you would go through if having to deal with the case: for example visit Mrs Clark, talk to her son, collect information and so on to fulfil your role as care manager. When you have done so reflect on which parts of Mrs Clark's system you would be in contact with.

3. From the perspective of a worker with an independent advocacy service for older people: write down the processes that you would go through to fulfil your role as advocate for Mrs Clark. You might want to use some of the website resources to see what they say about advocacy services for older people. When you have done so, reflect on which parts of Mrs Clark's system you would be in contact with.

4. Note in what way the different accounts that you have written are similar. In what ways are they different? Do the different roles and tasks involve different parts of Mrs Clark's system?

Further reading

Leadbetter, M. (2002) Chapters on 'Advocacy' and 'Advocacy and empowerment.' In R. Adams, L. Dominelli and M. Payne (eds) *Social Work: themes, issues and critical debates*. Basingstoke: Palgrave. These are two useful chapters that explore advocacy from the perspective of services users.

The Joseph Rowntree Foundation website provides a valuable resource in its Findings from research in social care. For example at: http:www.jrf.org.uk/knowledge/findings/ social care you can find reports such as: *Older People's Perspectives: devising information, advice and advocacy services* by Ann Quinn, Angela Snowling and Pam Denicolo – a report of research into older people's knowledge and views of advocacy services. Summaries can be downloaded and full reports are available for purchase.

There is a wealth of web pages to be consulted about advocacy services available for user and carer groups: see for example: http://www.ageconcernscotland.org.uk/

4 | Social work processes: communication

Introduction

The final chapter of this part on social work processes is about communication. This is because communication underpins both the processes of social work discussed so far and the interventions that are described in the following parts. Social workers might have extensive knowledge and understanding of theories of human behaviour and of a range of possible interventions to help resolve problems, but if they are unable to communicate, to instil confidence, listen and respond appropriately, then this knowledge is worthless. The centrality of communication to good social work practice was highlighted by the Rules and Requirements for Social Work devised to identify competencies required by social workers. The first competence students had to demonstrate was that they could 'communicate and engage' (CCETSW, 1989). These rules were superseded by the new Degree in Social Work (DoH, 2003). Arguments for a qualifying degree emphasised the growing amount of theory with which beginning social work practitioners had to become familiar. Nevertheless the degree has at its core the need for social workers to be able to apply that theory in practice, and to be able to communicate effectively with service users.

In individual work most communication takes place in the form of interviews where, either in the office or in the home of the service user, the interchanges are between two people. However the principles and skills involved in conducting interviews are relevant to family work, groupwork and community work. This is because in all of these situations social workers need to facilitate people to articulate their needs and to affirm that these needs have been heard, and attended to even if they have not directly been met.

It should be noted that reference has been made to 'conducting' interviews. That is because communication in social work does not happen spontaneously. A basic definition is that interviews are 'conversations with a purpose' (Davies, 1985). Whether the purpose is gathering information for an assessment or encouraging a bereaved person to speak about her/his grief, someone has to help structure the conversation to ensure the purpose is met. This chapter begins by examining the component parts of an interview, exploring differences when interviews are held for different purposes. It goes on to identify the skills that social workers need to facilitate communication. The emphasis in the chapter is on verbal communication rather than written, and it focuses on communication between service users and workers. That is not to deny the importance of written communications or the need for effective communication between workers.

Interviewing

In both early referrals and ongoing contact, much depends on the quality of interviewing. Guidance on interviewing is timeless, as evidenced by the popularity of texts such as Garrett (1972) and Kadushin (1972), but obviously interviews have to be relevant to the current context of the service user. As has been said, social work interviews have been described as conversations with a purpose, but they are more than this. An interview is a process that involves a combination of social psychology and sociology. In this process theories and information about people in their social circumstances, their motivations and their responses in interpersonal relationships can be used to help the worker understand the individual in his/her situation, gain relevant information and offer appropriate support.

Only by carefully listening and observing the way that people seek help can there be an effective interpersonal exchange that correctly receives overt and covert messages, decodes them and responds to the various levels of communication therein. People can say one thing but their behaviour may indicate the opposite. Advanced practitioners, such as those who are expert in family therapy, are able to use the literal message, alongside what is known as the 'metamessage' (that is messages about the message), as part of their interviewing. An illustration of this might be at the crucial stage of leaving home for adolescents; here mixed messages are frequently sent by them to their parents which the bracketed phrase, 'Can I [let you let me] leave?' reveals. Even if beginners cannot use this level of communication in interviews it is worth-while at least being able to spot these kinds of underlying motivation.

This is not to say that we should not believe what people say, but to recognise that often the messages that are given are complex. One criticism of social workers has been that at times they have used this capacity to interpret messages to disempower those who come to them for assistance. Feminist and radical critiques of social work have parodied such an approach as, 'What you are really saying is ...' suggesting that the worker knows best, and will refuse to accept the message that the person is claiming but will impute other meanings. This was a particular source of concern when social work was highly dependent on a psychosocial approach (discussed in the next chapter), and messages were interpreted as having subconscious meanings. Such responses, especially at the beginning of contact, can be off-putting to those who bring prob-lems and issues to the agency. Either they will experience the messages as not being heard, or, if the issue that is being brought is the beginning of a more complex problem, the person might not be ready to share all. Early interpretative approaches may lead to resistance to what might be seen to be an invasion into their privacy. Having said that, it is vital that in early interviews the person is helped to say as much as he/she wants to about the situation he/she is bringing to the social worker. Texts about inter-viewing and research into practice give numerous examples of people making initial contacts with request for community care assessments, but not being able to share their fears or concerns about the possible impact of such an assessment.

These examples recognise that initial contacts in social work are often screening processes. These are crucial in forming the basis for decisions about whether contact will continue and whether assess-ment for further services will be undertaken, but they are also crucial in establishing a beginning relationship with the person seeking help.

Initial interviews

The first meeting between a potential service user and a worker has four major aims. The first is to gather information that will be used jointly in decision-making about the nature of the difficulties and how to intervene. Second, it also is an opportunity to try to secure a 'treatment alliance' whereby the worker conveys a wish to understand the other's thoughts and feelings. The third aim is to try to include a sense of hopefulness about being able to tackle the circumstances. Finally, it demonstrates to the applicant some of the ways in which the social worker and the service work. Unless these factors are taken into consideration subsequent intervention could prove sterile; this is especially so when there is an apparently negative response to the interviewer.

At the beginning of contact in particular there is a fine line between inquiry and inquisition. By this is meant the need is recognised to gain enough information to make an appropriate assessment, and identify whether, and to what extent, help can be offered. However this has to be done without being seen to be inappropriately inquisitive, or not prepared to accept the explanation given. Let us just consider the daughter who approaches the social services office for help with day care for her elderly parent. In order to decide whether services can be allocated the worker has to assess both the level of need and the resources that are available. However, in doing this he/she may have to ask about the employment of adults in the family, and caring and other responsibilities of all concerned. Ultimately, there will also be questions about financial circumstances. Such information gathering has to be conducted in ways which do not invoke feelings of guilt, or make the daughter feel that she is becoming a 'client' of the agency, in the worst sense of the word.

Situations that involve those who are reluctant participants, that is, offenders, or parents who may be suspected of abusing their children, bring other dilemmas. In the former, the level of motivation for compliance with supervision or a community sentence has to be assessed, while it is recognised that a driving factor may be the desire to avoid a custodial sentence. When accusations and allegations of abuse have to be investigated, or suspicions followed up, information has to be acquired. But it must be remembered that the person being investigated may be innocent, and even if he or she is not, he/she will need a continuing relationship with a social work agency in order to ensure the appropriate outcome for all involved.

In other circumstances, where individuals have come of their own accord to the agency, they are motivated by all sorts of factors.

Practitioners can get frustrated or anxious when service users do not return after one interview, feeling that somehow they have failed. In fact, research has shown that up to 50 per cent of help-seekers do not return for a second interview, and while the quality of the initial session is related to a positive response, other reasons for non-continuation are possible (Marziali, 1988). Many people are quite satisfied with the first session and decide that they do not require further assistance. Others are not ready to commit themselves to ongoing intervention, while a high proportion of people prefer to ask for help on an as-needed basis rather than have a regular series of meetings. Finally, some people are so overwhelmed by the intensity or chronic nature of their problems that they cannot use the help that is offered.

In initial interviews for community care services the worker might have to operate eligibility criteria. In these circumstances it is possible that at the end of the interview the worker has to inform the person seeking help or support that services are not available. This may be because he or she has come to the wrong agency, and needs to be referred to a benefits agency or to a health service. Or it may be because he/she does not fit the eligibility criteria, or it is thought that the problem is not acute or sufficiently chronic to warrant further assessment at this stage. In these circumstances the person has to be given clear and full information why the decision is made. This has to be done in such a way that people feel validated and not rejected. In circumstances where people are involved in caring, it is likely that the situation will deteriorate and at some point in the future another referral will be made. It is therefore necessary to ensure that the person will feel able to come back to the agency.

There are ways of conducting an initial interview (or phone call) that are more likely to establish a favourable climate for a purposeful alliance. These involve ensuring that there is congruence, that is, agreement between worker and client about expectations of what can be done, and being open and honest about what cannot be done. From the outset all parties should be aware of why they are meeting (or talking). Successful interviews do not merely depend on content (what was said) or whether the client got what was asked for. A significant outcome for the first interview is for the worker to be perceived as someone who is able to understand what the client's concerns are and how he/she feels about his/her difficulties, and to be open about both the agency and the worker's own role within it. Additionally the worker will have demonstrated some of the basic values of social work, including acceptance and a non-judgmental attitude.

Skills in interviewing

Early accounts of social work identified basic skills in interviewing that involve ten principles:

1. Letting the interviewee know how much time there is.
2. Starting where the client is in his/her understanding of the situation.
3. Trying to be sympathetic so as to help make the atmosphere a relaxed one.
4. Trying to see things through the other person's eyes.
5. Knowing the danger of passing judgement rather than acceptance.
6. Developing social skills such as smiling to help open up communication at the outset.
7. Avoiding questions that can be answered 'yes' or 'no'.
8. Not putting answers in the client's mouth.
9. Not probing too deeply too quickly.
10. Learning to cope with silences (which are usually the interviewee's best thinking times).
    (Davies, 1985)

These 'principles' are based on core social work values such as respect for persons and 'starting where the client is'. The skill required in an interview is in how that respect is communicated irrespective of the circumstances or content of the interview. However this does not mean that the interview has to be aimless: respect also requires that the person is important enough for the worker to have prepared for the interview. Preparation involves understanding what happens in interviews.

Structure

Each interview tends to have a focus, such as an exploration of someone's financial needs, illnesses, offences, relationships or whatever; at the same time every interview ought to have a structure (that is a beginning, middle and end). There is a circularity in the interviewing process if it is to make sense to the person being interviewed and provide the necessary information. The person bringing the problem or issue will set the initial agenda, but the interviewer asking more questions helps to develop themes. Appropriate questions might lead to further information and other avenues to be explored. However, at the close of the interview the interviewer should ensure that the original topic is returned to, and reviewed in the light of the information that has emerged during the interview.

The first words at the beginning of any encounter are often quite significant, for example, 'My wife thought that you could help me' suggests reluctance on the part of the person coming to the agency. Equally the last things said could reveal what attitude the person leaves with, for instance, 'I think I can cope now I've got the information' recognises that the person leaves with reassurance as well as information. The language that is used often reveals emotions as, of course, do the bodily positions and non-verbal gestures displayed during the interviews. In single interviews and in a series of interviews, references to difficulties may be returned to, or repetition or even of denial that something is worrying may give clues to helping. Inconsistencies and gaps may be spotted, for instance mentioning one parent but never the other, or concealed meanings such as the sexually abused client who fears interference (being interfered with?). Also sudden changes in conversation topics may either reveal material that is too hurtful, or the person may have associated one idea with another, so these too are worth noting.

The above list of 'triggers' or cues indicates that each interview needs to be reflected upon, reviewing aspects of the content later, if possible via a detailed record or (in certain agencies such as those using family therapies) by means of a video recording. This reflection should include an awareness of the powerful role that the interviewer plays, both in helping the person explore the issues fully in a way that he/she wants to, and in the potential to block communication.

Sometimes students are worried when they encounter people who are uncooperative and who, despite saying that they want help, seem to do all that they can to block it. Often the reason for this is that approaching a stranger for help could be an occasion for shame, high expectations, a sense of failure and an admission of dependency. The worker does not have to reveal intimate, embarrassing or frightening facts about her or himself and so there is understandable reluctance and anger on the part of the interviewee, which may, indeed, remind him/her of times past when similar interpersonal contacts proved unhelpful.

Barriers to communication

A positive outcome in interviewing relies also on trying to eliminate some of the barriers to communication that can result in misunderstandings. Apart from clients who have evident comprehension, hearing or speech disorders (which may require study into alternative methods of communicating), errors which even experienced interviewers make include anticipating what the other person is going to say or assuming that he/she has understood the meaning of the words and non-verbal cues. It is better to let the client talk freely at first if possible; this can counteract any tendency to be sure in advance what the other is saying or is about to say. When people are allowed to tell their story in their own way it is surprising how often they come up with their own solutions.

Using interpreters

Interviewing through an interpreter raises particular aspects of communication. While this might be seen as something of a specialised and advanced skill, it would be wrong not to address it in an introductory text. It is important that all students and social workers are equipped to work in a multi-cultural and diverse society, and to acquire the necessary skills. Specialist texts have been written (see, for example, A. Ahmad, 1990; Freed, 1988; Baker et al., 1991; Robinson, 1998), and many health and social care organisations have developed specific policies and guidance on using interpreters. Freed (1988) saw the interpreter as a conduit, linking interviewer and interviewee, and thus careful preparation of the interpreter for this role is necessary, emphasising confidentiality, neutrality, conveying the emotional tone of the interview and transmitting accurately what is being communicated. As in all interviews, the social worker must pay attention to the seating arrangement. More significantly, the interpreter's presence has to be accepted and assurances of confidentiality given. The pace may be slow, and it is important to review the content and process later to ensure that a proper level of understanding was reached.

In using interpreters it is important to demonstrate respect by understanding attitudes to asking for help and about social work in the person's culture or country of origin. Significantly in the case of asylum seekers the fact that a social worker is an 'agent of the state' might have particular connotations. This might have implications for who is asked to provide the interpretation. Working through children or relatives is not acceptable, as this denies the person confidentiality and constrains the information that can be given. Agencies should fulfil their obligations to offer services to non-English-speaking clients by recruiting and training interpreters to function within that role, but this is not unproblematic.

The use of interpreters means that the person giving personal information has to give it to more than one person. The trained interpreter offers objectivity in a way that using a family member or friends does not. However the interpreter may still be experienced by the person needing help as in some way judging him or her. This might be particularly so where the crisis or problem has been precipitated by cultural dilemmas. For example Muslim women may feel reluctant to speak about domestic violence to an interpreter, because of cultural expectations of the role of women within marriage. Freed's (1988) paper is concerned with the unique skills of interviewing those who do not speak English. Much of what she writes could well refer to communicating through an interpreter for service users who have hearing and sight impairment.

Other barriers to communication include the attitudes and actions of workers who are unskilled, or unprepared. For example, stereotyping can lead to sets of assumptions that block the individual and this can create defences. Assuming that because someone is black, or middle class, or an asylum seeker he or she will have certain characteristics encourages premature judgements and hasty conclusions; people are too complex, subtle and dynamic to sum up rapidly. On the one hand, being antagonistic because someone is aggressive can exacerbate situations in ways that are not helpful for the user and could ultimately lead to risks for the worker (Brown *et al.*, 1986). On the other hand, warming to someone because of their charm, ability to verbalise and their seeming cooperation can lead to a false sense of positiveness, to collusion and denial of significant factors (for example child abuse or domestic violence).

Using jargon or technical terms is another obvious obstacle to good interviewing; it distances worker and client. Using the client's own words and phrases is often useful; it demonstrates that you are listening attentively and at the same time conveys acceptance and respect for his/her way of putting things (this is discussed in more detail below).

Interviewing children

Interviewing children and adolescents requires particular skills. Specialist literature for teaching and learning communication skills is available and should be consulted, and practice gained through experience, courses and maybe micro skills teaching via video and live supervision. Interviewers who are skilled in adult work can find it hard to communicate with children because of a tendency to concentrate too much on the formal elements of the interviewing task. For instance, using questions is different with children with whom, in fact-finding, one may need to be quite specific and direct. Letting the child talk freely while gaining facts takes expertise. Gaining cooperation, timing, overcoming confusion, managing hostility, being spontaneous, getting the right surroundings, communicating through 'third things' (toys and analogies), awareness of cultural appropriateness and so on, are perhaps more crucial than they already are when interviewing grown-ups.

Questioning

The purpose of interviewing is more often than not to gather information. This is especially so at the beginning of any contact and in the processes of assessment, review and quality assurance. Information can be gathered by observation and listening, but the most common way is to ask questions which get at both facts and feelings. As was discussed in the chapter on assessment there is an increasing use of schedules and pro formas to log information for a number of purposes. Social workers therefore need to be skilled in asking questions appropriately in order to get this information sensitively. Writers on interviewing have compared the different techniques associated with questions asked in classrooms, courtrooms and by researchers, clinicians and social workers (see Dillon, 1990), and these illustrate the ways in which the method can either hinder or aid the helping process.

An interviewer who poses questions accusingly or in a suspicious tone rather than in an interested and friendly way will arouse fear and antagonism. The wording of a question in this respect is less material than the manner and tone in which it is put. Try asking the question: 'Are you looking for work?' using a range of inflections to illustrate this.

Asking too many questions could sound nosey or interrogative. Asking too few questions may leave relevant features hidden. The pace at which questions are put needs to be the client's, otherwise more might be revealed than the person intended, resulting in annoyance or reluctance to return to the agency. However, it is sometimes possible to assist people to say what they want to, or give you the information you need to be able to help them by a process of funnelling. This encourages people to speak quite generally about a subject, encouraged by the prompt to 'Tell me about ...'. You can then ask them to give a specific example of what they are talking about, and then focus on that example, but also check out how frequently such events or experiences occur.

It is very common amongst inexperienced workers to avoid asking probing questions when clients hint at what they are worried about deep down. Failing to pursue some areas in an interview might be related to needing to protect ourselves from pain or fear of unearthing material that is threatening or distressing; over-cautiousness or reticence can be a hindrance. For example, if someone hints that he or she is so depressed that he/she wonders if life is worth living and then quickly moves on to another subject, it might be worthwhile coming back to that idea again later. This can be done by saying something like, 'Can you tell me more about that?' or 'I'm not sure I understood earlier when you said ...'. This allows for elaboration if the person wants this; it also lets the worker check out perceptions, and it conveys to the client that the worker can cope with the 'unacceptable' thoughts and feelings.

Avoidance can also occur when suspicions are raised about behaviour and attitudes that are unacceptable, inappropriate or even illegal. This is particularly sensitive in relationships where the worker has a responsibility for monitoring behaviour. For example the requirements in criminal justice work to confront offending behaviour, or for childcare workers to ensure the protection of children, can precipitate dilemmas for workers if they receive information in interviews that clearly indicates inappropriate or unacceptable behaviour. In these circumstances there is sometimes an appeal to confidentiality, an expectation that the worker will not act on the information. It is therefore important to be clear about the parameters; if the person then chooses to reveal information he/she does so knowing that the worker will have to act upon it.

The response of some workers to dealing with issues of race has been to avoid challenging black and ethnic minority people in the same way as white people might be challenged (A. Ahmad, 1990). It is appropriate to challenge the behaviour that is deemed to be unacceptable, as long as such workers have checked out that their judgement is not framed by cultural norms, which may lead them to misinterpret that behaviour and/or actions.

Open questions

Obviously questions have to be asked to get some information, especially when it has not been forthcoming in the interview. A general rule for social work is that more information is gleaned and more is learned about people's reaction by asking open questions. These are questions that require more than the answer 'yes' or 'no'. The question, 'Do you have any children?' will elicit the answer 'yes' or 'no'; the question, 'How many children do you have?' will get information about the number of children, and might also encourage the person to give details about them, thus avoiding the need for further questions about the sex and age of the children. It is often recommended that the 5WH (Why, What, Who, Where, When and How) are useful to help us think about open questions. A blend of enquiries that address these areas will reveal a lot of fundamental information: 'Why is this a problem?' 'When did it start?' 'Who could help?' 'What needs to be happen?' 'How do you think we can help?' Obviously these would not be asked all at once, or in quick succession!

Careful thought needs to be given even in the use of open questions. The overuse of the question 'Why?' might seem to imply that someone should explain their behaviour, and cause defences to go up. In any event, people often do not know 'Why?' and may be seeking help to understand themselves and their situation more clearly. A 'What?' alternative is preferable and may reveal information useful to all involved in the interchange, as happened when a worker, instead of asking an elderly person why she was afraid to go out, asked what she thought might happen if she did.

Probing questions

Skilful use of questions is sometimes overlooked in social work, as if it is something anyone can do. As an alternative to questions to collect information that appears to only have value to the organisation (which increases resistance, for example in involuntary clients in probation), probing questions are a way of actually starting off processes of change. It is worth studying the range of good questioning techniques that can help others identify their experience, raise consciousness, solve problems and so on. A number of these are written about in the literature: Henderson and Thomas (1980) describe how community workers will deliberately ask naive questions to prompt local residents to begin to question what they assume they cannot influence. Reporter-type questions can sometimes achieve the same goal, as can the devil's advocate approach. Here the respondent is intentionally confronted with the arguments of opponents in order to trigger a change. Other ways of employing questions that hold the germs of possible change involve taking a one-down stance by saying, 'I could be wrong but ... '; 'I wonder ...' or, 'I don't quite understand ...', all of which stimulate people to step outside of their usual frame of reference to consider new possibilities, without the worker dragging out information.

Another general guideline is to log awkward moments and return to them later when the client can cope with a specific question, perhaps acknowledging the awkwardness and underlining an earlier question by asking it again. Cognitive therapists, whose ideas stem from behaviour therapy, have expertise in asking questions that challenge negative thoughts or false assumptions to which those who are depressed are prone (see Scott, 1989). Thus a patient who says that he has no friends will be queried about this: 'When you say that you have no friends do you mean that, or do you mean that you have only one or two?' Another way to challenge would be to ask: 'Is it true to say that you are always depressed? Your diary indicates a slight lifting of mood in the mornings.' Questions can be used to slow people down, to check out the way that they automatically construe their world. These are somewhat specialised techniques, and the circumstances in which they are used will be dealt with in more detail in Chapter 8.

Circular questioning

Another style of asking good questions is that known as 'circular questioning'. Developed within the family therapy field, it assesses family functioning and interaction by asking one member of the family to comment on the relationship or behaviour of two other members. Thus, 'When your mother tries to get Andrew to go to school, what does your grandmother do?' and, 'Who do you think is closer to your father, your sister or your brother?' and so on. Circular questioning highlights different viewpoints, giving feedback to everyone present while introducing new information about how each third party views relations between other dyads (Penn, 1982). In essence, it sets behaviour within context.

Hypothetical questions, starting with, 'What if?' are additionally revealing for all, as are those that ask people to describe their ideal solution (giving clues to people's goals and the way in which work might move forward). They also provide a challenge to people's assumptions. An adolescent who is being fostered, but is in conflict with his family and threatening to leave home, could be encouraged to explore: 'What if you left home, what do you think would happen?' This could enable him to explain his worries or fears that his foster parents did not (and would not) care about what happened to him.

Problem-posing questions are preferable to those ready answers that undermine the competence of others. People often have their own ideas that can be 'unlocked'. For example, a despairing group of homeless people at a drop-in centre who said 'We can't change their policies' were induced to rethink their powerlessness by a worker who asked, 'Who are they, and what do we know of their policies?' In sum, asking good questions saves time, helps to engage rather than alienate clients, and can be a tool for actually beginning to change a situation.

Responding

Interviewing is not just a one-way process; it is not just about asking questions and listening to the answers. Nor is it about venturing opinions or advice-giving, as we shall see in Chapter 5 when we discuss counselling. Most people when they listen give some indication of the fact that they have heard; saying nothing can appear uninterested or even hostile. There are ways to demonstrate that you are listening: sitting attentively or nodding at appropriate points are two ways, but much more significant are the responses that are made. Five type of responses have been identified, not all of which are good practice.

Evaluative responses are those that say how you judge the person, or what is being told to you. Many remarks in ordinary conversation carry evaluative overtones. These are to be avoided. Good listeners will learn to accept people, and hear information without passing judgement about what they hear.

Interpretative responses analyse what the person has said, and give it new meaning. This is often an intellectual response, and can be attractive to students who are encouraged to link their practice to theory. Almost always interpretative responses lead away from what the person is saying, but represent what is going on in the listener's mind. Interpretations should be used sparingly – even when we are asked directly what we think.

Sympathetic responses might seem appropriate if people are sad or upset, or what they are talking about seems painful. However, there is a danger that in expressing sympathy you are reacting to how you think you might be feeling in the circumstances. Accurate empathy is listening to the emotions that people are expressing, however unexpected they might seem. If you name an emotion for someone, you might stop that person being able to express what he or she really feels, because he/she thinks the emotion is 'inappropriate'.

Probing responses are those that seek more detail about what is said, but often they are based on the listener's interpretation of the situation and seeking confirmation of this. As has been said, a good use of probing is when people are encouraged to explore their own feelings about what they are saying. This helps us to understand what they are experiencing.

Understanding responses are those needed to be a good listener. There are three kinds of understanding responses:

● *Reflection* – This is usually demonstrated by repeating what someone has said. This is not done merely in parrot fashion, but more as an echo of his/her thoughts. It acts as a prompt enabling that person to change or clarify the words that he/she has used and encouraging him/her to say more without directing or probing. It is also a clear indicator that you are actively hearing what the person says.

● *Paraphrase* – If you repeat back what someone has said, perhaps using different words, or joining together two or three things that he/she has said without changing the meaning, this is paraphrasing. It is important if summarising a complicated set of events or feelings that you do not interpret or evaluate them. It is also necessary to check out with the talker that what you have paraphrased is accurate.

● *Feedback* – This is given when you want to indicate that you have heard accurately what has been said, and that you accept the person, whatever the emotions expressed or information given. So, for example, it is possible to tell a bereaved person that it is all right to feel angry with the person who has died, if that is the emotion that he/she has expressed. But it is always important to check out with the person that you have fed back accurately.

At the outset of becoming a social worker it is difficult to remember all of these things at the same time. Often it feels as if concentrating on what you think you must and must not do gets in the way of what is important – letting people feel that they are valued and that you are concerned about them. In the short term you are unlikely to cause too much harm as long as you concentrate on listening and do not make precipitous interventions, give false reassurance or make unrealistic promises. In many cases there will be the opportunity to reflect on what you have heard, and what you have said, and to think about how future interviews can build on this. With this careful reflection and the opportunity to think about what worked in terms of what you did and said, there is the potential to become skilled. However no matter how many years experience you have and how skilled you feel, it is always necessary to build in time to consider the content and process of interviews. Among other things this will help to synthesise information that might be used in assessment. It will also help inform decisions about what method of intervention is most appropriate for the situation.

Conclusion

This chapter has focused on some of the basic skills required to facilitate communication in social work. It has underlined that effective communication is vital for good social work practice, and that it operates at all parts of the social work process. Importantly, effective communication has to be consistent with the value base of social work, that is, it has to reflect respect for persons and be non-oppressive and non-discriminatory. As will be seen in the next section, specific types of intervention, based on different theoretical approaches to social problems, all draw on these basic skills of communication, but develop them in different ways – depending on the function and purpose of the particular intervention.

---

putting it into practice

Practising communication skills is difficult on one's own, and it is better to do this in group settings. Also, the use of video and other feedback mechanisms is helpful, as long as the feedback is given in a helpful and constructive manner – we are all nervous when we are observed, and it is very easy to point out where things could be done better

However there are one or two exercises that can be done without the aid of technology:

1. Listen to conversations. If interviews are conversations with a purpose, it is revealing to listen to how unpurposeful seemingly aimless conversations can be. One of the best places to listen to conversations is on public transport. Without being too nosey or obtrusive listen in to snatches of conversation (between two people – not the one-sided ones on mobile phones!). Note the way that people do/do not listen to each other, how the conversation moves in unexpected directions and to what extent an individual does/does not dominate the conversation.

2. Now focus on yourself. Start listening to your own everyday conversations. This is not to suggest that you should be using social work skills in all your conversations. However it is useful to listen to oneself in different circumstances and with different people, and again to observe whether you get to say what you want in conversations, whether you really listen to friends, colleagues and

---

acquaintances. Are there some people with whom you have conversations where you feel more involved/engaged? If so, ask yourself 'Why'?

3. Use the media. Listen to different interviewing techniques on the radio and the television. This might be 'chat shows' or they may be news programmes or documentaries, all of which use interviews for different purposes. Note those techniques that you feel are effective, and write down what it is about the technique that is effective. Be clear about what 'effectiveness' is. Does the interviewer want information? Is he or she trying to 'catch out' someone (for example a politician)? Is he or she trying to encourage someone to talk about a painful experience in a documentary to explore a particular issue? Note what aspects of these interviews you find unacceptable. Why? Are there any aspects of particular interviewer's technique that you might adopt? If so what, and why?

Further reading

Lishman, J. (1995) *Communication in Social Work*. Basingstoke: BASW/Macmillan. A comprehensive text that is an important resource for social work students and practitioners and discusses written and verbal communication in specific social work processes.

Robinson, L. (1998) *Race: communication and the caring professions*. Buckingham: Open University Press. An important text in that it focuses solely on the way health and social care professions communicate with black and ethnic minority service users and carers.

Thompson, N. (2003) *Communication and Language: a handbook of theory and practice*. Basingstoke: Palgrave. Another text devoted to communication. This text focuses on the social psychology of communication, but has important material on linking this to practice.

Social Care Institute for Excellence (2004) *Teaching and Learning Communication Skills in Social Work Education*. London: Social Care Institute for Excellence. This review undertaken by Pamela Trevithick, Sally Richards, Gillian Ruch, Bernard Moss with Linda Line and Oded Manor provides an overview of writing about teaching and learning communication skills. It is a useful resource, as well as an example of how research is informing skills and practice. Available on the Scie website: http://www.scie.org.uk.

part **2** | # Methods of intervention

5 | Counselling

Introduction

This section on interventions opens with a discussion of counselling. There are two reasons for this. First, the processes of social work that have been discussed in Part I often draw upon the skills of counselling. As has been outlined in the previous chapter, effective communication is crucial in all social work intervention, whether it is with individuals, families, groups or communities. However social work needs more than good technical communication skills; it requires frameworks with which to comprehend the emotional and other meaning vested in communication, and it demands that workers reflect on the implications on their own and others' actions and reactions. Understandings drawn from these processes inform the decisions of workers about how to intervene. Second, skills in counselling, and the psychodynamic theory that underpins them, are core to other social work interventions, such as crisis intervention or behaviour modification. These are somewhat controversial statements, as some argue that with the changes in the organisation and delivery of social work, counselling has become redundant. This redundancy, it is argued, is in part because of the criticisms of counselling and its underpinning theories as being individually focused and oppressive. Another reason why such approaches are thought to be no longer relevant is that the changes in service delivery brought about by developments such as care management mean that counselling is no longer possible in statutory social work.

However this chapter illustrates that counselling takes place in specialist settings, such as palliative care, and that voluntary and independent agencies are increasingly providing counselling services. In addition, the principles of counselling also underpin a number of developments in social work.

The chapter therefore gives an introduction to theory underpinning counselling. Dealing briefly with the history, it outlines some classic approaches that draw predominantly on Freudian psychoanalytic theory. In discussing some criticisms the chapter then goes on to argue that counselling approaches have responded to these and can provide effective interventions in their own right, and that aspects of counselling contribute to other interventions. It also seeks to illustrate how counselling skills are key to effective social work practice, and are in part what makes social work a distinctive activity within the field of social care.

Counselling and social work

Psychosocial casework is one of the oldest methods in social work, and is usually linked to the writings of Mary Richmond (1922) and Florence Hollis (1964, 1970). The then-radical notion of formulating a 'social diagnosis' prior to deciding whether to give indirect treatment (that is relieving environmental distress) or direct treatment (that is, influencing the thoughts and feelings of individuals) became known as the diagnostic school of social work. Throughout the 1950s and 1960s Freudian psychoanalytic ideas, particularly personality theory, began to feed into what became known as psychodynamic casework. The 1970s and 1980s saw much debate about this method of social work. For example, the separate phases of study, diagnosis and treatment were thought to lead to too much concentration on the first two, at the expense of actually doing anything. Also, it was thought that workers sometimes relied on the client–worker relationship as an end in itself, spending a lot of time with people which, research suggested, was ineffective (Fischer, 1976).

During the 1970s and 1980s the radical critique of social work brought into question methods that were individually focused, suggesting that they were oppressive and failed to address the broader socio-economic issues that contributed to the problems experienced by clients, or service users. This was followed in the 1990s by major changes in the delivery of social work services. The debate within this period was twofold. On the one hand there were questions about whether it was appropriate for social workers to be involved in counselling. On the other, there was the suggestion that what social workers did was not counselling. This debate had been crystallised in the Barclay Report (Barclay, 1982), but has continued in a variety of fora.

Uses of counselling

As Seden (1999) points out, counselling is a generic term which covers a number of different schools or approaches. Also it is often used as a shorthand for any form of interaction to help people. She suggests that counselling techniques can be used in many tasks that are undertaken by social workers (for example community care assessment, pre-sentence reports, and assessments of children and families). Analysing the introduction of care management, Orme and Glastonbury (1993) argued that it required many skills of social work, and that the ability to respond to people in a variety of circumstances is core to these skills. It is worth remembering that even when there are resources available, there are situations that are difficult to change, as well as people whose behaviour leaves even experienced workers puzzled and floundering. Assessment and intervention in such cases usually cannot be brief and straightforward. Methods of helping service users acknowledge their emotional problems have to be found because some people need to understand themselves and why they feel powerless to change, or respond to change in unpredictable ways. There are others for whom self-knowledge could be damaging, or where such insight would seem to make no difference.

In these situations social workers do not necessarily have to undertake in-depth counselling, but they do have to acquire the skills of making relationships. Such skills are not only about technical proficiency; they also require appropriate attitudes and style (Seden, 1999, p. 12). Just as importantly social workers need to have knowledge of, and understand the differences between, different approaches to counselling so that when they refer service users to other agencies, or when commissioning services from these agencies, they are able to make informed judgements about the appropriateness.

There is an irony that while statutory social work becomes more dependent upon approaches that help workers contain situations and operate in the mixed economy of welfare to commission services from other organisations, there is also a growing tendency within society as a whole to turn to counselling. In areas of work such as palliative care the principles of counselling are core (Sheldon, 1997). In working with children there has been a resurgence of interest in psychosocial theories, and attachment theory in particular (see Howe, 1995; 1997). Often after natural disasters, horrific violent offences, war and other events that involve groups of people it is reported that teams of counsellors are enlisted to help those involved in the experience (see Chapter 6 for further discussion of work in these situations). It is apparent that these teams of counsellors are enlisted from somewhere. Their existence is testament that in voluntary sector organisations, and increasingly in the private sector, opportunities for counselling are increasing. This is, according to the sociologist Anthony Giddens, because in the period that he calls 'high modernity' people have a more heightened sense of self, and the search for self is a therapeutic activity that involves making sense of our biographies (Giddens, 1991, p. 33).

It would appear therefore that there is a role for counselling. Seden (1999) draws on the work of Marsh and Triseliotis (1996) to argue that social work students want more teaching on counselling. She suggests that there is a lack of clarity in social work training about counselling, and that the difference between counselling and social work should be clarified. In particular she emphasises that legal, procedural and resourcing frameworks affect the boundaries and responsibilities of social workers in ways that affect their capacity to counsel. 'Counsellors do not have to engage in service delivery or directly with their clients' social environments' (Seden, 1999, p. 14).

The psychosocial approach as a method of understanding

Everyone, and that includes social workers, has vulnerabilities; we sometimes do not know why certain events upset us or remind us of a part of the past that we would rather forget. As part of our duties, too, we could unconsciously slip into favouring one client group, for example children or women, over others, thereby risking neglect of less 'attractive' clients on our workloads. This is why social workers need to attempt self-understanding and why, moreover, there is a need to try to understand others so that we may accurately understand the person as well as the problem. If we accept, and are to take into account, that people have inner worlds and outer realities, then we have to understand the 'person in-situation' whole (the psychosocial). Practice that automatically accepts that the presenting problem *is* the problem may, on some occasions, miss the point. If initial coping strategies or solutions do not seem to alleviate the distress, or in some cases seem to exacerbate the anxieties, then it may be worth taking time to explore other explanations.

The psychosocial approach helps us to develop a healthy questioning of the obvious. An open mind, imagination and knowledge of personality functioning, human behaviour and emotional suffering are inherent in the ideas; they assist in reaching 'differential diagnoses and treatment plans'. This is another way of saying that clients interact with their environment in unique ways, and if we are to give service that is accurately targeted then, when appropriate, we have to comprehend underlying feelings and motives that can block people from making optimum use of such help.

Many situations in social work cause us to ask what is going on for the person when he/she acts in angry ways or misses or avoids appointments. But that does not mean every missed appointment has to be analysed. Understandings based on the psychosocial approach highlight that we should not be too precipitous in dismissing behaviour as just 'difficult' or 'non-compliant'. Trying to make intelligible how people behave and feel means there is a decreased likelihood of wasting time or dismissing someone as beyond help. It might be that, to some degree, the psychosocial approach is less a system of therapy and more an approach to understanding.

Framework for understanding the psychosocial approach

The theoretical base for psychosocial work is Freudian personality theory, with an emphasis on the ego's capacity for adaptation and problem-solving.

Assessing ego strengths

Basic to the psychosocial approach is knowledge of psychosexual development (see Howe, 1987). Freud emphasised the importance of early development, delineating several major stages: oral (first year of life), anal (ages 1–3), phallic (ages 3–6), latency (ages 6–12) and genital (continuing from 12 for the rest of life). The origins of faulty personality development were thought to stem from childhood adjustment problems, resulting in unhealthy uses of *ego-defence mechanisms*. These are a further key feature of the psychosocial approach, since defences help individuals to cope with anxiety, thereby preventing the ego from being overwhelmed: these are normal behaviours but they can frustrate coping with reality. Common ego defences are repression, whereby painful thoughts and feelings are excluded from awareness, denial, where again people 'close their eyes' to threatening actuality but on a more conscious level than repression, and regression, where there is a return to behaviour which is immature. In order to assess how realistic and logical the person is in coping with problems and inner conflicts, that is, to reveal which method of helping is indicated, elements of personality structure are assessed.

According to the psychoanalytic view, the personality consists of three systems: the id, the ego and the superego, which interact dynamically both with each other and with the environment, that is, the individual's living situation (see Milner and O'Byrne, 2002, for an excellent discussion of this). The impulses originating from the id are governed by the pleasure principle, while the 'conscience', the superego, strives to inhibit these chaotic drives. The ego, in touch with outer reality, tries to mediate between instincts and the outer environment, thinking through ways of satisfying needs, anticipating consequences and rationally working out solutions. The capacity to do this depends on the strength of the ego.

Ego strengths are not a fixed condition but an ever-changing capacity to cope with frustration, control impulses, make mature relationships and use defence mechanisms appropriately. In general, an individual's age, capacity to work through early traumas and the intensity of pressures all affect ego functioning. A truly mature person in this sense is someone who does not need to rely on others for positive self-esteem and who has a deep understanding of who he/she is. It is to this that Giddens (1991) is referring when exploring the notion of self-identity. In community care a worker's focus may be on reducing environmental change, or bringing about change as a way of giving hope and comfort to a person, but many of the situations dealt with involve challenges to how a person sees himself or herself. In such situations, which often involve loss, individuals might not desire self-awareness or could not cope with it, but it is still useful to be able to gauge ego strengths. This assists in understanding how motivated or reluctant the person is likely to be and what kind of relationship is likely to develop. Kenny and Kenny give the example of an older woman whose husband has developed dementia. They point out that the worker's task is to find a nursing home for the husband, but that worker also has to be responsive to the woman's capacity to cope with what amounts to the death of her husband as she has known him (2000, p. 38).

When helping adults who appear to have 'infantile' needs, or whose behaviour is baffling (for example those who intellectually understand what to do but who do not connect this to their feelings or actions), it might be useful to assess at what stage of psycho-sexual development they might be stuck. Especially when there has been a past trauma, for instance, loss of a parent at a vulnerable age; then, when there is internal or external pressure, the client frequently regresses to the stage where these earlier issues were not resolved.

Equally, those clients who seem totally unable to manage their lives (Kaufman, 1966) can be helped to gradually mature with a worker who feels comfortable in a nurturing, restitutive parent–child relationship, where dependency is accepted and worked through. Normally, these are the adults who antagonise agencies because of their neediness and their inability to care for anyone else (until they have been cared for). Examples include the parent who forgets to have food in the house and who spends the money she is given on cigarettes; the patient who is over-concerned with illness but whose numerous tests reveal no abnormality; the person who insists on seeing the social worker at all hours and then is aggressive when limits are imposed. Some time ago Wittenberg said that:

> The caseworker acts as a kind of mother who takes away the mess that the child produces and cleans it up and helps him to do so gradually himself.
> (Wittenberg, 1970, p. 155)

With clients whose lives may have been marked by inconsistency, desertion, the intrusion of too many figures of authority or attacks on self-esteem, workers have to provide understanding, holding and containment.

That said, it should not be assumed that it is always necessary to introduce self-awareness and re-education. Ego strengths must be

assessed particularly when dealing with those who have been diagnosed psychotic or when working with the immature ego of the
child. In such situations indiscriminate 'laying bare' of feelings can
prove overwhelming to the personality, and interpretation and
insight would probably be harmful. Indeed, the immature ego may
need help to increase rather than decrease defences to prevent
repressed (unconscious) material from threatening the fragile
personality.

Psychosocial techniques

Building on Freud's concepts of defence mechanisms, personality
structure, transference and counter-transference, resistance and
early trauma, Hollis (1970) suggests that the interplay between the
'psycho' and the social aspects lead to clear identification of
systems that include:

Problems: are intra-psychic, interpersonal or environmental.
They relate to meeting basic needs, for example love, trust, dependence, separateness and autonomy. Problems can be unconscious in
origin: the 'cause' of a problem, the 'why?' is seen as important.

Goals: are to understand and change the person, the situation or
both; that is, direct and indirect intervention. Specific, proximate
goals help people with focused aspects of their lives, while ultimate
goals might be more vague and relate to self-understanding.

The *client's role* is somewhat passive, a patient role almost.
Where indicated, the person talks about thoughts and feelings. By
bringing these into the open or into conscious awareness, the client
begins to understand him/herself better.

The *worker's role* is to study, diagnose and treat the 'person-in-
situation' whole. The worker may or may not share the assessment
with the client, dependent on the client's ego capacity for self-
understanding. (This can be viewed as professional omnipotence,
since we can never know all there is to know about someone's
history or the workings of his/her mind.) Treatment processes
include establishing a relationship, building ego support via the
client's identification with the worker's strengths, helping the client
to grow in terms of identity and self-awareness, and working
through previously unsettled inner conflicts. A major contribution
is obtaining needed practical resources and advocating with others
to reduce pressure such that personality change may occur.

Techniques: two main procedures are used, sustaining and modifying (Hollis, 1964). These need a little more explanation.

Sustaining procedures: are those techniques familiar to practitioners who talk about 'offering support' or 'building a relationship'. They sustain the ego and include:

● *Ventilation*: this unburdening of feelings and thoughts allows the overwhelmed ego to concentrate on problem-solving.

● *Realistic reassurance*: by keeping the person in touch with actuality, not promising what cannot be done, keeping an appraisal of external facts to the forefront, and in other ways, the ego's capacity for reality testing is strengthened.

● *Acceptance* in the relationship allows the superego to 'soften'; 'bad' feelings need not be defended against; the person lessens self-criticism, overwork, rigidity, shame at having a problem, and so on.

● *Logical discussion* gives the worker scope to assess someone's ability to reason and confront reality without needing to retreat into fantasy, symptoms of physical illness, pessimism and so on.

● *Demonstrating behaviour* whereby the worker models coping. He/she can be trusted and depended upon to be able to tolerate frustration, set limits, keep perspective and to reason – ego strengths a client may need to 'borrow', that is, copy or internalise, for a time.

● *Giving information* increases the motivation of the ego to handle problem-solving, for instance because it sustains hope, separates the facts of what is 'inside' the person and 'outside' in relation to facts and resources, and prevents magical expectations.

● *Offering advice and guidance*: in psychosocial terms this enlarges understanding, sustaining the client's own efforts to keep control; reducing doubt and fear of the unknown introduces hope and assists ego capacity for reflection, adaptation and readiness to cope.

● *Environmental manipulation*: helping with rehousing, money, advocacy. Obtaining needed resources; the worker shares the burden of handling practical problems. Reducing anxiety increases self-confidence. (Deprivation produces irrational feelings of shame and guilt; or anger becomes explosive, using up needed, productive mental energy.)

Modifying procedures: these also aim to reduce outer pressures while increasing ego awareness of previously unrecognised aspects of personality dynamics. In social work terms this involves the client gaining insight. Provided that the diagnosis of ego strengths has confirmed that self-scrutiny can be tolerated, techniques include:

- *Reflective communications* to enlarge clients' self-understanding: within this is a set of methods which involve sustaining clients while they consider in a new light their opinions, attitudes, behaviour, present feelings, past traumas, early life experiences, using the relationship with the worker as a corrective emotional experience.
- *Confrontation techniques* include pointing out patterns of thinking, feeling and doing. Confrontation may show clients how they respond in stereotyped ways in their relationships, using an example of the client–worker relationship itself. For example, a person who has had bad experience of dependency could find difficulty accepting anything that the worker says.
- *Clarification techniques* similarly include the use of interpretations to point out, for example, when a person's use of defence mechanisms is getting in the way of change, making him/her resistant. (For example, 'Whenever we get around to talking about your father you change the topic.') Or the past may inappropriately be influencing the present; for instance, a successful doctor felt very guilty because his father, a car worker, had always been ambitious for another son who became a manual worker. The doctor felt he had betrayed his father who had always said, 'You'll go nowhere, like me.'

Interpretation, as implied, is a major procedure. Usually it comprises an observation that helps clients to link their present circumstances in their lives 'out there' to the feelings that they have 'in here', that is, the relationship with the helper to what went on 'back there', the past (Jacobs, 1986). This forms a 'triangle of conflict'. An example is a person who is unable to stay in any job without becoming resentful and challenging towards female managers. The worker might interpret it like this. 'You say you get anxious with women in authority. I remember you saying your mother was the boss at home. I wonder if you feel worried now because I am a woman who seems to be telling you what to do?'

Interpretations might be necessary when symptoms are used as a diversion away from painful conflicts in life and in an individual's inner world.

While there is some doubt about the effectiveness of this kind of interpretation (insight does not necessarily lead to change), these methods are often no more than a reflective discussion of making sense with and for the individual – helping to answer, 'Why am I like this?' This does not involve elucidating unconscious motives or what has been called 'archaeological digging' using dreams or free association. The aim is that the person might see things a little differently and feel that he/she has more control over his/her problems in the present.

Criticisms of the psychosocial approach

In the UK the psychosocial approach has been a controversial aspect of social work practice. Wootton (1959) attacked social caseworkers for posing as miniature psychoanalysts, declaring that, rather than search for underlying reasons for behaviour, the social worker would do better to 'look superficially on top', especially if practical help was sought. Consequently, a great deal of 'looking superficially on top' took place, workers were content to provide services and respond to problems as presented. Interestingly in the discussion of the application of theory in Chapter 1 it was suggested that social workers need to do more than just 'look on top'. The psychosocial approach provides one theoretical approach that could be part of reflexive considerations.

However there are other criticisms of the psychosocial approach. One is that clinical and obscure jargon may be off-putting. Also it can be dismissed as being too time-consuming for both worker and service user. More significant are the criticisms that highlight the potential for the method to be oppressive. As Kenny and Kenny (2000) point out, there is an element of psychic determinism inherent in the tendency to construe cause and effect, often simplistically blaming the past for the present. This aspect led to growing tension between critical sociologists and social work theorists, because the latter ostensibly favoured the status quo rather than struggle, through collective action, to change society. The aim of the psychosocial school was said to be to make people fit into a given environment (Jordan, 1987).

Oppressive potential

Furthermore, notions of a therapeutic relationship, self-disclosure, individualisation and self-awareness, plus the power of the worker to make the diagnosis, were antipathetic to the needs of black clients. Dominelli (1988) has suggested that casework 'pathologised' blackness and diverted workers' attention away from racist organisational policies. Middle-class social workers were criticised by radical sociologists and social policy analysts for concentrating on intra-psychic forces and 'insight giving' while ignoring the effects of harsh, competitive, capitalist systems (Bailey and Brake, 1975). Freud's theories were said to lack a materialist understanding of the individual (Corrigan and Leonard, 1978). Feminist critics (Brook and Davis, 1985) suggested psychosocial approaches pathologised women in the same way as they oppressed black people, often perceiving the cause of women's experiences and behaviour as being in themselves rather than in their economic and social circumstances. More recently, in discussing her work with women, Milner (2001) has pointed out the negative impact of psychosocial work was that it is obsessed with asking the question 'Why?'

Others point out that the models of human development on which the theories are based can be oppressive to gay, lesbian and bisexual people. The heterosexist bias in theories of development reinforces homophobia (Milner and O'Byrne, 2002).

Behind the censure of the psychosocial approach and its base in psychoanalytic ideas may lie a presumption that the method is practised by authoritarian caseworkers, who are unable to reflect upon and question what they do. Also the therapeutic techniques of ventilation and reflexive discussion rest on white, middle-class norms regarding the desirability of self-growth and self-awareness (Milner and O'Byrne, 2002, p. 97). It is possible that there are rigid believers who do not tolerate ambiguity, diversity and uncertainty about human behaviour, and who fail to locate their practice in a socio-economic or linguistic context. It is for this reason that moves to monitor, register and regulate social work and the growth of 'independent' counsellors are so important. In professional social work there is recognition that all forms of helping are really forms of power. However, Payne also sees one criterion of professionalism as acknowledging the influence of past experiences (of both clients and workers) to account for irrational aspects to the progress of the relationship (Payne, 1997, p. 89). The tension seems to be between 'good' collective struggles and 'bad' individual work.

False divisions between private and public worlds ignore the interaction between them. Many attempts have been made to integrate psychoanalysis with various sociological and political theories (see the valuable overview by Pearson *et al.*, 1988). Feminism has responded in a variety of ways. Some recognise only the potential for oppression. Others (Yelloly, 1980; Eichenbaum and Orbach, 1983; Mitchell, 1984; Chaplin, 1988) see the value and the drawbacks of theory which, at one and the same time, implies the inferiority of women and provides a key to understanding women's psychology, and their oppression under patriarchy. Featherstone has written extensively on the use of psychoanalytic theories in working with women and men who have abused children (see Featherstone, 1997, for a discussion of the implications of this for women social workers).

Some benefits and some techniques of the psychosocial approach

Kenny and Kenny (2000), while recognising the patriarchal and oppressive potential of psychosocial approaches, also highlight that there is one true constant among all diversity and that is the social worker–client relationship. Echoing constructivist approaches to assessment, they suggest that when clients and workers make sense together, this leads to a shared or empathic understanding (Kenny and Kenny, 2000, p. 33). This sense-making acknowledges that in many social work interactions, no matter what the reason for being involved, workers need to contemplate ideas such as loss, attachment, individual development, anxiety, transference and so on. We find it easy to accept as normal regressed behaviour, for instance of those recently bereaved, who are afraid to be alone or who are convinced they have seen or heard their lost loved one. Knowledge of child personality development is a cornerstone for those involved in childcare and child guidance work. It is commonplace to meet clients who transfer feelings and attitudes on to us that derive from someone else, just as, in counter-transference, we unconsciously respond to the client 'as if' we were that person. For example, clients may relate to us as if we are the all-giving, all-powerful parent they need; if we live up to this fantasy we become unable to say 'no' and to be honest about our limitations. A more subtle illustration of transference happened to a residential social worker who winked at one of the young boys in his unit when they were having a meal. The child became hysterical. It transpired that this had reminded the boy of earlier sexual abuse from a swimming instructor.

Just when social workers think they are getting somewhere, they too might need assistance in supervision to 'stay with' someone who seems to be rejecting their help. Maximé (1986) talks about the confused self-concept and identity of black children brought up in care (who have internalised images and feedback that 'black is bad'). These children express rage to others in their environment, especially black social workers, whom they view negatively. Self-rejection through self-destructiveness is another symptom of introjecting (taking in) negative external images of 'black is bad'.

Having said that, Milner and O'Byrne urge caution when translating psychosocial concepts into situations of racial oppression:

> Tinkering with the theory to incorporate ethnic sensibilities is never enough to surmount the hurdle posed by attempting to translate the effects of racism into an individual psychological problem requiring psychotherapy.
> (Milner and O'Byrne, 2002, p. 97)

The strengths of the psychosocial approach are in the emphasis on listening, accepting and avoiding giving direction. The understandings provide a map for directing conversations. For Payne (1997), psychodynamic social work fulfils one of the purposes of social work; it is a method for improving relationships among people within their life situations. While it is important to understandings in social work, 'classic' psychosocial work is practised less in the UK but has been developed into a number of approaches that draw on the theory and skills.

Counselling

The British Association for Counselling defines counselling as:

> when a person, occupying regularly or temporarily the role of counsellor, offers and agrees explicitly to give time, attention and respect to another person, or persons, who will temporarily be in the role of client.
> (*Membership Notes*, 1990)

The task is to give the client an opportunity to explore, discover and clarify ways of living more resourcefully and with a greater sense of well-being. This is a very broad description that allows for the fact that counselling has many schools – behavioural, psychodynamic and humanistic, as well as feminist and transcultural versions.

The focus of this section will be on counselling that draws on some of the principles of psychodynamic work. Specifically two models of counselling that have had prominence in social work will be discussed, those of Carl Rogers and Gerard Egan. Both of these reflect the social work values of accepting the individual, use skills in listening and attending to the information that is given, and work towards joint understanding and decision-making about ways forward.

Whatever the school of thought or model of counselling followed, generically workers need to be able to listen, observe and respond. As was outlined in the previous chapter, the communication skills needed are attending, specifying, confronting, questioning, reflecting feelings and content, personalising, problem-solving and action planning. Nelson-Jones (1983) recommends that it requires more than being caring and understanding to become a skilled counsellor. Technical expertise is needed as well. Once acquired constant use of the skills is necessary to prevent them becoming 'rusty'. In order to be effective in active listening and appropriate responses, counsellors must own the following seven qualities:

1. *Empathy or understanding* – the effort to see the world through the other person's eyes.
2. *Respect* – responding in a way that conveys a belief in the other's ability to tackle the problem.
3. *Concreteness or being specific* – so that the counselee can be enabled to reduce confusion about what he/she means.
4. *Self-knowledge and self-acceptance* – ready to help others with this.
5. *Genuineness* – being real in a relationship.
6. *Congruence* – so that the words we use match our body language.
7. *Immediacy* – dealing with what is going on in the present moment of the counselling session, as a sample of what is going on in someone's everyday life.

Counselling and diversity

These qualities enable counsellors to instil confidence in others that they are being accepted and listened to, but also allow other people to be different from ourselves. Counselling relies on empathic understanding of others' experience and frame of reference. When the counsellor comes from a different background it might therefore be assumed that empathic understanding is not possible. There are problems with this assumption. Differences and diversity might include age, class, disability, gender, race and sexual orientation, but there are many other aspects of people's experience that might separate them. Indeed it is probably more problematic to assume that just because both counsellor and client are female, or black, they will necessarily understand each other. White social workers might be influenced by their own cultural assumptions and fail to recognise diverse black and ethnic minority cultures. As Stuart (1996) acknowledges, the heterogenous nature of black and other ethnic minority users of community care services suggests that no one can 'know' everything about them and it would be foolish to assume they did. The skills of counselling, the careful listening to the views of users and carers, are fundamental to avoiding stereotyping and false assumptions about how people understand their experiences in the world.

Bandana Ahmad (1990) asks how relevant is the aspect of the client's culture to recognising his or her needs and the nature of the counselling interaction. Do we check the cultural realities of all our clients? How do we guard against over-simplistic explanations which ignore underlying emotional (and, indeed, structural) factors that, for example, contribute to someone's depression? In interpersonal contacts where the worker is white and the client black, while both are aware of this significant factor, both participants possibly agree to a conspiracy of silence, the worker feeling guilty about being the 'oppressor'. Alternatively, assuming that being black is a disadvantage could result in ignoring clients' strengths.

The major element in counselling, particularly Rogers' 'client-centred' approach, which aims to facilitate the self-actualising potential of people, is about equalising the distribution of power. This requires white workers to accept clients, correct their own preconceptions and be open to confrontation: for example that they could never know what it is like to live continually with rejection, humiliation and discrimination, which can so undermine self-respect.

Black workers similarly may feel uncomfortable with white clients, concerned that they will never be able to understand the other's realities. If both worker and client are black this could create barriers to openness and self-disclosure, especially if the client believes that the worker has 'sold out' to the establishment, or if the worker over-identifies because of the common bond of racial experience. On the other hand, beneficial counselling opportunities exist when white clients welcome the chance to share feelings of exploitation with black helpers, or when a black counsellor's positive self-concept offers a sense of hope to the black client (Maximé, 1986).

This said, the very notion of counselling as a model of helping, developed according to Western values, beliefs and perspectives, could be inappropriate to different cultures. For instance, the concepts of self-determination, individualisation, independence and self-disclosure may conflict with values such as interdependence, acceptance and self-control. Because of this some writers (Hirayama and Cetingok, 1988) favour empowerment of the family or whole community rather than focus on an individual: goals would then reflect loyalty, solidarity and cooperation, the worker taking a more active role as teacher, resource consultant and mediator.

Gender differences

When considering gender differences, some feminist literature has stressed that female therapists should see women clients, as only women can understand women. However sometimes gender is not the significant factor, and classic counselling even when provided by women does not necessarily espouse feminism. Also some feminist counselling has not incorporated black perspectives (Dominelli and McLeod, 1989). Early feminist social work literature provided some guidelines for working with women. Hanmer and Statham (1988) for example suggest an exercise that helps the female worker identify commonalities and diversities with the woman she is working with. This can be effective in facilitating an empathic and genuine response and can draw attention to the power balances within counselling relationships. In doing so it helps to avoid stereotypical assumptions about, for example, sexual orientation.

However developments in feminist approaches to social work recognise that assuming that there is an 'essential' femaleness can restrict women's opportunities (Orme, 1998). Also failing to recognise the complexities of women's behaviour might put them, and others, at risk. For example if it is assumed that women are non-violent, children and older people for whom they care are put at risk (Wise, 1990).

Other blanket assumptions about working with women relate to the gender of the worker. There is vital evidence that in the initial stages of counselling women who have been beaten, raped or subject to incest, there is a preference for women counsellors. However in later stages the female client may gain more from a male counsellor who provides a different role model. Such decisions should not be forced on women, but should be arrived at as part of the counselling relationship. Recently developments in feminism have explored the work that has to be done in challenging aspects of masculinity, especially violent behaviour (see Orme, 1995; Cavanagh and Cree, 1996). While it is recognised that having a woman counsellor allows men to develop skills in making positive relationships with women, this has at times been oppressive for women workers. The need for male workers to offer more positive models of masculinity to male clients has been recognised (Thompson, 1995; Christie, 2001). This brief discussion illustrates that research into gender matching, and matching client and worker more generally, is complex, but it should not be ignored. The literature quoted here is an introduction to looking at this phenomenon in more depth.

Older people

Another group for whom counselling is important, but whose needs are sometimes ignored, is older people. Too frequently we assume that problems occur merely because of old age rather than the unique conflicts that face each of us at any age. Ageism makes us fail to see when older people are depressed, abusing alcohol and drugs, having sexual problems, wanting to develop self-awareness or trying to modify behaviour and attitudes (see Hughes, 1995, for discussions of discrimination experienced by older people).

This discussion of diversity is core to all counselling approaches, and should be seen as a backdrop to the following discussions about specific counselling methods. Attention to difference and diversity should be part of any approach to counselling, and it is a yardstick against which counselling methods can be evaluated. It should be kept in mind when reading the following accounts of specific methods.

Client-centred counselling

Client-centred (also called person-centred) counselling (Rogers, 1980) is based on the premise that those who seek help are responsible people with power to direct their own lives, and is grounded in the belief that the client is the only natural authority about her or himself. The goal of this approach is the greater integration and independence of the individual: the focus is on the person rather than on solving the presenting problem. Through the counsellor's attitudes of genuine caring, respect and understanding and by demonstrating empathy, congruence and positive regard, people are able to loosen their defences and open themselves to new experiences and revised perceptions. As the helping relationship progresses, clients are able to express deeper feelings such as shame, anger and guilt, previously deemed too frightening to incorporate into their sense of self.

The goal of client-centred work is to help the individual move away from 'oughts' and 'shoulds', that is, living up to the expectations of others. People decide their own standards and independently validate the choices and decisions made. In a climate of acceptance clients have the opportunity to experience the whole range of their feelings, thereby becoming less defensive about their hidden, negative aspects. They develop 'a way of being'.

This is achieved by a therapeutic relationship that communicates acceptance, respect, understanding and sharing. The counsellor does not use techniques in the creation of an accepting climate, as this would depersonalise the encounter and the counsellor would not be genuine. In some ways this approach has built-in safety features for novices who do not have to offer interpretations: staying within the other's frame of reference offers some assurance that clients will not be harmed by this caring approach, which thereby encourages clients to care for themselves.

Egan's systematic helping

Egan's (1981) work has been found helpful by social work students, not only because of his framework but also because he has provided material to help students develop the methods.

Figure 5.1 Four stages of Egan's model

Each of the stages *exploration, understanding, action* and *evaluation* is represented diagrammatically by four adjacent diamond shapes; these signify the widening and narrowing of focus within each interview and along the total helping process.

Stage 1: Exploration skills. The worker aims to establish rapport, assisting in the exploration of thoughts, feelings and behaviour relevant to the problem in hand. Asking 'What is the difficulty?' the counsellor tries to build trust and a working alliance, using active listening, reflecting, paraphrasing and summarising skills. Open questions are used before the client is asked to say which concrete problem he/she and the helper need to understand.

Stage 2: Understanding skills. The counsellor continues to be facilitative, using Stage I skills, and in addition helps the person to piece together the picture that has emerged. Themes and patterns may be pointed out to assist in gaining new perspectives: this alternative point of view aids clearer understanding of what the person's goals are and identifies strengths and resources. The skills lie in offering an alternative frame of reference, using disclosure appropriately, staying in touch with what is happening here-and-now and using confrontation. This latter skill is not to be misunderstood as an attack. It is an act of caring, of encouraging clients to consider what they are doing or not doing, challenging inconsistencies and conflicting ideas in order to tap people's unused resources. Egan would view confrontation without support as disastrous, and support without confrontation as anaemic. The timing of confrontation is vital when the relationship can endure such a challenge.

Stage 3: Action skills. The worker and the counselee begin to identify and develop resources for resolving or coping with the causes of concern, based on a thorough understanding of self and situation. The skills lie in setting goals, providing support and resources, teaching problem-solving if necessary, agreeing purposes and using decision-making abilities.

Stage 4: Evaluation. An action plan having been chosen and tried, all ideas are reviewed and measured for effectiveness. The counsellor's skills rely again on active listening plus all those of the previous stages.

If necessary in a circular fashion, the first stage of wide exploration is resumed as part of the helping process.

In Egan's approach the worker's use of influence and expert authority is acknowledged. This contrasts with what was said about the Rogerian school of thought. Not all clients are willing ones; in social service and criminal justice social work departments, despite critical argument (see Rojek *et al.*, 1988), whether we admit it or not, we act as agents of control. Even when help is sought, there is natural resistance to dependency and the power of professionals. Social workers use authority that stems from their statutory powers, their position in an organisation, as well as the authority that derives from their knowledge and skill. Apart from abuse of power, supposedly anathema in our profession but not unheard of, authority can be used in counselling for setting limits, just as staff in Young Offender projects do to help teenage offenders to gain control over themselves. Equally, we gain authority on occasion from the strength of our relationships and skills in persuading and negotiating, Yet it needs to be remembered that in using all kinds of authority, we are only as powerful as others allow us to be: influence has to be validated by others. There are ways, furthermore, of sharing power with users by explaining the skills and techniques that are used, for instance in counselling, networking and other interventions.

Transactional analysis

Frequent comparisons have been made in this chapter of the worker/client relationship with that of parent/child. This has been systematically explored in the techniques of Transactional Analysis (usually referred to as TA). While there are significant differences in approach between TA and other psychosocial approaches, the common ground is the recognition of ego states. Developed out of the work of Eric Berne (1961), TA accepts a Freudian notion of ego states, where the ego is the conscious part of the personality, and the id and the superego are largely unconscious. However, Berne related these ego states to consistent patterns of behaviour that are labelled Parent, Adult and Child. These descriptions bear no relation to age or role, but are, according to Berne, structures of the human personality. The Child state carries thoughts, feelings and behaviours of childhood; the Parent holds all the messages, positive and negative, that are given by parents or other authority figures, and behaviours that provide models, while the Adult assesses situations and decides how to respond information received. This initial description is further subdivided by Berne into more descriptive subcategories, for example, Critical Parent and Nurturing Parent, Adapted Child and Free Child.

What is significant is that these ego states have observable behaviours attached to them, and recognisable inner feelings. In working with a TA model, workers will recognise behaviour and 'scripts' when clients are responding using a particular ego state. These responses lead to certain kinds of communication or transactions (a transaction being defined as a unit of social action). Berne argues that all transactions are designed to achieve 'strokes' or responses, and that primary need is for positive strokes (for being and doing), but if positive strokes are not forthcoming, then negative strokes are better than no strokes at all. The two main types of transaction in ordinary conversations are:

● *Complementary*: this is where the transactional stimulus and the transactional response involve the same two ego states. This can be Adult to Adult, Parent to Child; the critical aspect is that the stimulus and the response are complementary.
● *Crossed*: is where the stimulus and response may involve three or four ego states and one person is responding in one ego state (Child) to the other's Adult communication.

Much more significant for Berne are those transactions that reflect what is going on under the surface, which are revealed by incongruities of speech and behaviour. These are *Ulterior* transactions and are also described by Berne as 'games people play'. Games are ulterior transactions used repeatedly to achieve certain outcomes. Often the outcomes that are achieved are negative because the 'games' are not being played with the person, but with the parents or parental figures of childhood. Attempts to resolve past conflicts or misunderstandings are fruitless because the person in the current relationship does not comprehend, and may well respond in a way that is part of his/her own earlier transactions. The only way to resolve leftover transactions is to deal with them oneself, or with help from someone who does not engage with them.

An example of an ulterior transaction is where a client will constantly present problems, however minor, for the worker to resolve. This might be construed as attention-seeking behaviour, but often can lead to frustration that the client is always complaining. Such a reaction could well replicate past parental responses; but what the client (or the Child part of the client) is seeking is a demonstration that the parental figure (the worker) cares enough to 'put things right'; this would constitute positive strokes. The frustration could be construed as negative strokes, but even that is better than being ignored. It is important to emphasise that the client is not being childish, but the Child part of his or her personality is operating in the transaction.

TA differs from other psychosocial techniques in that it is an educational therapy where the desired outcome is behavioural change: the focus is on behaviour and not feelings or therapeutic insights. In this way TA has some things in common with behaviour modification, which we discuss in the next chapter. The difference is that TA requires an understanding of ego states and defence mechanisms in order to bring about changes in behaviour. These can be utilised in exercises, games, structured fantasies, as well as straightforward interviews to bring about understandings of the way that past transactions influence behaviour in the 'here and now'. The way that people use different scripts in their daily lives is written up in an amusing way by Berne in his *Games People Play* (1968). However, at times this might seem to trivialise some very significant transactions. For example, some of the marital 'games' described are often ways of avoiding, or may even contribute to, situations of domestic violence. However, an important outcome of Berne's work is acknowledging the way that all of us in day-to-day transactions can have crossed communications.

Narrative approaches

Those who have been the exponents of narrative approaches (Parton, 2000; Payne, 2000; Milner, 2001; Milner and O'Byrne, 2002; Fook, 2002) might be surprised to find their ideas discussed in a chapter on counselling. However there is a clear rationale for dealing with them here. Although focusing more on service users' futures rather than their past, narrative approaches are, it is suggested, another form of counselling. Indeed in some instances the term used is narrative *therapy* (White and Epston, 1990; Payne, 2000). Although Milner and O'Byrne argue that externalising the internalised story differs from the insight-giving of psychodynamic approaches (Milner and O'Byrne, 2002, p. 161), there are many points of congruence. For example, while the significant difference is said to be that the focus is not on the person as the problem, but how people become ensnared by problems (Milner and O'Byrne, 2002), to do this requires looking at the past before going on to the future. Also concepts are reconstructed: *interpretation* is how service users can make meaning of their lives; *resistance* is the way in which service users can resist the influence of problems on their lives (Milner and O'Byrne, 2002, p. 53).

That said, it is important to note that putting narrative approaches with counselling risks recognising only the things that are similar, rather than emphasising differences (Milner, 2001). Milner is clear that narrative approaches, in that they are based on the solution-focused therapy of de Shazer (1988), are future-oriented. It is not necessary to understand the causes of a problem to arrive at its solution. Moreover narrative therapy challenges the belief that a problem speaks the identity of people who need help. Hence people should not be thought of *as* problems because they *have* problems.

Narrative approaches are seen to be a necessary and important outcome of the response of social work to postmodernism (Parton and O'Byrne, 2000). This response recognises the oppressive effects of dominant narratives and the ambiguities, contradictions and contingencies of any account of events, and therefore emphasises the need to deconstruct and reconstruct stories with service users. All accounts are perceived to be versions of reality (Fook, 2002), and analysing the narrative is a key factor in how people construct their lives. Importantly, as was said in the discussion of constructivist approaches to assessment, the purpose is not to get at a single truth, but to get meanings from different perspectives. Equally, ways of interacting with people described in the narratives are not revealed as, for example, maladaptive attachment patterns (Milner, 2001). In deconstructing and reconstructing narratives there are positive ways forward for service users: 'new narratives yield a new vocabulary and construct new meaning, new possibilities and new self agency' (Milner and O'Byrne, 2002, p. 159).

As with all counselling approaches the role of the worker is vital. The way that he/she asks questions can influence the way narratives are presented. Significantly, in the light of discussions in the previous chapter, for Fook (2002) the emphasis is on 'Tell me about your experiences' rather than on the 'Why?' and the 'What?' questions. She also outlines techniques to aid the reconstruction of the narrative. These include:

- uncovering narratives
- challenging assumptions that are unhelpful
- externalising the problem narrative
- shifting the story to narratives that are enabling and empowering
- creating an audience.
  (Fook, 2002, pp. 139–41)

Presenting such a stark outline suggests a rather programmatic approach, but this is not how narrative approaches operate. The significance of the method is not just in the role of the worker but also in the processes of the method. These include:

- externalising the internalised narrative
- naming the problem
- discussing the relationship with the problem
- thickening the plot
- giving narrative feedback.
  (Milner and O'Byrne, 2002)

Hence while the emphasis is very different – concentrating on the discourse rather than the person – narrative approaches offer opportunities to understand people's interpretation of both the internal and external world. Also, in that they offer a relationship over time and are based on respect for the person, they do incorporate some aspects of counselling. As Parton and O'Byrne comment in their introduction to what they see as a new social work practice:

> It may be that the psycho-dynamic approach's greatest contribution had little to do with providing an understanding of the functioning of the ego, the super ego and the id but the importance of the validation that a person receives simply in telling their story to an attentive listener.
> (Parton and O'Byrne, 2000, p. 12)

Conclusion

As was said at the outset, this chapter leads the section on interventions because both chronologically and in terms of the importance of the theories outlined it is fundamental to all social work interventions. It is suggested that psychosocial approaches based on psychodynamic theory have provided more than a point of reference. In focusing on the need to find explanations for the way people feel, the way they behave and indeed the way they feel about the way they behave, psychosocial approaches enable social workers to begin to explore the interrelationship between the individual and the environment. Admittedly this was initially a very narrow view, and the focus on the individual meant that service users, or clients, tended to be pathologised: the problem was seen to rest in them. However in moving away from the pathologising tendencies it is vital that social work does not abandon the individual totally. As the rest of the book will illustrate, whether social workers are working with individuals, groups, families or communities it is important to try to discern how the individual makes sense of his/her experiences. This is not to deny that political and socio-economic forces, together with the organisation of social work agencies, are powerful influences in the way that social problems, and those who experience them, are constructed. However to ensure that we work in a non-oppressive way we need to ensure that we do not make assumptions about how people experience this. As we will see in the following chapters theories of interventions can help us try to understand people's reactions without stereotyping or constraining individuals.

---

putting it into practice

Practising counselling is difficult. As has been said, putting counselling theory into practice usually involves feedback through supervision, often using video links or special interviewing rooms. However there are things that we can do to help make us more aware of some of the processes that take place in the helping relationship. The practice of writing a process recording is very useful.

1. In this the worker/student writes a very detailed account of what happens in an interview interaction. It is important to choose an interview that for whatever reason was significant for you. It might have been difficult because it was demanding or you might feel that you did not handle it as well as you might have. Also when choosing an interview, focus on only a part of it, otherwise the account will be too long and/or too superficial. Again, choose the part that was significant to you, whatever the reason. Write down everything that happens in the part of the interview that you are focusing on: who said what, the words that are used, the silences, the non-verbal signals – everything you can remember about your own interventions and those of the service user (and anyone else who might have been involved).

2. Now re-read the account and write down what you think was going on for the service user, bearing in mind some of the ideas and theories that have been discussed in this chapter. What do the words used mean? What story is the person telling? How is the person reacting to you? Is he or she relating to you in ways that are unexpected? Why might this be so?

3. Now read the account again and write down what was happening for you in the interview/interaction. Why have you chosen this section of this interview? How did you react to the situation? How did you react to the things that were said? Why do you think you reacted in that way? What made you decide to do the things that you did/said?

4. Now read all three accounts see if you can relate what is recorded (and what happened) to the theories that have been discussed in this chapter.

Further reading

Cossis-Brown, H. (2002) 'Counselling'. In R. Adams, L. Dominelli and M. Payne (eds) *Social Work: themes, issues and critical debates*. Basingstoke: Palgrave. An introductory chapter that gives an overview of counselling and its place in social work.

Seden, J. (1999) *Counselling Skills in Social Work Practice*. Buckingham: Open University Press. A useful text that discusses the basic principles and practices of counselling and their implications for social work practice.

Milner, J. (2001) *Women and Social Work: narrative approaches*. Basingstoke: Palgrave. While not specifically about counselling in the 'traditional sense' this book develops the narrative approach, and focuses on working with women.

6 | Working with loss and change

Introduction

In this chapter we explore ways of intervening that draw on the theories and skills of counselling in specific situations. Individuals who come to social work agencies have experienced or are experiencing trauma and loss. This loss may be actual, for example as a result of bereavement, divorce or illness. Others may seem to be experiencing crises because of homelessness, debt, difficulties with looking after children, the onset of dementia or other aspects of living. In these circumstances it is necessary to understand what is meant by the word 'crisis' as it relates to social work intervention. Such circumstances could be, for some people, a permanent way of living, and they develop mechanisms for coping. For others, one seemingly small event might precipitate feelings of helplessness and render the person incapable of acting.

This chapter will explore how theory has helped to explain different reactions to crises. It will highlight the necessity of focusing on how the individual is experiencing the world, or his/her part of it. The stages of crisis resolution, the signs and symptoms to look for and the difference between stress and crisis are noted. A framework that summarises the main ideas of crisis intervention is followed by a detailed description of the techniques that may be used in the initial, continuing and closing phases of intervention. In that crises usually involve loss and change, literature associated with bereavement is introduced. Increasingly agencies have to prepare co-ordinated aftercare systems and preventive intervention services in the event of disasters, so this is also addressed.

What do we mean by 'crisis'?

Social work interventions repeatedly occur with clients in crisis, and yet the word is generally misunderstood and used in something of a dragnet fashion, indefinitely describing a variety of problems, needs, stresses and emergency states. Teams talk about crises when they mean that an urgent referral has come in or that they can only 'do crisis work', that is, engage in minimal activity because of over-work. This signifies a lack of understanding of the concept of crisis and methods of intervention: inaccurate use of the term may have actually prevented a more thorough testing of the model such that we cannot yet dignify the crisis approach with the status of 'theory'. It is hoped that, having read this, practitioners will avoid uncritical and undifferentiated use of the concept but try to understand the particular circumstances being experienced, and apply and develop the processes associated with what is called crisis intervention or crisis work.

Defining crisis is difficult (O'Hagan, 1986), hampered further by the layperson's portrayal of crisis as a drama, panic, chaos, the 'economic crisis' and so on. Erich Lindemann and Gerald Caplan in the 1940s and the 1950s were the first to study the ways in which individuals reacted to psychologically hazardous situations, and formulated the concept of crisis. Their work led Rapoport to conclude that '*a crisis is an upset in a steady state*' (Rapoport, 1970, p. 276).

This is a simple way of portraying how a sense of loss associ-ated with accidental or developmental life transitions throws an individual into a state of helplessness, where coping strategies are no longer successful in overcoming problems and where the person's psychological defences are weakened. The steady state (also called 'homeostasis' or 'equilibrium') is maintained by human beings through a series of adaptations and problem-solving processes – Charles Darwin might have expressed this as a biological survival mechanism since new solutions are usually needed to manage the hazardous event that precipitated such dis-equilibrium. Crises are not necessarily unusual or tragic events; they can form a normal part of our development and maturation. What happens in a crisis is that our habitual strengths and ways of coping do not work; we fail to adjust because the situation is new to us, or it has not been anticipated, or a series of events become too overwhelming.

If a human being is overpowered by external, interpersonal or intrapsychic forces (in other words, conflicting needs) then harmony is lost for a time. One important thing to remember is that crises are self-limiting; they also have a beginning, middle and end. Caplan (1964) postulated that this period lasts for up to six weeks. In the initial phase there is a rise in tension as a reaction to the impact of stress; during this time habitual ways of trying to solve problems are called on. If first efforts fail this makes tension rise even further, as the person gets upset at his/her ineffectiveness (the middle phase). This state of mind results in the final phase, when either the problem is solved or the individual, needing to rid him/herself of the problem, redefines it for instance as something less threatening; or, alternatively, the problem is avoided altogether, for example by distancing oneself from it. (The same phenomenon of protest, despair and detachment is familiar to workers who understand the separation traumas of young children.) It can be seen that crises have a peak or turning point; as this peak approaches, tension mounts and energy for coping is mobilised – we 'rise to the occasion' (Parad and Caplan, 1965, p. 57).

As indicated, during the disorganised recovery stage people are more receptive to being helped because they are less defensive and need to restore the predictability of their worlds; we all seek some kind of balance in our daily lives. This said, there are some families and clients who seem to thrive on living in a constant state of crisis; they lurch from one seemingly appalling state of chaos to another, on the precipice of eviction, fuel disconnection, abandonment and despair. This chronic state may be part of the lifestyle and not to be confused with concepts of crisis discussed so far.

Crises can be perceived as a threat, a loss or a challenge. The threat can be to one's self-esteem or to one's sense of trust; for instance, the loss might be an actual one or may be an inner feeling of emptiness and isolation. When viewed as a challenge, a crisis can encompass not only danger but also an opportunity for growth. This is especially so when new methods of solving problems are found or when the person finds that he/she can cope. Similarly, because crises can revive old, unresolved issues from the past, they can add to the sense of being overwhelmed and overburdened (a double dose); at the same time however they can offer a second chance to correct non-adjustment to a past event. Two case examples help illustrate this vulnerability, which runs alongside increased mental energy made available for coping when it is no longer being used to repress ill-resolved old problems.

Case examples

Mrs Todd was admitted to an elder care home following the death of her husband and at the request of her daughter, aged 70, who could no longer manage. Six months after admission Mrs Todd refused to get out of bed for a week, saying that there was no point. Physical explanations were ruled out. Sensitive questioning by the residential social worker revealed that Mrs Todd had never come to terms with the loss of her husband. On top of this she had been unable to put into words her feelings of being abandoned by her family. Mrs Todd's denial of her grief, plus the perception that she had lost control and independence, despite high-quality care in the home, had resulted in confused thinking, distortion of grief and withdrawal.

The ward sister of a nearby hospital contacted the field social worker who had spent some months working intensively with the Smith family in order to plan the return home of their nine-year-old daughter who had become disabled following a road accident. Adaptations and equipment were installed in the home and community care services organised. On being given a definite discharge date, perhaps the first impact of reality, Mr Smith had become uncontrollably tearful, refusing to take his young child home, saying that he could not cope. In working through this period of crisis, the social worker helped Mr Smith to recognise his emotional outpourings as normal and to explore all the resources that would be made available. This little bit of help, given at the right time, prevented Mr Smith from drifting into worries that the family would be abandoned once the little girl was home, or abandoning his daughter. In fact, the specificity of a discharge date had triggered off inner conflicts in Mr Smith, only partially resolved, that his wife would leave him, as she had done many years before.

Rather than seek help with their unhappy marriage, the couple had resigned themselves to their disappointment in each other, never talking about the past and trying to pretend that their problems had never existed. Their efforts and emotions had then been focused on their daughter. In order to uncouple the symbolic links between past and present needs and fears, the social worker renegotiated her agreement with the Smiths; following short-term crisis intervention a longer-term, more open-ended approach to marital counselling was offered.

Neither of these referrals would have been high priority on many caseload weightings; they were not the stuff of drama or danger. A 'fire-fighting' response was not called for and yet these clients were in crisis. They perceived themselves as having no autonomy or command over their problems, tension had mounted and thinking had become disintegrated so that little mental energy was left over to use inner and outer resources. Without help, either of these clients could deteriorate into a major state of personality and behavioural pathology – what is commonly termed a 'nervous breakdown' could have occurred. Magical thinking such as 'If I don't think about it the problem will disappear' could have led to a loss of touch with reality or a serious medical condition (a broken heart?). Because of this, it is important for all social workers to be aware of crisis theory and to be attentive to it in all interactions. However it is also important to be aware of Thompson's criticism (1991) that often pure crisis 'theory' is dissociated from structural factors of oppression and relies on clinical terms that can pathologise the individual experiencing trauma. For both Mrs Todd and Mr Smith their reactions might have been exacerbated by societal expectations of 'normality' in family relationships and in physical appearance.

Before we compare stress with crisis and learn to recognise the signs of someone in crisis we need to sum up. Crises occur throughout life, they are not illnesses; we constantly make adaptive manoeuvres in order to cope and maintain our steady state. If we meet a novel situation, experience too many life events, or become overloaded with old, unresolved conflicts, then a crisis occurs. This is a time-limited process during which we become disorganised in thinking and behaving. Mounting tension can result in the generation of mental energy for getting the problem solved. Crises can be perceived as a threat, a loss or a challenge; the concept encompasses danger together with opportunity. On a positive note, the outcome can include improved mental health, when new methods of coping are found or when there is a second chance to tackle an earlier hazardous event. It should be remembered that the outcome of the crisis can depend not just on skilled intervention but also on the quality of the person's social support network (Parry, 1990).

Crisis and stress

Occasionally, the word 'stress' is used interchangeably with crisis. However, the concept of stress tends to evoke only negative connotations, for instance that stress is a burden or a load under which people can crack. In comparison, we have seen that the state of crisis need not have this harmful outcome. Crisis contains a growth-promoting possibility; it can be a catalyst, raising the level of mental health by changing old habits of problem-solving and evolving new ways of coping. In addition, the concept of stress carries within it a sense of longer-term pressures, which may largely derive from external pressure as opposed to internal conflict. Crisis, on the other hand, appears as a short-term phenomenon where the individual rapidly tries to re-establish previous harmony. Earlier levels of functioning may have been inadequate, but that is where the person's perception of equanimity lay: where crisis resolution is less than optimum, lower levels of coping may result.

Nevertheless, there is a relationship between life events and stress, as research shows (Schless *et al.*, 1977). A state of crisis can occur when making social readjustments such as moving house, having a first child or becoming unemployed. What is important is that what constitutes unbearable stress for one person may not be so for another. Students are always surprised when they compare their views of stressful events with their colleagues; some dread Christmas, others lose their sense of coping when faced with academic work. Thus, it is the meaning that people attach to these 'uneventful' events that matters – maybe someone links Christmas symbolically to an unsatisfactory time in the past, or someone whose self-esteem was bound up with academic success attaches great significance to results. The same is true when we meet clients; what the event means to them is what matters, not whether we think it is serious or not.

Stress and mental health

Anyone working in the mental health field should be interested in discriminating between stress and crisis. Specifically, when working in crisis intervention mental health teams, where there is a request for compulsory removal to hospital or other safe place, it is vital that a correct assessment is made. Where the situation involves black clients, or those from ethnic minority backgrounds, disturbing evidence has emerged of stress being misinterpreted as mental ill health. One analysis (Aros-Atolagbe, 1990) is that second-generation black people in the UK suffer tremendous crises of cultural identification; alienation produces more stress, which may precipitate a temporary breakdown.

Although individual and ethnic-group variations exist, many immigrants similarly go through a pattern of adaptation to an unfamiliar, and probably discriminating, environment. The loss of support networks together with a sense of powerlessness means that the process of emigrating goes through critical phases such as:

excitement – disenchantment – perception of discrimination – identification crisis – and marginal acceptance.

(See Hirayama and Cetingok, 1988, and Marris, 1986, who discuss the loss of one's homeland.) Such feelings are exacerbated when the reasons for leaving the homeland have been traumatic, for example war-torn countries.

In the case of asylum seekers the situation arises more immediately. Levels of stress caused by the sense of dislocation can exacerbate a state of crisis when this stress is either ignored or denied. Excitement might be more a sense of hope, which often turns to despair when officials who deal with applications take no account of these experiences or emotions.

Alternative explanations for the misdiagnosis of people from different cultural backgrounds include the misinterpretation by workers of reactions to crisis and loss. On the one hand, some groups may be able to express their reactions by overt demonstrations of emotion. In some cultures holding a wake or similar event to allow the outward expression of personal grief is the norm, while in the UK open displays of emotion, although becoming more acceptable, are still frowned upon in some generations. On the other hand, cultural expectations of what has to be tolerated without comment or expression of emotion may be interpreted as depression by workers who expect clients to be prepared to 'talk through' situations (Hong Chui and Ford, 2000). Similar misinterpretations may occur on the basis of gender, where stereotypical assumptions lead workers to expect that men and women cope with difficult situations in different ways. The social worker in the case of Mr Smith, for example, was able to accept that his uncontrollable tears were a perfectly normal reaction to the events with which he had to cope. This is an important message in a culture that has deterred men from using tears as an appropriate means of stress relief.

Therefore we can see that the signs of someone in crisis actually might be difficult to spot, or the behaviour may be open to different interpretations. However, like grief, some of the responses follow a typical or classical pathway, and this can give us some clues. We know that in the period of distress the person is striving to gain control, and is open to suggestions which will aid recovery: phrases may include 'I can't cope', 'I feel a failure', 'I don't know where to turn' or 'It is hopeless'. With Paula (the case example in Chapter 3), she did not even know which words would express her crisis. Often thoughts and behaviour are agitated, confused, hostile, ashamed or helpless. People may become irritable or withdrawn from their friends and relatives. Attempts to solve difficulties seem chaotic and unfocused. One client, unhappy in his new department at work, walked around all day muttering to himself; this could have been mistaken for a form of mental illness rather than the man's anxiety at losing his previous well-known routines. Other signs may be physiological, so that complaints about sleeplessness, tension and headaches (see Parry, 1990) may be mentioned by someone in crisis.

Techniques of crisis intervention

Techniques for intervening in crisis situations help in the initial, ongoing and final stages. In the first interview it is essential that the focus be kept on the present circumstances of the crisis event. Asking 'What happened?' thereby encourages the person's cognitive grasp of the situation. Comments such as 'You must feel awful' or 'No wonder you are upset' help to draw out the affective responses (that is, feelings) which block thinking. The worker and client together try to make an assessment of the actual event and the causes that seem to have triggered it. It is necessary to gauge what ego strengths (see previous chapter) someone has so that his/her normal coping resources can be gleaned. Often asking how the person has reacted in other, similar, situations can do this.

Having gained some idea of available and potential resources, the worker outlines the next step, asking 'What is the most pressing problem?' or 'What is bothering you most?' The client is then asked to settle on one target area, the worker confirming this by saying

'So the most important thing is ...? Obviously, these are not formulae for copying, they are suggestions as to what to cover in the initial period of disorganisation when the worker conveys hope, shows commitment to persevering while cutting the overwhelming problem down into manageable bits (known as partialising the problem). A contract for further work is spelled out in specific, concrete terms such as 'Let's concentrate on .... You do .... I'll do ....' These are not problem-solving contracts such as those used in task-centred work, but help give the person some agency, some influence and/or control over what seems an uncontrollable situation. Optimism is used to reduce the client's anxiety and perception of hopelessness, concreteness helps to keep the person in touch with reality. The aim at this early stage is to start to build a relationship based, not on time, but on the worker's expertise and authenticity, again to restore the client's sense of trust. Because of this it might be necessary to have a number of short meetings at regular intervals (even daily). This may appear to create a sense of dependence, but the worker should always be clear that this is just an interim period.

As the client's thinking is clarified, it is necessary to re-establish a sense of autonomy, by giving him/her something to do before the next meeting. This can be achieved, for instance with someone frozen into inaction, by getting him/her to say when next you need to meet again. In any event, letting individuals decide on the schedule for help such as 'I think I need to see you four more times over the next two weeks' builds self-reliance into the agreement and prevents undue dependence in the longer term.

Further contact in the middle phase sees the worker centring on obtaining missing data, for example, 'Can you tell me more about ...?' Although the emphasis is still on the here-and-now there may be links with past conflicts not recognised in the earlier phase of staying with the presenting issues. Pointing out possible connections helps the person to correct cognitive perception while keeping the problem, rather than fantasy or distortion, in the foreground. Also, one way of helping people keep a perspective is to recognise that he/she has had past crises and has coped with these. Discussing those coping mechanisms sometimes gives good indications about what approaches might work in the current situation. The helper has to be the voice of reality (Golan, 1978), showing the difference between 'what is' (real) and 'If only'. Maybe the client Mr Smith would have wished he could have his 'whole' daughter back as if the accident had not happened; but that was not possible and plans had to be made to assist her and others to live with her disability.

Letting the person talk helps to relieve tension; ventilating feelings can release mental energy for tackling past worries. Help is given to sort out what worked and did not work in attempting to solve the problems; 'So you did .... Did it work? ' Alternative solutions are weighed; exploring overlooked resources assists in restoring equilibrium and also develops a pattern (that is, new habits) in being able to use such help in the future. By sorting out specific tasks together, aiming for achievable goals, the social worker acts as a role model for competent problem-solving; for instance, setting homework, 'Before we next meet I'd like you to think how you could ...', sets the stage for encouraging a change in thinking, feeling and action.

The termination phase of crisis intervention, perhaps the last two interviews, should have been built into the original agreement. Once the state of crisis is overcome and homeostasis restored, it would be harmful to prolong this type of approach as it could ignore the natural growth potential present in all human beings. Reminding the client how much time there is left, reviewing progress and planning for the future prevent dependency (that is, lowered functioning). However, premature termination, 'I can cope now, so I don't want to see you any more', could be a 'flight into health' (Rapoport, 1970) not a well thought-through decision. We shall explore endings in more detail in the final chapter.

Bereavement and loss

Throughout this chapter we have made reference to the fact that crises are not necessarily dramatic or unusual events. Developmental crises might be avoided by anticipatory grief work. In work with pregnant women attention can be paid to the crisis of childbirth, not as a biological event, but in terms of the changes that will occur in the social situation. As we have said crises can be associated with loss. For women who are giving up work there is loss of economic independence and loss of the social environment of the work place. For women who plan to return to work, there are other losses to face; loss of independence and freedom and, if in a relationship, the loss of intimacy. Similar senses of loss occur in other crisis situations. In the case of Mr Smith above, he mourned the daughter he had previously known, and this precipitated confusing emotions and other senses of crisis.

It is this concept of loss present in many crisis situations that makes bereavement theory so important for helping understand crisis and to anticipate the reactions in some of the developmental crises: birth, marriage, retirement and, of course, death. Other situations, often more difficult to anticipate, similarly involve loss and therefore the sense of being bereaved. These include divorce, separation from children or partners, disability by either accident or the onset of illness such as dementia, stroke or multiple sclerosis. Workers therefore have to be prepared to deal with the range and complexity of emotions associated with bereavement.

Situations that involve change, no matter how much that change is welcomed, usually involve losing something, giving up something. As Timms and Timms (1977) suggested, one of the basic functions of social work is conducting interviews with those who are facing loss and change. For this reason, the theories of bereavement are explored here.

In one of the earliest texts to discuss the physical and emotional effects of grief and bereavement Murray Parkes (1986) identified five stages of typical reactions to grief. In identifying these it is not intended that they should be used in a mechanical way to chart people's progress through them. They are an aid to understanding people's reactions to loss, and provide a basis for formulating the kinds of intervention that are empathic and facilitative to people in crisis.

The stages are:

- alarm
- searching
- mitigation
- anger and guilt
- gaining a new identity.

In each of these stages physical and emotional changes occur which are associated with coming to terms with the loss, with the separation from the person who has died, or left. Symptoms occur which are physical such as disturbance of appetite and/or sleep, palpitations and breathlessness. Behaviour is displayed which may seem bizarre or morbid, such as searching for the person, denying his/her death and continuing to live life as if he/she was still present. Emotions expressed can be extreme and include anger with self, the deceased person and professionals who may be held responsible for the loss, guilt at not being able to prevent the loss, or at feelings and behaviour just prior to the death. These can be painful and powerful.

The importance of the work of Murray Parkes (and others, including Lily Pincus, 1976) in identifying the range of experiences associated with grief and bereavement is that workers can accept the bereaved person with all his/her ambivalences, contradictions and complexities. In accepting and understanding the stages of grief work, they can give reassurance that while each grief experienced is personal and unique, the person experiencing it is not abnormal in the ways that he/she expresses it. Having said that, there are occasions when people, for a variety of reasons, become fixed in a particular grief reaction or display extremes of behaviour. In these circumstances having a framework to help assess an individual's coping strategies and to identify particular ways of working with these to develop and strengthen the person's own resources is helpful. Knowing when to stay with a person and listen, when to offer practical tasks and when to introduce them to a support group such as Cruse, or to more specialised help, is part of understanding the stages of grief and bereavement.

The above analyses of the 'stages' of grief have been criticised for being too programmatic and rooted in attachment theory. In particular they are seen to ignore differences in grief reactions and behaviour based on race and gender. However the most significant observation is that the stage 'gaining a new identity' suggests that individuals are encouraged to 'move on' and 'get over' bereavement by becoming detached from the person they have lost. It may be that the new identity is more to do with having to cope with life without the presence of the other person, that the bereaved person has to relocate him/herself in the world. This has led to recognition that work might include a 'dual process model' of coping with bereavement (Currer, 2002) that recognises both the stress of the loss and the changes that result from it. This leads to a dual orientation for the work – loss and orientation. Most people require both, but Currer (2002) suggests that social workers working with a 'staged' model might be more focused on restoration, helping people with practical changes and adjustments, and opportunities to focus on loss might be missed. She suggests that oscillation is the key to adaptive behaviour (Currer, 2002, p. 216), but this does not constitute 'getting over' the lost person. To aid this she identifies that at the point of immediate loss it is important for the bereaved person to be helped to give 'witness' to the relationship. This requires workers to:

● recognise the need to grieve
● give accompaniment to the grieving person
● give support in relation to re-engagement.

Throughout any support that is given workers should always recognise that there may be future need to grieve. Hence the notion of being 'fixed' at a particular stage might not be helpful. Nevertheless, the 'stages' of the process are still a means of understanding the swings in emotion, and the sometimes-unexpected emotions experienced in grief work. A case example helps to illustrate aspects of bereavement and grief work.

Case example

Tom, aged 32 and living at home with his family, was referred to a specialist service dealing with post-traumatic stress disorders. He was a soldier who had served in the Iraq war where he had confronted with the deaths and disfiguring injuries of others, although he had been physically unharmed. However these kinds of experiences do not easily go away and do not fade readily from mind. Tom felt that he had encountered hell on earth. Stressors such as words or places brought back all the intensity of the violence. This was not helped by the fact that discussion of the war was frequently in the media, that violence was continuing in Iraq and there were questions about the fact that the war had been unnecessary. He had recurrent dreams of the events, was hyper alert and gradually became irritable and aggressive with his family.

When he had first returned home everyone was elated that he had survived and returned. He initially was only too glad to join in the celebration and forget what he had gone through. After several weeks his family expected him to get on with living and to 'put it all behind him'. Unfortunately, Tom could not do this: he had endured terrible smells, sounds and seen the mutilation of others; encountering violent death for the first time in his life he was preoccupied with death and the war, which after a time, no one wanted to listen to. He buried the intrusive images of his experiences and tried to get on with his life.

What was worse, Tom had actually shut out the fact that he had been exposed to the killing of his closest comrade. Both had been under fire when his friend was killed at his side. Tom had carried on as if it had never happened. So effective was his denial that he joined with the other soldiers to rejoice when the attack was over; this psychic numbness helped him through, protecting him from what is dreadful about war – that killing may be necessary for personal survival. It stopped feeling then, and he continued to block it out on his return home. Veterans of other wars have complained, 'I can't feel for people like I used to.' Thus, on discharge, he continued to protect his ego, his defence against death anxiety and guilt. His family became tired of his inability to 'pull himself together' and, relieved that he was safe, did not want to listen to his accounts. He therefore became isolated, depressed and withdrawn, and was referred to mental health workers skilled in treating post-traumatic stress disorder.

Usually, treatment methods include individual, family and group approaches, using behavioural techniques and counselling. Tom was helped in abreactive sessions, that is, to try to remember the blur of events on the day that his friend was killed. In a group, he and other survivors drew on their anger and their pain in order to externalise their feelings about traumatic events. After some weeks, Tom was helped to face the detail of what had happened on the day of loss, what he had been doing and so on in detail.

A breakthrough occurred when he at last was able to shed tears for the first time. Like other people who want to give testimony to what the experience meant and how others may gain from it, Tom wrote about his recovery. His account begins:

> I think now that at last the war is over for me, though it will always be there for me for the rest of my days. Looking back I have come to realise that we fight our battles on two fronts; one against the enemy in our sights, the other against the enemy within ourselves.

Framework for understanding crisis intervention

Having explored some of the theory of bereavement and its links with loss, change and crisis we can return to crisis intervention. A framework for understanding crisis intervention includes:

- *Theories* and important concepts, which contribute to the identification of crisis, developed from:
  (a) Psychoanalytic theories of personality (see Chapter 5) where the ego directs energy for problem-solving, appraises reality and helps us to cope, adapt and master conflicts.
  (b) Erikson (1965), building on ego psychology, suggests that we grow by managing psychosocial crisis points, which are transitional points in our life cycle towards maturity.
  (c) Learning theory contributes in relation to ideas about cognitive perception, role modelling and repetitive rehearsal of effective problem-solving (see Chapter 8).
  (d) These contributions fuse with those from research into grief reactions (Lindemann, 1965) and those of time-limited, task-focused work dealt with in the following chapter.
- *Problems* for which this approach is applicable may not even seem like problems. They can be changes such as becoming a teenager, as well as situational or unanticipated crises such as promotion or illness. Furthermore, as we have seen, crises can occur at any time when a person perceives a threat to his/her life goals. It is the meaning of the event to the unique individual that matters. Problems are usually current and pressing ones; routine early history taking would be inappropriate. So too would organisational arrangements such as waiting lists or long-drawn-out allocation procedures. Chronic crisis situations cannot be dealt with by this approach – longer-term, in-depth work is often necessary.
- *Goals* are kept to a minimum. They include relief of current life stressors, restoration to the previous level of coping, learning to understand what precipitated the condition, planning what the client can do to maintain maximum autonomy and contact with reality, and finding out what other resources could be used. When current stresses have their origins in past life experiences, the goal might be to help the person to come to terms with earlier losses to reduce the risk of future vulnerability.
- *The client's role* is to review and question the hazardous event in order to understand how the state of crisis occurred. At times, clients take unwise decisions or make inappropriate suggestions for solving the problem, so the worker takes advantage of the person's lowered defences and willingness to take advice, thereby

inhibiting flight, for example premature plans for the future. Indeed, a lot of the work for clients is to remember that there is a future. By 'telling the story to themselves' cognitive awareness is improved. Sharing the experience and the feelings with family or others in the support network strengthens these resources which, in their distress, some clients forget are there. Disintegration is also prevented when the client assumes responsibility for some small practical task.

● *The worker's role* is to give information and advice, to be active, directive and systematic, if need be. It is essential to be authentic as part of the promotion of reality testing and adjustment. Setting time limits, for example four to six contacts, encourages the person to face up to the future without fear or shame that he/she will never be independent again. While cognitive restructuring and release of tension are the aims of this approach, self-understanding need not be part of the worker's plan for the client. Teaching how to split problems into manageable pieces and acting as a role model for effective problem-solving in the acute stage is what is required. To do this workers must put themselves into a position of 'standing still', that is, remaining calm and being able to 'bear it' when confronted with someone in crisis. The danger in crisis intervention is that the caregivers, surrounded by people who want something done, usually a 'plea to remove someone' (O'Hagan, 1986), will almost go into crisis themselves, not thinking clearly about what needs to be done.

Prevention

Preventive work is a neglected aspect of crisis intervention. If there are two types of crisis, those that can be foreseen, such as lifecycle transitions, and those that are accidental or unforeseen, such as sudden bereavement, then there is scope in the former to prepare for the change. Because maturational crises can be anticipated, public health systems that operate services to maintain mental health could be developed to respond to these. Of course, politically, any preventive service is likely to be threatened when there are cutbacks. But it is somewhat shortsighted of social policy planners and social services to simply react to crises on a case-by-case basis.

When tragedies such as those considered below occur, many are actually 'human-made', such as wars, traffic accidents and toxic waste disasters. Here too, preventive action, known as *primary prevention*, is possible, with coordinated services made ready to prevent long-term psychological and other effects. We know that on an individual level, 'anticipatory worry work' helps later grieving, as do ceremonial rituals practised for a long time after a death by some cultures (Raphael, 1984; Parkes, 1986). Services need to be geared to lowering the incidence of mental disorder precipitated by stress or unresolved grief.

Crisis intervention at a *secondary preventive level*, that is, help geared to people who are actually in crisis, is equally at risk from unenlightened policy-makers. For instance, funding threats continually face organisations such as women's refuges, rape crisis services, suicide prevention centres, and substance abuse rehabilitation units. The changes brought about by the community care legislation mean that voluntary sector agencies are concentrating on providing services that are commissioned as part of community care planning, to ensure they receive funding. Government grants to voluntary sector organisations are now replaced by spot- or block purchasing, which means services are reactive. One consequence of this is that some preventive work, for example individual counselling, is now being offered in the private sector. Anyone can set up as a therapist, charging for services. This means that access to such services is only available to those who have the means to purchase them. It also means that there is no regulation of the provision, or accountability of those offering it.

As we have seen, help given at the right time, when a person is psychologically amenable, can prevent long-term use of any of these systems. Fortunately, some recognition of how we can set up *tertiary prevention* services (the help given to those people who have actually been made worse by earlier intervention), can be seen in the efforts to re-establish long-term patients from psychiatric hospitals back in the community. Community development approaches, discussed in Chapter 11, could provide the opportunity to practise primary, preventive crisis intervention, not simply by putting right harmful interventions but by intervening in ways to counteract destructive forces that affect health. Communities can not only provide services, they can also provide the action, as can be seen in the reaction when communities experience crises.

Coping with catastrophe

The case study of Tom reminds us that other forms of crisis involve not just individuals, but communities, and even whole countries. These crises are those experienced when major catastrophic events occur, requiring coordination of services (Raphael, 1986; Hodgkinson and Stewart, 1991; Newburn, 1996). Hong Chui and Ford (2000) highlight the 1990s as a decade of disaster that includes tragedies such as that at Hillsborough football ground, the Lockerbie air disaster, the sinking of the ferry *Herald of Free Enterprise* and the Dunblane massacre. These have been compounded by terrorist attacks, child abduction and murder (such as those of James Bulger, Sarah Payne, Holly Wells and Jessica Chapman), numerous rail disasters and, of course, wars. While the horrors of famine, floods, fires, epidemics, earthquakes, mass murder, transport and technology accidents and terrorism are not new, since September 11 2001 awareness of the potential for disaster and trauma has heightened. The tsunami created by the earthquake in 2004 was a devastating reminder of the unpredictability of natural phenomena.

Such a list illustrates that communities can be in crisis either because everyone is threatened, or because everyone is affected by what happens to individuals. At both national and local level there is an expectation that social service organisations constantly monitor their disaster plans. Reflections on these various events have revealed that there can be long-term psychological effects of trauma, and how early counselling of survivors, bereaved relatives and friends and those in the rescue services can prevent pathological outcomes in the years that follow.

The definitions of disaster imply extraordinary seriousness and great human suffering. However there are many overlapping characteristics relevant to both crisis and catastrophe: both are marked by rapid time sequences, disruption of usual coping responses, perceptions of threat and helplessness, major changes in behaviour and a turning to others for help (Raphael, 1986). Similarly, personal tragedies such as the loss of a loved one by violent means or someone who has been diagnosed with a terminal illness will produce reactions such as shock, disbelief, denial, magical thinking, depersonalisation, sleep disorders, depression, anger, guilt and isolation. Sudden death or losses of any kind produce syndromes characteristic of disaster responses.

The time phases of disaster:

threat – impact – taking stock of the effects – rescue and recovery

resemble those of crisis reactions, though there tends to be post-disaster euphoria at having survived and immediate convergence from far and wide to help the stricken community. Nevertheless, the predominant need for people in states of crisis and those affected by disaster is for *information* by which to make meaning of such overpowering experiences, seeking to understand by describing what happened, and trying to restore some sense of command over the powerlessness which the very thought of extraordinary destruction brings.

So, even though many practitioners may never encounter catastrophes, they are of interest to any agency interested in providing sensitive, compassionate treatment and drawing up preventive programmes alongside those that manage psychosocial care in the aftermath. (That we know so much about the dimensions of grief is due partly to people like Lindemann, quoted above, who studied survivors of a nightclub fire.) Raphael (1986) suggests that we should study these phenomena because:

- they give an insight into the common responses of individuals and groups, revealing universal themes of survival, loss and long-term adaptation
- prediction and counter-disaster activities together with guidelines for coordinating help can be drawn up
- knowledge can be applied to individual, everyday disasters, stress and life events.

Also, with the more interventionist approaches of the media, images of such tragedies and disasters are being made more imminent for all of us. The sense of grief and outrage that can be felt at the reporting of events may well trigger unresolved grief reactions in individuals who then present at GPs' surgeries or even social work agencies because they do not understand the strength of their own reactions. The events of the tragic massacre of schoolchildren at Dunblane led to a renewal of grief reactions in those who had suffered loss in similar circumstances at the Hungerford massacre.

When setting up post-disaster aftercare those involved in counselling the survivors need to assess and understand background variables related to the nature of the community that has suffered the impact. Their patterns of communication and access to it; their view towards the authorities and agencies that give direction; cultural and ethnic issues; how dependent/independent and urban/rural the community is; how integrated/loose-knit are networks; the interpretations made of the disaster; any special individuals whose qualities could influence responses, are some of the factors to be taken into account. An overview of welfare systems is required, as is epidemiological data such as mortality and morbidity rates so that public health planning and coordination of the relief services such as police and ambulance is effective.

There are many different ways in which people attempt to gain command in the immediate post-disaster phase. These can include:

● *Talking through*, putting into words (and therefore outside oneself), the meaning of the experience. On the other hand, someone who tells his or her story again and again with no emotional abreaction can become locked into the experience.

● *Giving testimony*, wanting to write about or talk on the media about the process is a further attempt to gain control over the events and to guide others in the future. Such testimony has also led to people becoming actively involved in campaigning to help prevent the situations that led to the disaster recurring. The involvement of the parents of children killed in shootings in the anti-gun lobby is just one example of this.

● *Feelings* are often the most difficult to release, perhaps only coming later when the catastrophe is safely behind. Long after impact, sensory perceptions may remain as frightening memories. For instance, the awful noise accompanying any event or the terrible silence and stillness, vivid visual experiences and the smell of the disaster haunt those who survived the terrorist attacks on the Twin Towers in New York in September 2001.

● *Tears* are important in the release of feelings, maybe triggered by others' grief and distress, though, as we have said, sometimes difficult for some men or cultures where they are viewed as weakness. Caregivers, such as ambulance personnel, doctors or social workers, are sometimes hidden victims of disasters when they are assumed to be invulnerable. Communal rituals and public acknowledgement of suffering may also help tears and anger, but generally feelings have to come out bit by bit when the person can gradually test out how he/she feels.

● *Perception of the future* and the need to get on with the demands of living is a signal that recovery has started, some trust in the world and hope returns; certain survivors become more aware of what matters to them and have a greater insight into their coping resources (see Raphael, 1986).

As mentioned earlier, care for workers and helpers is an important component of any treatment approach. Psychological debriefing to lessen the stress of encounters with death and devastation prevents illness that can arise out of feelings of depression at not being able to do more. Lack of preparation for the role, whether through lack of training or shock, may mean that those involved require support. Many of the helpers in the Liverpool/Hillsborough teams found that they had to relearn counselling skills so that they could empathise with large numbers of people unloading all their grief and anger upon them. Support groups are useful, especially because they do not make the helpers feel that they have failed or that they are themselves somehow being psychoanalysed. Group processes help members to explore their reactions, reviewing positive and negative aspects in order to integrate (that is, be able to look at a distance and retrospectively) what was learned for oneself, for others and for the future.

Conclusion

This chapter has described how research and practice have helped identify the range of emotions that occur in reaction to crises, either developmental crises or trauma and sudden loss. It urges practitioners to remember that many of these reactions are normal and understandable and that staying with people while they experience them is an important skill. Opinion is split on what has been seen as a 'rush' to counselling for those involved directly or indirectly in traumatic events. What is important is that increasingly as part of social services involvement in planning for response to disasters, the possibility to offer counselling is kept open, and that people can avail themselves of it without feeling stigmatised or aberrant because they need to express their emotions.

putting it into practice

Asking people to undertake exercises related to grief, bereavement and crises is always difficult. Working with crises can precipitate feelings associated with our own losses. However it is for this reason that it is important for workers to be aware of ways in which they may be affected by their own experiences. This can help bring new insights as well as avoiding blocks. What follow therefore are some ways of reflecting on our own strengths and vulnerabilities.

1. Experiencing loss. Think about a time when you lost something. This can be as simple as losing your keys or your diary or you may choose to focus on a more significant loss. The choice is yours. Write down all the emotions you went through and the different behaviours – disbelief, searching, anger, sweating, and so on. Think about how these divide up into:
   - 'somatic' reactions: that is, bodily reactions
   - 'emotional' or some say 'psychic' reactions: that is, how we feel and what we think
   - behavioural reactions: what we do.

   This analysis will help illustrate some of the theories related to crisis, grief and bereavement that have been discussed in this chapter.

2. Coping with loss. If you feel able focus now on a more significant loss. Again you should choose something that you feel able to think and talk about. Using a tape recorder, 'tell yourself' how you coped with this loss. That is describe to the tape recorder, Using sentences starting with, for example, 'I did ...', I felt ...', what you did, how you felt, and so on. This is 'telling yourself' because only you will listen to the tape.

3. Listen to the tape recorder and note down the words that you are using. What do they tell you about the way you felt about the experience? If you feel able, listen to the tape recorder again and again looking out for different things. For example, what seem to be the significant things that helped you cope? How much did you share with other people?

These exercises will help you to reflect on how you have coped with loss and this will provide strength for you when dealing with other people's loss. However remember that this might be a difficult or painful experience for you. You should ensure that, if it becomes too difficult, you stop the exercise and talk with someone else, either a close friend, a tutor or a counsellor if you feel that would help. Such self-reflection and the ability to recognise painful areas is an indication of strength.

Further reading

Sheldon, F. (1997) *Psychosocial Palliative Care: good practice in the care of the bereaved and dying*. Cheltenham: Stanley Thornes. An excellent introduction to the theory, practice and emotions involved in working with those experiencing loss through terminal illness.

Payne, S., Horn, S. and Relf, M. (1999) *Loss and Bereavement*. Buckingham: Open University Press. Although written primarily for nurses this book is extremely useful for social work students. It draws on research and other literature to explain the practices and processes of loss and bereavement.

7 | Task-centred practice

Introduction

Task-centred practice, also known as brief therapy, short-term or contract work has had a significant impact on both social work practice and the organisation of services. It is one of the most popular and frequently cited methods of working by students and workers. However, because it is so popular, task-centred work is often misunderstood and misrepresented as being simplistic, nothing more than making agreements with service users about what is to be done and who is to do it. Also, because it shares with crisis intervention the notion of being time-limited there is often confusion between task-centred work and crisis intervention.

This chapter explores how emphasis on substantive factors and concrete problems has been developed into a well-specified set of procedures associated with task-centred practice. Undertaken effectively task-centred practice has the potential to empower, but there are also criticisms that its focus on outcomes could make it attractive to a managerialist agenda. Discussion of some of the research into the effectiveness of task-centred casework will help to highlight the main ideas and to explore the advantages and risks of utilising this approach. A framework for understanding is offered, summarising the components of task-centred work, while case examples illustrate the method in action. This will help clarify how it differs from crisis intervention.

Context

As the various names suggest, task-centred practice is focused work that is time-limited and offers approaches to problem-solving that take into account the needs of individuals to bring about change in their situations, and the requirements of agencies that work is targeted and effective. An account of the development of the method shows that its introduction challenged some of the principles of casework. As Doel (2002) points out, task-centred work has maintained its popularity through changes in social work practice that have included approaches based on behaviourism, systems theory, problem-solving and user rights and empowerment. At various times it has been seen to complement these approaches, while at the same time being seen as a method of intervention in its own right. It is a method that has been tried and tested in a wide variety of agencies, with a range of problems and with people from diverse cultures and backgrounds. It has been subject to more evaluation and scrutiny than any other method and is significant in that it derives from research and lends itself to research (Ford and Postle, 2001).

The significant contribution made by task-centred practice is that it moves workers from individualised therapeutic approaches to problem-solving techniques. It acknowledges that the person with the problem also has the means to resolve it, and that social work intervention should become more of a partnership. In this way task-centred casework can be seen to be a method that empowers users of social work services. It offers an optimistic approach that moves the focus away from the person as the problem, to practical and positive ways of dealing with difficult situations.

Just as importantly its introduction led to changes in the way that services are delivered. The most common organisation of services now includes some kind of referral or intake point, where people can present their problems and receive short-term help to alleviate immediate pressures. If appropriate, they can then be referred on to other agencies or to other long-term service provision within the agency. This organisation grew out of the adoption of methods of task-centred casework by many social work agencies. Doel (2002) has suggested that because of both the time-limited nature of the intervention and its capacity to demonstrate outcomes, task-centred work offers an answer to survival for social work in the changing organisational context. However this is both a positive and a negative, as Ford and Postle (2001) point out. The problem-solving focus of task-centred work could lead to assumptions that it is synonymous with care management. However this is a superficial correlation, and workers have to ensure that they fully understand and apply the principles of task-centred work to ensure that care management is both user-focused and leads to effective problem-solving.

How the task-centred approach developed

It seems hard to believe, in this era of short-term work, contracts with clients and setting up evaluations of projects, that for many years between 1920 and the 1960s practitioners tended to concentrate less on problem-solving processes and more on in-depth assessment and the client–worker relationship. Models of practice therefore tended to involve long-term work, exploration of clients' feelings, a tendency to talk about, rather than take action on difficulties, and an interest in underlying, rather than presenting problems. Consequently some clients received help for years, and compulsive care-giving by helpers often resulted in the difficulties becoming the responsibility and 'property' of the worker (Buckle, 1981).

This model meant cases were kept open indefinitely: visiting was done on a friendly but aimless basis; providing pre-care or after-care services was the global aim but there were few specific goals to be accomplished, with or without the clients' agreement. This led Davies (1985) to call social workers 'maintenance mechanics': he says this is a key social work role and suggests that craving for change is textbook idealism. However, proponents of task-centred practice would disagree. They propose that social work should be a focused activity and, owing a debt to Perlman (1957), should educate clients to become good at problem-solving. Furthermore, emphasis on efficiency, effectiveness and economy means that social workers have to justify their services and prove to those who provide funds that social work works.

So, how did we reach this position of being able to show the relationship between inputs and outcomes? In North America, in 1969, a four-year study into brief versus extended casework was published (Reid and Shyne, 1969). Clients in a large voluntary agency dealing with family welfare were offered two contrasting 'packages' of social work intervention: one was an experimental brief service of planned short-term treatment (PSTT), consisting of eight interviews; the other was the usual practice in the agency of long-term service lasting up to 18 months. To everyone's surprise, the clients in the short-term group improved more than those given the continued service. In fact the latter tended to deteriorate! The authors hypothesised that a law of diminishing returns was operating. For both workers and clients, the closer we reach a deadline the more motivated we are. Once help is extended beyond a certain point, clients may lose confidence in their own ability to cope (as intimated in crisis intervention) and become dependent on the worker or the agency, with which they may develop a kind of negative attachment. In addition, when improvement or change does occur, the study revealed that this is likely to occur early on in 'treatment', regardless of the worker's implicit long-term goals.

The initial Reid and Shyne research was a curtailed form of long-term work. The results appeared to show that brief periods of service, concentrating on limited goals chosen by the client, were often more effective and more durable than open-ended work. It seemed that setting a time limit led to the expectation that rapid change would occur, thus increasing the motivation and energy of all the participants. The North American projects in the 1960s concentrated on advice-giving and active exploration of problems. They aimed for unambitious, specified goals. Moreover, their performance was committed and hopeful although these might have been placebo effects, adding to the success.

The first book implementing a specific task-centred 'therapy' translated the results of research into the elements of the approach that seemed to be linked to its success (Reid and Epstein, 1972). By that time, an even more systematic and goal-directed framework had been produced which suggested that there should be a maximum of 12 interviews within three months, focusing on limited, achievable goals which are chosen by the client. From then on, social workers who tried out the idea were instrumental in helping to further refine the model (Reid and Epstein, 1977). This refinement has continued with Reid developing a guide to task 'menus' (see Doel, 2002, p. 195).

The UK context

Throughout the development of the approach in North America, parallel research was being conducted in the UK by Matilda Goldberg and her colleagues (Goldberg *et al.*, 1977). They found that the model used by a social service department area team in

Buckinghamshire applied to only a minority of clients, at least in its 'pure' form. Those with a need for practical resources who acknowledged that they had a problem fared best. Involuntary/unwilling clients or those who had chronic, complex problems were less amenable. Having said this, there were positive gains for the workers in the project, who improved their capacity for clearer thinking and forward planning. Tackling small, manageable objectives, rather than vague global ones, proved more realistic. For example, a contract set up by a student social worker with a 14-year-old boy to behave himself was breached when he committed offences. The contract stated that the goal would be to stop offending; not only is this a negative way of putting things (doing something positive is preferred), but the objective was too ambitious and stated in 'world-wide' terms. Far better to aim low, for instance, a weekly contract that he will visit his 'gran' and try to keep out of trouble – for example not steal cars. Also, social workers in the project found themselves feeling less guilty about being unable to sort out everything, the Utopian cure-all that we all foolishly try to cope with.

Subsequently, Goldberg's team set up three experimental projects using task-centred work in a probation department, in two intake teams and in a hospital social work department (Goldberg *et al.*, 1985). Task-centred methods proved applicable to between half and two-thirds of all cases. The remaining groups largely ended the attempt to be task-centred after the problem search (phase 1) resulted in no agreement about the target problem. On the other hand, most clients who completed all five phases were pleased with the approach and said that their problems were reduced (see below for explanation of the five phases). The clients who could not be helped included those whose lifestyle centred on chronic 'cliff-hanging' episodes and those whose difficulties were deep-seated and longer-term. Other groups who were not amenable to this approach are those who are not in touch with reality. For example people involved in substance abuse and those with severe mental disorders are not likely to respond to a task-centred approach.

The skills required of the workers included:

- an ability to listen and grasp what the client was truly bothered about
- to know when to use systematic communication styles and when to be responsive (this is analysed below)

● to have the ability to renegotiate the contract or agreement
● to act as an empowering partner, not just a service provider
● to be explicit about time limits, and to give reminders about ending the contact, without harping on this.

Difficulties were encountered by social workers who recognised that it was not authentic to treat clients as equals when they have no control over resources or when people were under surveillance as part of statutory duties such as a probation order.

Communication

Returning to the point about having to acquire the technique of simultaneously using two styles of communicating, it is specified in Reid and Epstein (1972) that communication be systematic and responsive. This means that as well as having to keep the client to the agreed task in hand, so as to reach the target problem, the worker also has to remain empathic to the client's messages, respecting his/her right to self-determination. On occasions this feels to be something of a paradoxical expectation. The worker's responses should ensure that the client's problem-solving does not become diffuse, but clients have a tendency to wander from the point, discussing matters that are not part of the agreed focus. If, for instance, a client has a chosen objective to control his/her children's behaviour and each time he/she meets with the social worker the discussion wanders on to marital circumstances, this might cause the worker a dilemma. Is communication becoming unsystematic or is the marital disharmony a more important problem? Or is it connected to the children's behaviour and therefore a central feature of the problem being worked on?

There is always a possibility that the original problem search and agreed target problems are no longer valid, that goals will have to be redefined. Of course, in practice, it is permissible to allow for some wider discussion and then, in view of the limited time available, to bring the client back to the task. Alternatively, it would be robot-like and unresponsive to cling to the contract and it might be necessary to say, 'We often seem to get around to talking about your marriage. Do you think we should look again at what we've decided to do?' Of itself responsiveness will not bring about change; structuring the work may. Ensuring that we have really understood what a problem means to someone requires, as we have

seen in earlier chapters, giving attention to the client's communications and not introducing ideas that are only of interest to the
worker. Combining this with a structured use of time and planned
strategies helps to accomplish change in a step-by-step fashion.

To give some idea of how both qualities, of systematic and
responsive communications, can be preserved it is important to
convey an understanding that there are many other difficulties. But
a start has to be made somewhere if the person does not want to
become overwhelmed. An explanation could be given at the beginning of the process that each area selected by the client will
eventually be discussed in detail. The point is to remain flexible;
sometimes a passing remark seemingly unconnected to the task
focus might be worth looking into rather than letting it pass or
changing the subject. Thus, a woman who is worrying about her
rent arrears may hint that her partner gets out of control when
disciplining her children. Or, a person might say, 'I'm confused ...'.
Such an incomplete sentence could hide many meanings that are
worth bringing to the surface by asking, 'About what?' It is always
useful to spot when clients and others translate, mediate or generalise their experiences using words such as nobody, never, always
and so on. Having said that, it is important to remember that a
fundamental principle is that the focus for the task-centred work is
agreed by both client and worker, and not imposed by the worker's
interpretation of 'what the real problem is'.

The task-centred approach

The research by Reid and Epstein suggested that task-centred practice deals with eight problem areas (which cover most of the
referrals met with by practitioners). They are:

Interpersonal conflict
Dissatisfaction in social relations
Problems with formal organisations
Difficulties in role performance
Problems of social transition
Reactive emotional distress
Inadequate resources
Behavioural problems
(Reid, 1978; Reid and Hanrahan, 1981)

There are definite steps to be taken in the process of problem-solving. These are five phases in helping clients to achieve their own modest goals:

1. *Problem exploration or entry* – when clients' concerns are elicited, clarified, defined in explicit terms and ranked in order of importance to the client. In certain circumstances (for example where there is a court order) there may be mandated problems and/or tasks.
2. *Agreement* is reached with the client on the target for change, which is then classified by the worker under the previous eight categories. In this stage sometimes problems can be confused with goals. For example not having somewhere to live can be framed as a problem but finding somewhere to live is a goal.
3. *Formulating an objective* that has been decided jointly. Agreement is reached on the frequency and duration of the contract. (In respect of contracts that are written, it is as well to clarify the traditions of certain social classes and minority ethnic groups, as the 'legal' concept may be misunderstood. Of course, such contracts in social work are not legally binding but simply clarify respective tasks and roles.) The tasks to be undertaken do not always have to be 'physical doings' but they can include tasks such as cognitive reflections (Doel, 2002).
4. *Achieving the task(s)*, for which no prescribed methods or techniques are proposed within task-centred literature.
5. *Termination* is built in from the beginning. When reviewing the achievements, the worker's efforts are examined, not merely those of the client or the other helping networks.

Some techniques in each of the five phases

Once again, these are not recipes for action, merely some notion of what is likely to crop up in the sequence of phases towards problem resolution.

Phases 1 and 2

In the initial contract, exploration and agreement phases (say between one and six contacts), if the client is not self-referred:

● find out what the referrer's goals are

- negotiate specific goals and if these can be time-limited
- negotiate with the referrer what resources will be offered to achieve these goals.

If the client applies independently and voluntarily:

- encourage the client to articulate his/her problems
- encourage ventilation of feelings about these
- step in with immediate practical help if necessary
- assist the person to take some action on his or her own, something small and achievable
- elicit the array of problems with which the client is currently concerned
- explain how the task-centred approach works, for example time limits; priority focus; schedule for interviews; anyone else who needs to be involved, such as family member
- define the stated problems in specific, behavioural terms
- tentatively determine target problems with client
- choose a maximum of three problems ranked for priority by the client
- classify the problems under the eight categories
- list the problems in a written contract, if used.

Phases 3 and 4

In formulating objectives and achieving the tasks (say between the fourth and tenth contact):

- Make the task selection phase short. If the targeting of problems has been done carefully this will indicate what/who needs to change;
- Get the client to think out her/his own tasks and what effects will be likely, helping if the client's assessment looks unrealistic, will make things worse or cannot be achieved in the time.
- If other people are involved, get their agreement too.
- If need be, help the client to generate alternatives and identify what resources are around.
- Support task performance by a variety of problem-solving means. For instance: refer to a specialised source if this is required (for example debt counselling, vocational guidance, classes to learn a language); demonstrate or use games/ simulations/video; rehearse problem-solving; report back how it

went; accompany client for moral support; discuss client's fears, plans, resources; regularly record the status of the problem; examine obstacles and failures in detail.

● If other areas of concern emerge, decide in collaboration with the client if these are worth pursuing.

● Always ask about all the tasks in case failures are not mentioned.

● If the method has been modified as partially task-centred (for example for assessment only, or time limits are not part of the contract) consider what follow-up or alternatives will be used.

Phase 5

In the termination phase (hard to predict how long the process takes in each situation but say the final two to three contacts):

● talk about what will be the effect of ending the contact
● find ways of helping clients to cope with anxieties
● review progress and give encouragement
● help clients to identify further areas of work
● extend time limits only if clients feel that they need extra time and have shown commitment to working on tasks
● monitor only when mandated by agency or legal requirements or if part of a community care 'package'
● evaluate each person's inputs and record outcomes
● say goodbye sensitively.

For further information on task-centred processes, Epstein (1980) offers a detailed map of the model in action. Significantly Milner and O'Byrne refer to this method of intervention as a 'tourist map' because it involves no complex theory and social workers use its elements, without naming them, as a guide to where they want to go (Milner and O'Byrne, 2002, p. 117). They offer such aids as a 'Want sheet' and a 'Problem scale' to assist workers in using the method.

Framework for understanding task-centred practice

Effective task-centred practice requires understanding not only what has to be done but also why. This is not about trying to analyse the cause of problems in order to work on them, but more about knowing what makes the method effective. Critical reflection on each piece of work will help workers understand more about what has contributed to its success or failure. In this way workers can mirror what they need to do when they are using the method, as the purpose of task-centred work is to provide a form of training session for service users, helping them to discover what works and does not work for them (Doel, 2002).

That said, it is useful to provide a synthesis of the characteristics of the method:

● *Theories* that underlie the task-centred practice are really only concepts: they include the crisis notion that focused help given at the right time is as effective as long-term service. Also, task accomplishment is viewed as an essential process in human coping endeavours: the choice of tasks and success in tackling them motivates people towards improved problem-solving. Becoming effective in certain situations strengthens the ego; success breeds success. Though no specific problem-oriented theory exists at this point, nevertheless the underlying values that guide this approach are that workers should state what they are trying to achieve and clients' self-esteem and independence is preserved when they are seen as experts of their own lives. The use of time limits conveys the message that change is possible in the time agreed, and working to deadlines sometimes inspires commitment.

● *Problems* are psychosocial in nature. This does not mean that they rest in the individual but that there is a subtle relationship between the individual's experience of the problem and the structural circumstances in which the problem is situated. The eight categories describe problem situations rather than client types.

● *Goals* are modest, achievable, specific and often framed in behavioural terms; they are chosen by the client in collaboration with the worker. Goals are inherent in each of the five phases, completion of which would qualify the approach as fully task-centred. However, a partially task-centred approach is possible when only some of these phases are reached: an example of this would be task-centred assessment.

● *The client's role* is to identify desirable and feasible goals and to specify tasks and sub-tasks, prioritised in a working agreement with the social worker.

- *The worker's role* is to make explicit the time limits to the client and the agencies involved and to assist in the problem search, target and task setting by which problems are reduced and some solutions found.
- *Techniques* are really activities, examples of which are:

  (a) *Problem specification*, for example, 'When you try to get your son to go to school, what does he do? Who helps you? How do you react? What happens then?' and so on.

  (b) *Task planning* which incorporates agreeing tasks, planning detailed implementation, generating alternative solutions and summarising, for example, 'So what else could you try? Could you do this before we meet next time? Will you ask your husband to back you up? Are we clear about what we've agreed?' and so on.

  (c) *Analysing obstacles and failures* such as 'It sounds as though your husband says nothing when you try to get your son to go to school. What could we do to get him to help you more?'

  (d) *Planning tasks*, the detail of 'Who will do what?'

  (e) *Structuring interview time*, asking 'How long do you think we need?' and 'Our time is coming to an end. We have agreed ...'.

  (f) *Reviewing and ending*, for example, 'What did you think of the time limits? Did they help or not in what you achieved?'

Case example

Mr Singh is a 67-year-old widower. He has spent his adult life in England but his work had involved travelling and this means he has no friends in the locality in which he eventually settled. His married sons, who live many miles away, only visit him two or three times a year. Following a stroke Mr Singh has been accommodated in a facility for disabled people, but during the six months he has been there he has become reclusive and uncooperative. Rehabilitation efforts have ceased because staff complained that Mr Singh was unmotivated and aggressive; they even wondered if he was clinically depressed, as he slumped all day in a wheelchair, keeping himself to himself.

The social worker received a referral from the care staff to sort out the numerous debts that had accrued because Mr Singh had not claimed any benefits. She found that, far from being hostile, Mr Singh was a gentle, shy man who was not used to discussing his private affairs. She also considered that there were cultural differences in the way that Mr Singh might react to strangers knowing about his personal affairs. Culture might also affect the way that Mr Singh reacted to female carers.

The social worker considered recommending a change of worker, but before doing this she suggested that they try to deal with his debts by using a task-centred approach, which would not pry into his background but would focus on what needed to be done. He seemed more able to talk about concrete problems. He defined these as 'problems with formal organisations' and 'inadequate resources'. His goal was to become more independent. The contract was agreed that they would meet weekly to work on two target problems:

1. To pay off rent, telephone and fuel bills within the following three months.
2. To claim outstanding benefits from social security, insurance companies and salary from previous employers.

General tasks, such as writing letters, listing the debts, making phone calls and deciding who would do what were dealt with in the first two meetings. A schedule was drawn up about the frequency and duration of the meetings (mornings and for 25 minutes as Mr Singh tired easily). They agreed also to let the centre staff know what would happen.

Every Monday at the same time the social worker wheeled Mr Singh to a pleasant spot where they discussed how the debts could be cleared and which were the most pressing. Responsibilities were allocated, and each week they reviewed each other's task accomplishments. Sometimes the worker had to obtain necessary forms and give Mr Singh assistance in completing them. This was in part because although Mr Singh was fluent in spoken English, the technical language of the forms was not always easy to understand. Although there were minor changes to what was initially agreed, no revision of the contract was needed.

Mr Singh, in one of the task-centred discussions, confided to the worker his fear of returning home to live alone, and his loneliness at not knowing any neighbours. He talked about his shyness, which had even stopped him getting to know anyone in the unit. He also recognised that he would like to be able to share with people from his own cultural back-ground. Accepting that he had overcome his shyness with the worker, they examined ways in which to start a conversation, renegotiating a further task-centred working agreement that:

1. He would start a conversation with one of his companions at lunch every day.
2. He would write to his sons telling them how he had sorted out his finances, and ask if they would visit him some time.

Because Mr Singh became more outgoing, physiotherapy and occupational therapy were restarted, resulting in him being able to try walking with a tripod. One of Mr Singh's sons made a visit and offered to have his father home with him for a period to assess if this could be a long-term arrangement.

The benefits of undertaking task-centred practice

The case study helps to illustrate some of the benefits of using task-centred practice. First, and most importantly, task-centred does not mean simply assigning tasks, or setting 'homework' such as is common in behavioural and family therapies. It is a well-researched, feasible, and cost-effective method of working, which consumer feedback indicates is very helpful to the majority of parties (Butler *et al.*, 1978; Gibbons *et al.*, 1979). It offers a specific set of procedures where service users are helped to carry out problem-alleviating tasks within agreed periods of time. Tasks are not just activities; they have meaning because of the overall structure in which they take place. The person is the main change agent, helping the worker to assess and choose what the priorities for change ought to be (even if the worker has other ideas) and then agreeing who is going to do what. The movement from problem to goal is by tasks that are as diverse and varied as the problems, goals, users and services that generate them (Marsh, 2002).

Task-centred practice fitted well into intake teams (Buckle, 1981), and even though these may be disappearing in the light of organisational reforms, most social services departments will retain some kind of duty system and short-term projects. Interdisciplinary teams set up to establish community care may use a form of task-centred practice, basing their goals on what is worked out with service users, in addition to having a pre-planned exit time.

Debate has taken place about the use of task-centred methods in work that has been mandated by the courts, specifically in criminal justice work. Supervision is already time-limited in that it is defined by the sentence of the court or by the length of a licence. However, task-centred work is more than just working to a short timescale. The possibility of using task-centred practice within the duration of a supervision order, and arguing for early discharge once the identified and agreed goals have been achieved, is obviously an option. Aspects of the method have therefore been adopted by Trotter (1999) in his work with 'involuntary clients' discussed in the next chapter. However, the nature of the problems presented by offenders, in that they may be out of touch with reality by virtue of substance abuse or mental disorder, sometimes mean that this method is not appropriate.

Any practice that ensures that there is no misunderstanding about why contact is taking place is likely to be more successful – if only because it is more honest and does not build up false expectations. It also means that where the social worker is acting as an agent of social control, or is intent upon offering protection, there is no ambiguity about this.

The use of task-centred ideas is welcomed also by black practitioners (Devore and Schlesinger, 1981) and black and ethnic minority service users. Many social work methods have been experienced as eurocentric (Milner and O'Byrne, 2002). However, as can be seen from the case study, task-centred practice requires that the worker actively consider the implications of culture on both the problems experienced and the methods used to solve them. The methods do not further oppress people by taking over their lives or implying that the worker knows best. There is no mystery about what the worker is doing because he/she is as accountable as the client in carrying out agreed tasks. This lessens the sense of powerlessness when faced with 'authority' figures. Similarly, in women-centred practice, this method gives power to women clients to identify the source of problems, and some means of influencing them. In issues of childcare this might mean that the focus is on finding a support group or network, rather than a critique of the woman's parenting skills.

Apart from the somewhat rigid time limits, which possibly ignore certain ethnic traditions which prefer slow entry into family and community relations, task-centred work is beneficial in that it:

- Takes into account not only individual but also collective experiences during the stages of problem search, agreement and setting tasks. The source of the problem is not presumed to reside in the client; as much attention is paid to external factors, such as welfare rights and housing, where there is scope for supplying 'power' resources such as information and knowledge (Hirayama and Cetingok, 1988). The role for the worker is one of resource consultant.
- Focuses on individuals, couples, families, groups and/or organisations. Practical advice on how to approach problems and systems can be rehearsed, modified and copied in groups; peers, as well as social workers, can act as teacher/trainers in problem-solving (Northen, 1982).
- Addresses the strengths of people and their networks. For instance, it is an antidote to the process of labelling which assumes that being black is a problem. There is scope to valorise black people's strengths and use the resources of black communities (B. Ahmad, 1990). One aim of the method is to enhance self-esteem as well as problem-solving.
- Provides positive feedback for people who are not used to success. Setting achievable goals and do-able tasks means that people are more likely to fulfil them. The goals also have to be something to which the service user is motivated. Even though achieving the ultimate goal might take time, identifiable progress towards a desired goal provides motivation for further success.
- Does not rely on the notion of self-disclosure via a one-way, vertical helping relationship. It tries to put worker and client on the same footing.

Obviously the practice does not always go smoothly but nevertheless this approach has an over-arching usefulness; it does not require a search for 'suitable referrals' as even those that look as though they will not 'fit' may benefit from task-centred assessments. Here, the first two phases of problem exploration and classification can help everyone to see things more clearly and know what the work will entail. Similarly, some clients find it difficult to actually pinpoint the source of their distress or difficulty. Again a partially task-centred approach could offer clearer definition, from whence clients may choose not to go ahead or to be helped using an alternative method such as those found elsewhere in this book.

It was mentioned earlier that it could also be useful in working with organisations. The management technology called management by objectives (MBO) resembles task-centred practice, having agreed goals within a time-limited perspective (Coulshed and Mullender, 1999). In relation to staff and student supervision, also, some practitioners find it valuable having agreed set tasks and in-built mechanisms for mutual evaluation.

Last, we should not overlook the use of time itself as a therapeutic agent; working within a time limit pushes forward the process. As one client expressed it, 'A good idea, can't depend on someone all my life' (Butler *et al.*, 1978, p. 407).

The limitations of using task-centred practice

That said, there are limitations. Or more accurately there is concern that task-centred practice might lead to workers attempting to pigeonhole service users, or require them to adopt certain patterns or standards of behaviour. In fact at its worst task-centred work might be seen as a form of behaviour modification in that only certain forms of problem-solving behaviour will be acceptable.

A task-centred approach might have the capacity to facilitate empowerment but service organisation and performance management might lead to other pressures. The negative impact of MBO is management by results, and there are concerns that the imperative to use this method might be influenced more by the need to meet 'targets' for dealing with cases than by the needs of the service users. There are obvious benefits to management to dealing with cases quickly and reducing waiting lists. Of course, client self-determination and respect for persons are the accepted values of our profession, though hotly debated (see Webb and McBeath, 1990). They are also compromised by other imperatives. For example, in situations where there are perceived risks, agencies are loath to impose time limits. Cases are often kept open even if, as the various child abuse enquiries indicate, the work is not necessarily effective.

There nevertheless remain possibilities inherent in task-centred work of changing from service provision to service brokerage as community care plans show (DoH, 1989a), and for the method to achieve some of the goals outlined in Chapter 3. For example, the accounts of creative problem-solving with elderly people (Challis *et al.*, 1990) would indicate that this method of practice might be appropriate within the process of care management.

Comparison with crisis intervention

As a postscript to this chapter and the previous one it is necessary to consider how this approach differs from crisis intervention. Both encompass brief, focal work and may be used when clients are temporarily unable to sort out their own problems and are better able to use help to improve coping in a time-limited framework. This is as far as the similarity goes. Some of the research into the effectiveness of task-centred practice seems to have been tried with people who were in a state of crisis. We recognised in the previous chapter that people in crisis often cannot 'think straight', they cannot easily conceptualise their problems or the solutions without fairly heavy dependency on the worker in the initial and mid-way stages. Certainly, those in crisis are not ready for an energetic, problem-solving, equitable relationship with a worker and able to agree to a detailed contract that needs to be carefully thought through and planned.

It may be that both methods handle significant social, emotional and practical difficulties – but these need not be crises in the accepted sense. We know that, even with some flexibility, the work under discussion in this chapter tends to involve a systematic, structural approach. This involves focusing on one task at a time; goals are behaviourally specified, the whole programme tightly scheduled to fit a maximum of 12 to 14 interviews, the ending predetermined rather than dependent on the psychological recovery of the person in crisis. Turbulent change can occur in crises. These call for worker responsiveness that is not necessarily goal-directed. In sum, people in crisis are unlikely to be able to cope with the demands of a fully task-centred approach.

Conclusion

Task-centred practice is a significant method of intervention in social work. It came about as a result of empirical research and its aim is to bring about change. The fact that it is time limited and focuses on the problem rather than the person means that it is experienced positively by service users. They feel that they have some agency in their lives, they have the means to influence their situation. As such it can be empowering.

However, like all methods of intervention it is open to misuse and abuse. Workers might use it as a short cut and ignore the complexities of the situation with which they are faced. The emphasis on the short-term contract means that it might be incorporated into managerialist agendas that require rapid throughput of work. As with all methods of intervention it is necessary for practitioners to study them, understand them and reflect on their use in particular situations and not just assume that they are adopting 'quick fix' solutions.

---

putting it into practice

The best way to think about putting task-centred methods into practice is to reflect on your work with service users, but it is important when thinking about putting theory into practice that you do not inappropriately use methods with service users for your own ends. Choose a situation from practice that seems to have some clear indications that something has to change.

1. The essence of effective task-centred work is in the assessment. It is important to listen carefully to what is being said about the situation and to discern what the service user says he/she wants changing.
2. Once you have identified what the service user wants changing it is important to work with him/her to clarify what tasks need to be done to bring about the necessary change. Remember tasks need to be small manageable pieces of work that will be undertaken either by the service user or by you.
3. As you identify what needs to change, and work out what has to be done, and who does what it is helpful to write these down – both for yourself and for the service user.

4. Obviously you will now work with the service user to ensure that you both complete the agreement. However at this point it is also useful to do some reflective work on your own with the agreement. Think about when you first encountered the situation: does the agreement or contract reflect what you thought about the situation? Would you have chosen to focus on the tasks that the service user has chosen? What do you think the hurdles will be? What do you think are the strengths of the situation?

5. Once you have completed the time-limited piece of work with the service user it will be useful to go back to this list and see how the work that developed compared with your assessment. In doing so try to be honest about how much you influenced the situation and to what extent you were able to let the service user make his or her own decisions.

Further reading

Doel, M. and Marsh, P. (1992) *Task-centred Social Work*. Aldershot: Ashgate. A comprehensive text that expands on the introductory ideas contained in this chapter offering clear and practical guidelines.

Ford, P. and Postle, K. (2001) 'Task-centred practice and care management'. In P. Stepney and D. Ford (eds) *Social Work Models, Methods and Theories*. Lyme Regis: Russell House. A useful chapter that discusses the association of task-centred work with the principles and practice of care management, based on research.

Doel, M. (2002) 'Task centred practice'. In R. Adams, L. Dominelli and M. Payne (eds) *Social Work: themes, issues and critical debates*. Basingstoke: Palgrave. An excellent summary of task-centred work incorporating some new research and development undertaken by one of the originators, William Reed.

8 | Cognitive-behavioural work

Introduction

The final chapter in this section looks at methods that have been developed from psychology, but which are playing an increasingly important part in social work practice. The basic tenet of behavioural approaches is that behaviour is learned and unlearned. Much of the work was developed in psychology but behaviourism has influenced social work practice in a number of ways. In working with people with learning difficulties the principles of 'normalisation' or age-appropriate behaviour involve the basic principles of learning theory. Programmes working with offenders, especially those who are dependent upon substances such as drugs or alcohol, involve cognitive behaviour therapy, as do those working with people experiencing depression.

It could be argued that much of social work, in that it is about changing behaviour, has aspects of behaviourism. There are for example similarities between behavioural approaches and task-centred practice, in that both focus on a particular problem, follow specific procedures, test out approaches to problems and impose time limits. However there are also significant differences. In groupwork, aspects of learning theory operate in most group situations but there have also been developments, for example in criminal justice work, that rely specifically on behavioural approaches. In recent years social work educators and researchers have helped to make the concepts relevant and more accessible to social work (Hudson and Macdonald, 1986; Sheldon, 1995). Importantly they have illustrated that behavioural approaches fit well into the climate of evidence-based practice. Learning theory, on which behavioural principles are based, is a vast, well-researched field (Sheldon, 2000). Also there are a number of examples of how it is possible to evaluate behavioural methods by observing behavioural change (Trotter, 1999). However, despite the existence of this evidence, the implications for social work are complex.

This chapter therefore explores the theoretical basis of learning theory, and some techniques and procedures that developed from the application of this theory in social work practice. Because it is of growing interest to social workers, cognitive-behaviour therapy will be examined in some detail. Some of the advantages and disadvantages of behavioural approaches will be discussed, with a specific focus on the ethical implications of this work.

Background

The behavioural approach to therapy grew rapidly in the 1950s and 1960s, partly to get away from the dominance of the psychoanalytic perspective. It was imported from social psychology and is an example of the way in which social work can adopt theories from other disciplines and apply them in practice to formulate different ways of helping people. One of the significant differences between earlier practice and behavioural work is that those who take a psychosocial approach would say that behaviour, thoughts and attitudes, and feelings are influenced largely by the past and by internal conflict. As we saw in the chapter on 'counselling' even Transactional Analysis, with its focus on behaviour, sees the roots of that behaviour in past experiences. Skinner (1938), the theorist responsible for developing behaviourism, would have contested this by saying that behaviour and personality are determined mainly by current events in the external environment. More recent approaches in social work that emphasise focusing on solutions rather than causes also challenge the emphasis on the past, but in focusing on the future they do not necessarily advocate behaviourist methods (Parton and O'Byrne, 2000; Milner and O'Byrne, 2002).

As has been said, fundamental to the behaviourist school is the acceptance that if behaviour is learned then it can be unlearned, and new behaviours can be learned. There are however different types of learning.

Four types of learning

Psychologists have identified four types of learning, which are basic to an understanding of behavioural therapeutic approaches.

Respondent (classical) and *operant* conditioning were developed in work with animals. The former explained simple reflex behaviours such as blinking when a light flashes, while the latter model, developed by Skinner (1938), examined non-reflexive, active, trial-and-error learning. Experiments on *observational learning* showed that we also learn by watching other people, while more recent approaches recognise that that private self-talk and thoughts govern our behaviour too and contribute to *cognitive learning*. Let us take each of these four types of learning in turn.

Respondent conditioning

Howe (1987) gives an amusing set of examples that help to illustrate how behaviour that is out of conscious control can become controlled. He reminds us that Pavlov's dogs were taught to salivate at the sound of a tuning fork just before food was presented; thus the stimulus that evoked the response (fork sound) became the conditioned stimulus (S) and the saliva the conditioned response (R). Textbooks represent this as S – R.

Howe evokes the stimulus of a dog biting an unwary social worker. This will evoke a fear response, resulting perhaps in the worker avoiding all the places where dogs may lurk (in this event, the dog stimulus has widened and become *generalised* to a fear of all dogs). In other words, something happens and a specific *response* occurs. This gives a clue, moreover, to how the connection might be broken in therapy. Systematic desensitisation (also called reciprocal inhibition) is based on this principle of respondent conditioning. It is used primarily for anxiety and avoidance reactions. Once the stimuli that provoke anxiety have been assessed, relaxation techniques are taught and the client helped to establish an 'anxiety hierarchy'. So, for example, a person who is afraid to leave the house will be asked to rank which situations he/she finds easy and which most difficult when trying to go outdoors. While the client relaxes, each situation, say from putting out the milk bottles to going to the shops, is imagined progressively up the 'ladder' of feeling. *In vivo*, that is, real-life experience, is probably one familiar to education social workers who may help a pupil to return to school by gradually getting used to the bus route, the playground and finally the classroom with the other children.

Operant conditioning

This consists of actions that operate on the environment to produce consequences. The key feature is that behaviour is altered by its consequences. If the changes brought about by the behaviour are reinforcing (that is, bring about a reward or eliminate something unpleasant for the person) then there is more chance that that behaviour will occur again. Thus, operant behaviour therapy has been useful in returning long-stay hospital patients to the community, because token economy systems and verbal praise rewarded desired behaviour such as self-help and social skills and reduced unwanted, bizarre actions. Unlike insight giving and the psychoanalytic approach, this method has been found appropriate for people who are diagnosed psychotic, since no interpretation of 'why' the behaviour occurs is necessary. (See Sheldon, 1984, for further examples of this method with those who are mentally ill.)

Positive reinforcement, known as the ABC of behaviour (Hudson and Macdonald, 1986), is most useful for social workers, especially those dealing with parents whose children misbehave. Parents find it fascinating to discover that they may inadvertently have been reinforcing the 'wrong' behaviour. Thus, the child screams and gets a sweet to keep him/her quiet: this behaviour is more likely to occur again because of the reward. To understand the sequence of events it is necessary to examine the Antecedents of the Behaviour and its Consequences (ABC). This is shown diagrammatically below.

Antecedents	Behaviour	Consequences
Mother and sweet refusal	Child screams	Receives sweet

An important aspect of giving reinforcers, for example in encouraging children in residential accommodation to clear away their games, is that the reward, say a smile or thanks from the staff, should be given *immediately and consistently* by the whole team. This consistent response has to continue until such behaviour is occurring naturally and need not be so systematically commented upon (because the reward tends to lose some of its value over time). Here, 'correct' behaviour is rewarded and undesirable behaviour ignored. Using a visual aid to record positive gains such as 'star charts' can reward achievements. Randall (1990) used a similar device to boost an older person as she began to do household chores.

Chaining and backward chaining are operant procedures too; they can be used to teach new behaviours and have been successful in work with people with learning difficulties (Tsoi and Yule, 1982). Teaching self-help skills such as dressing or brushing one's teeth is not as simple as it sounds, though, because each successive step to achieve such behaviour has to be separately analysed and progressively tracked. An example of backward chaining was that used by foster parents to teach their foster son, who had a learning difficulty, to make his own bed. The foster mother performed all but the last link in the chain, and then reinforced the child for carrying out the last step of tucking in the sheet. Then the last two links were left for him to master, and so on backwards. He needed a lengthy programme but eventually gained the satisfaction of fully completing the tasks himself.

The termination of something unpleasant is called negative reinforcement and is aimed at reinforcing wanted behaviour, so that children may keep quiet if only to avoid the pain of being shouted at. This is not to be confused with punishment, a confusion that has blighted recent social work practice when 'pin down' procedures have been adopted in residential homes as a means of changing behaviour.

This strategy is not as welcome as a positive reward because it does little to increase new behaviour, and shouting can sometimes become rewarding when some attention is preferred to none. A combined strategy is preferred if the aim is to decrease or extinguish unacceptable behaviour. Accordingly, when staff in a unit for disabled people wanted to stop a 10-year-old girl from whining, they collectively ignored her when she whined, and played bubbles and gave her a much-loved mirror when she was quiet.

'Time out' (that is, from reinforcement), is an extinction procedure which, when used properly and ethically, can be successful. Some agencies mistakenly control aggressive behaviour by isolating people for lengthy periods – this is not time out but dubious punishment. The procedure should follow within seconds of the misbehaviour, clear explanations should have been given in advance about what would happen and why, and the person should be taken to a time-out area, such as the corner of the room where there are no pleasant distractions or harmful objects for between three and five minutes. When working with groups of parents whose children were 'driving them up the wall', Scott (1983) found it necessary to keep parents motivated by using humour (a relaxation technique, in essence), teaching them the 'when ... then' technique ('When you have cleared away your toys then you can watch television'), modelling the use of praise and time out and, most importantly, warning that target behaviours usually get worse before they get better!

Observational learning

By copying what other people do we can learn something without having to go through a process of trial and error. Bandura (1977) says that there are three different effects of what is known as modelling: we can learn new skills or ideas; social skills can be imitated and practised; and fear responses can be inhibited, for example sitting next to someone on a plane who enjoys the experience. The main difference from the previous two types of learning is that reinforcement is not viewed as essential. Learning can be deliberate, such as the groups set up to teach social skills or assertiveness via role play and video films; or it can be unplanned, when, for instance, clients copy the way workers talk to social security officials on the telephone. Imitative learning is even more likely when there is a good working relationship or where the model is perceived as competent and of high status. Black staff in nurseries for black children (see Morgan, 1986) are deliberately chosen to counter images of white people as superior. Play materials that portray successful black people, music, art and literature provide positive symbolic models for the children. This active modelling (pro social modelling) has been developed by Trotter (1999) as one aspect of work with involuntary clients, for example those in the criminal justice system on court orders. This is discussed in more detail below.

Cognitive learning

Traditionally, learning theory has been concerned with outward behaviour, fixing people as passive beings whose behaviour can be altered by environmental controls. However, it has been recognised by cognitive behaviourists that we also feel and think, that we attach meaning to events. Bandura's work, mentioned above, paved the way inasmuch as some kind of internalisation of images can influence behaviour. Beck (1989) made a major contribution; working with depressed and emotionally disordered people he suggested that negative thoughts about themselves, their situation and their prospects brought about their emotional disorders. In the same way, Meichenbaum (1978) suggested that the way that we talk to ourselves, 'inner speech', affects our behaviour. Thus, if we keep telling ourselves that we shall not cope, there is a likelihood that we shall not.

However, in an excellent book on this topic (Scott, 1989), Mike Scott reminds us that the idea that thought processes can have an impact on emotions and behaviour is not a new one. For example Kelly's Personal Construct Theory (Kelly, 1955) showed how people construct their own view of the world, and work is only effective if we can try to understand that view. Ellis's (1962) Rational Emotive Therapy (RET) maintains that we upset ourselves by our irrational thoughts – we are upset, not by events, but by the view we take of them. Modern cognitive-behaviour therapy incorporates ideas from Kelly and Ellis. As a social worker, Scott has found these theories to be appropriate when working with depression, anxiety, marital work and work with children. The processes used in the practice of cognitive-behaviour therapy will be explored in some detail towards the end of this chapter.

Some techniques and procedures

The different approaches to learning mean that various ways of changing behaviour, and an increasing number of response options (that is, new skills), are employed by those using a behavioural approach. It is an action-oriented approach; people are helped to take a specific action to change observable behaviour; goals are spelled out in concrete terms and the procedure is almost scientifically evaluated by questioning what was done, how often, by whom, for what specific problem and under which particular circumstances. In the cognitive field, private or subjective meanings are the key to a person learning to understand how his or her cognitions (thoughts) have distorted reality and how, therefore, the individual has the responsibility and the capacity to unravel disturbances, regardless of their origin.

There are various comparisons with the psychosocial approach. For example, the client selects goals; the relationship is seen as important but not sufficient to achieve change; work is a joint effort; a written plan of action may be signed and the worker functions typically as a teacher who helps the client to understand the method to perpetuate self-help.

The initial stage of work is to do a behavioural assessment. The implications for assessment are vital because without a baseline the effectiveness of the intervention cannot be judged (Milner and O'Byrne, 2002). Hence assessment involves a detailed account of exactly what happens before, during and after a problematic event. The client may keep a diary so that all the factors that could affect outcomes are taken into account. Next, the client says which behaviour is to be increased/decreased. The worker clarifies who or what else in the environment could assist or prevent the change effort (for instance sometimes a partner might subtly reinforce a woman's drinking pattern; slippery floors and high toilets can deter frail elderly people from using the toilet). Each goal is framed in behavioural terms: as with task-centred practice, it is insufficient to say something like, 'John will do as his parents tell him.' Far better to state that John will be home by 9 pm during the week and 10 pm at weekends, what the reward will be and what will happen if he arrives later.

A handout or explanatory leaflet may sustain the person's efforts. For example, in challenging depressive thoughts a client may complete a sheet recording thoughts; the emotions these aroused; the automatic dysfunctional thought that accompanied this, such as 'I am worthless'; what rational thought response he or she tried and the degree of success he or she achieved. Or it could be that the strategy is to increase a person's behavioural repertoire; for instance helping to assert oneself with an authority figure. The techniques would follow the following steps:

1. Identify what behaviour is to be learned.
2. Instruct or demonstrate what this behaviour looks like.
3. Ask the person to role-play or copy the behaviour.
4. Provide feedback and reward desired responses.
5. Rehearse and practise again, modelling again if necessary.
6. Desired behaviour may need to be shaped gradually using praise.
7. Assign homework – 'practice makes perfect'.
8. Evaluate 'before and after' ratings of the behaviour.

This focused and programmatic approach could be seen to challenge the mystique of a psychosocial approach, but overall it does little to move us away from a 'treatment' model.

The growth of cognitive-behaviour therapy

As stated earlier, the field of cognitive-behaviour therapy owes much to the work of Kelly (1955). The basic premise is that we each bring 'theories' about the world, unique ways of anticipating events and relationships, which colour our cognitive processes. These approaches have been developed effectively in work with perpetrators of domestic violence, where male 'theories' of women and women's behaviour have been challenged (Macrae and Andrews, 2000). Similarly, Ellis's (1962) work attempted to show that people's aberrations in thinking, such as self-defeating beliefs, create disturbances in the way we feel about things. Ellis would propose that if someone is unhappy after a divorce, it is not the divorce itself that causes this but the person's beliefs about being a failure or losing a partner, or whatever. Beck's application of these ideas to treating depression (see Beck, 1989) in the 1970s contributed significantly to the growth of the cognitive-therapy movement.

By developing a system of psychotherapy that helped people to overcome their blocks and the way they reacted to situations, he educated them to understand their cognitive styles and underlying cognitive structures (or unconscious philosophies) that were activated by particular events. Methods to correct erroneous beliefs included:

● An *intellectual* approach, which identified misconceptions, tested how valid these were and then substituted more appropriate concepts.
● An *experiential* approach, which motivated people to experience situations powerfully which could modify assumptions, and a behavioural approach which encouraged the development of new coping techniques, for instance, systematic desensitisation procedures described earlier.

So Beck worked not only on clients' thoughts, but also on outward behaviour and feelings. Most practitioners use the term cognitive-behavioural nowadays to illustrate that problem reduction involves a wide variety of modalities.

For a time, critics of such methods pointed out that workers seemed to ignore clients' stories and how they felt. Early films of Albert Ellis show him humourously disputing clients' philosophies and crisply dismissing the importance of their early history and relentlessly repeating that, 'You feel bad because you think it's bad.'

Although sensitivity and acceptance are seen as part of the thera-peutic alliance, once a few goals have been identified with a client, techniques could involve rapid-fire questioning which tries to reveal the absurdity and self-destructiveness of those irrational 'shoulds' and 'oughts' which block change. However, Beck (1989) warns against dogmatism and ignoring when clients disagree; he ensures that his interpretation is accepted, saying, 'You've heard my view of the problem, what do you think of it?' If there are reservations the person is encouraged to offer other interpretations and consider the consequences of his or her ideas.

The stages followed in cognitive-behaviour therapy are:

1. *Engagement*. The client's expectations of help are explored in a leisurely fashion, conveying the message that there is time to listen and that the worker cares. The use of open questions allows the person to talk freely.
2. *Problem focus*. Having identified some problems that could be targeted for exploration, the worker asks, 'Which problems do you most want help with?', that is, prioritises.
3. *Problem assessment*. Here one specific example is examined in detail. The client is asked to describe an event, his/her underlying assumptions or inferences from it, his/her feelings, thoughts and behaviours towards the event, and 'In what ways would you like to feel, think and behave differently than you do now?', that is, goals.
4. *Teach cognitive principles* and practices of the therapy and get the person to look at his/her own thoughts; for example, teach the client to spot when he/she uses the words 'should' and 'ought', 'I should (not) have done that' or 'I ought to feel guilty' and so on.
5. *Dispute and challenge* these target assumptions.
6. *Encourage the client's self-disputing* through the use of questions. For instance, 'What evidence do you have? Is there another way of looking at this? Are your thoughts logical?'
7. *Set behavioural homework* to carry on this process and keep a diary of distorted inferences and self-evaluations.
8. *Ending*. Teach self-therapy to maintain improvement.

Currently within the cognitive-behaviourist arena there is acknowl-edgement that 'thought' is a much more complicated notion. Chomsky undertook a study of the relationship between thought and language. He critiqued behavioural psychology, arguing that we are not lumps of clay, shaped by punishment and reward. He asks how is it that very young children, without being taught deliberately, master the complexities of language (see Magee, 1982; Lyons, 1977). In other words, there is probably an intimate relationship between the deep structure of language and the workings of the mind. We almost come full circle again to Kelly's theories of how we each construct our worlds.

Motivational interviewing

In criminal justice work this interrelationship between thought and action has been the subject of much analysis in working with addictive forms of behaviour, especially alcohol addiction. Approaches to addictive behaviour have included counselling and alcohol education. Behavioural therapies originally depended upon the use of Antabuse as a form of respondent conditioning. This involved administering a drug that created a nauseous reaction when alcohol was consumed. Ultimately the person addicted would associate the consumption of alcohol with nausea and would be deterred. More recently research in the area of clinical psychology led to the development of treatments based on cognitive-behavioural approaches.

The most widely used approach is based on the work of Prochaska and DiClemente (*The Transtheoretical Approach: crossing the traditional boundaries of therapy*, 1984), where stages of change in the motivation of the person experiencing the addiction are identified and seen as forming the motivational cycle. When working with clients who are addicted to alcohol, probation officers organise their intervention around the stages of the cycle. The interventions involve work that is close to individual counselling, but also utilises some of the basic behavioural approaches outlined above.

The stages of the cycle are:

● *The precontemplative stage* where change is not necessarily desired by clients at a personal or psychological level but their circumstances cause them to consider it. Often offenders who have been sentenced for alcohol-related offences, or who identify alcohol as contributing to their offending behaviour, are at this stage.

- *The contemplation stage* involves an active structured evaluation with the worker of the pros and cons of changing and not changing. What would be the consequences of not drinking?
- *The action stage* will be a conscious and planned attempt at controlling the addictive behaviour.
- *The maintenance stage* is when the drinking is under control, but behavioural and cognitive strategies are employed to resist pressure or temptation to drink, thus avoiding the
- *Relapse stage*, which is when there is a resumption of the addictive behaviour.

Those who are able to respond positively to the maintenance stage may move to a state where drinking is no longer seen as problematic behaviour to be consciously controlled. However many people move between stages of the cycle several times before they reach that outcome. In that there are no rules about the organisation of the cycle people may relapse to precontemplation or contemplation.

Acknowledging this enables the worker to see such relapses as a normal part of the change cycle, and he/she will employ different forms of intervention at different stages, thus avoiding frustration and depression on the part of worker and client who might otherwise view relapses as failure. Techniques of *motivational interviewing* help the client move through the stages, which involve a series of non-confrontational practices to help people recognise for themselves the need for change by identifying the positive and negative consequences of their drinking behaviour. Uncomfortable ambivalences revealed at this stage may be resolved by acting to change the drinking pattern. In this way the desire to change has been identified by the person him or herself, which moves him/her from the pre-contemplative stage, although it can be revisited at different stages in the cycle.

Within motivational interviewing other techniques include behavioural assessment methods. These involve realistic appraisal of drinking patterns, consumption level and factors that precipitate drinking. Simple versions of drink diaries or other reporting methods are used in the initial stages, but more complex recording methods can be adopted later. In discussing the use of motivational interviewing in a project with the probation service, Remington and Barron (1991) describe another specific technique – a *constructional approach to social casework*. This emphasises the need to reinforce positive motivation as well as eliminate negative behaviour. In working with the client on his/her strengths and abilities, treatment decisions are made and achievable goals identified, taking into account the function of the drinking in the person's life and trying to find other means of fulfilling that function. These techniques, and the way they have been used effectively by probation officers, are described comprehensively in their article in the *Probation Journal* (Remington and Barron, 1991). It concludes by arguing that the general principles of this composite approach are relevant to a whole range of what they call 'appetite' problems, which include gambling, eating disorders, sex-related offending and the use of illegal drugs.

Apart from the positive outcomes of such approaches outlined in evaluations, a method (or collection of methods) that focuses on both the behaviour and the person's understanding of the behaviour gives some responsibility to the individual for wanting to change. Also important in making choices is an understanding of the effects of that change, both positive and negative. In this way the individual is participating throughout the process, and can make informed choices about his/her participation, rather than having to conform to a set of behaviours imposed by the worker. Also because the past is not seen as important; nor is the 'why', that is, the 'cause' of the problem pursued, some have argued that structured behavioural approaches go some way to user/client participation. Labelling is discouraged and accountability is made more evident (Milner and O'Byrne, 2002).

Of course, the consequences of not changing may be that he/she commits further offences, or fails to comply with the supervision order, but these outcomes become part of the considerations that either do, or do not motivate the person to change his/her behaviour.

Pro social modelling

Another application of cognitive-behavioural approaches is that developed by Trotter (1999) using the results of evaluative research into working with involuntary clients. Involuntary clients are those who either have not chosen to receive services, or have been court-mandated to receive services. Such clients challenge workers, who have the dual responsibility of legal duty or surveillance role and a commitment to helping and/or problem-solving. Trotter suggests that with this group of clients a combination of accurate role clarification, working with problems and goals that are defined by the client, and modelling and reinforcing pro social values have been found to be effective. For example, he found in research into the work of probation officers in Australia with offenders that using a pro social modelling approach was reduced their offending behaviour.

Pro social modelling draws on aspects of cognitive-behaviour therapy that focus on thought patterns and changing distorted thinking. Trotter suggests that people are influenced by behaviour that is modelled by others and by positive and negative reinforcement of their own behaviour. Pro social behaviour is developed by exposure to pro social role models, and reinforcing and rewarding pro social behaviour. As was said earlier in the chapter, an important factor is the nature of the rewards, the timing of the rewards and the consistency of the rewards.

In working with involuntary clients Trotter suggests that the worker has to:

- identify pro social comments and behaviour
- reward these with praise
- present him or herself as a pro social model – by demonstrating respect and self-revelation
- challenge anti-social or pro-criminal behaviour and attitudes.

It is apparent that in this work the worker–client relationship is crucial. Trotter acknowledges that in his training courses workers often claim that they already operate in this way. However it is suggested that without proper training and without being aware of the theoretical background, and need for consistency, social workers might apply some of these aspects erratically and might end up reinforcing the wrong behaviour. Trotter recognises that there are dilemmas connected to the use of power in relationships, but he asserts that, from his research and training courses, a careful and thoughtful approach can be achieved.

Overview for understanding behavioural approaches

- *The theoretical base* for behavioural approaches is learning theory, which includes respondent and operant conditioning, observational and cognitive learning.

● *Problems* that respond well to this approach include phobias, habits, anxiety, depression and obsessive–compulsive disorders (perhaps with drug treatment in tandem). Also, behavioural deficits such as social skills are treated through behavioural regimes.

● *Goals* are specific, observable (or self-reported in the case of something like a sexual difficulty). Goals must be stated in behavioural terms.

● *The client's role.* The person helps to measure the baseline behaviour, its frequency, intensity, duration and the context within which it occurs (see Sheldon, 1983). Diaries and other records may be kept. The client's view of what is a reward for him/her is vital, as are their goals for change. The person usually must be motivated or helped to be motivated. Where a child is the client, the carer or other change agent needs to be motivated.

● *The worker's role* is to help with the behavioural assessment and to mobilise any necessary resources. A contract may be drawn up. Strategies must be capable of being evaluated and measured for effectiveness. A concerned, genuine and hopeful relationship is necessary, if not sufficient, for change. The worker is active, sometimes directive and challenging, and an educator.

● *Techniques* include systematic desensitisation, extinction procedures and positive reinforcement, teaching self-control and thought-stopping techniques, motivating through positive construction, disputing irrational thoughts and giving information to other agents such as teachers, parents and colleagues involved in the programme.

Case example using cognitive-behaviour therapy

Velma is a 33-year-old woman whose mother was white British and father black American. She has been diagnosed as suffering from schizophrenia. She is an intelligent woman but has had limited formal education. Her turbulent childhood included episodes of abuse by her stepfather, although this was not acknowledged until she was an adult. During her adolescence she demonstrated behaviour that led to her spending a great deal of time in residential care, although she was never charged with any offences. Frequently it was stated that she was 'at risk' because she would run away from foster homes. Eventually she was confined to a secure mental hospital, having been sectioned under the Mental Health Act when she attempted arson on her mother's house.

On discharge from hospital Velma was accommodated away from her family in a semi-secure hostel. As part of her care programme she attended a day centre, was seen by a psychologist, a psychiatrist, and had a mental health social worker as well as a key worker at the hostel. It was her hope that she would be eventually given her own accommodation in the community.

However Velma was prone to outbursts of violent behaviour when she experienced frustration. This was not directed at other people but either at herself (self-harm by cutting herself) or at objects (for example she would kick doors, break windows or smash objects). On one occasion this behaviour had led to her spending a night in the police cells, and Velma was aware that because of her previous history she was at risk of losing her liberty if the behaviour continued. She was working with the psychologist to identify factors that precipitated the violence. They had identified that it occurred when Velma thought people were ignoring her, or she felt she was unfairly treated. The psychologist introduced Velma to ways of trying to think differently about the situations. Although her resentment was understandable she had to recognise that when she reacted angrily it was she who was punished, not others. She was encouraged to 'take time out' and control her breathing to try and stay calm in these situations.

Meanwhile, as part of her care planning approach, the hostel staff were also working with Velma to modify behaviour that was seen to be unacceptable. For example, Velma would get very attached to particular staff and want to spend time with them, getting frustrated and angry if they were not available for her. The staff, with Velma's agreement, devised a points system. She was allocated a number of points each month, and if she behaved in ways that were deemed unacceptable by the staff she would lose points. If she went below a certain threshold she would lose privileges, such as participating in social outings or being allowed to go out by herself. The aim of this was to extinguish the 'antisocial' behaviour rather than reward good behaviour.

Velma complied and overall her behaviour did improve. However at times she suggested to her social worker that she resented the fact that she thought some staff would deduct points unnecessarily.

Ethical considerations

The case of Velma not only illustrates the use of two different behavioural approaches, it also highlights some of the ethical problems that have been raised in connection with using behaviourist approaches.

In an early text describing *Learning Theory and Social Work*, Jehu (1967) discusses ethical issues raised by approaches that seek to change people's behaviour. He points out that to encourage people to behave in certain ways, or to attempt to extinguish behaviour that is deemed to be inappropriate or maladaptive, presents many dilemmas. The debate about the term 'normalisation' in working with people with learning difficulties highlights some of these (Wolfensberger, 1983). It is assumed that there are 'normal' ways of behaving, which are common to us all and should be used as some sort of yardstick for deciding whether someone is ready to live in the community. Whatever group of people we are working with, definitions of 'normal' must reflect the wide variety of behaviours demonstrated by those of us who are not subject to social work intervention. Otherwise social workers are at risk of abusing their power and influence, and of setting inappropriate standards. This was certainly how Velma experienced the actions of some of the hostel staff.

The alternative term for normalisation – age-appropriate behaviour – begs all sorts of questions about what is 'appropriate'. Such definitions must reflect differences based on, for example, class, race, ethnic background and gender, as well as age itself.

That said, it has been suggested that social workers do have power and they influence their clients in all sorts of subtle ways. For some the fact that the aim of the intervention is made explicit is more honest than the more 'therapeutic' interventions. As Sheldon (2000) argues, at the political level there are always concerns about which behaviour is to be reinforced, or extinguished, but on a case-by-case basis it is usually obvious, especially when anti-social or self-destructive behaviour is being demonstrated. As has been said, the principles of client involvement and consent can act as safeguards. In working with offenders or those demonstrating addictive behaviour it is sometimes argued that informed consent can be linked to principles of self-determination. If someone knows the consequences of continuing to offend, or continuing to abuse harmful substances, then he or she can actively choose to be involved in a behavioural approach. However, if the alternative is the threat of a custodial sentence, or continued incarceration in either a prison or a mental hospital, then it is questionable how free such choices are.

Those who support behavioural approaches have argued that because of the structured approach, and the overwhelming evidence of its success (Sheldon, 2000), then it would be immoral not to use these methods. Hudson and Macdonald (1986) argue that behavioural work is usually effective because it is prepared to measure what is achieved and engages clients in working on overt behaviour which they choose to change, not covert goals which the worker thinks would be 'good' for them. It could be argued that being prepared to share skills with clients, teaching them to avoid inappropriate dependence on workers, gives clients more opportunities to achieve social acceptability.

However like most individual approaches the major criticism of the approach is that it focuses on the individual and holds the individual responsible for his/her behaviour and circumstances. In this way it is supporting the status quo (Trotter, 1999). Although these approaches may give the individual agency, in other ways they reflect a reductionist approach that does not take into account the social and economic circumstances that contribute to the individual's behaviour. For example in the case of Velma the race and gender considerations that are part of both her history and her current circumstances are not addressed. She has to learn to 'cope' by reacting to them in a different way.

Conclusion

This chapter has demonstrated that behavioural approaches adopted from psychology influence social work practice in a number of ways. As a structured way of working with emphasis on demonstrating changes these approaches fit in well with an evidence-based approach to social work practice, or, as it is commonly known, the 'what works' approach. The chapter has also illustrated that the approaches can be used in different social work settings and with different user groups.

Although there is thought to be merit in the fact that the desired outcomes of intervention are transparent, and usually negotiated, it is apparent that the methods do precipitate some ethical challenges.

However it may be that these challenges exist for all social work intervention.

---

putting it into practice

Behaviour modification can operate in a variety of ways – both formally and informally – so it is important that you are aware of the way that you can influence situations.

1. Thinking about Trotter's pro social modelling, identify a piece of work that you have been involved in. Reflect on the way that you behaved with this case. You can do this by thinking about your work over time, or by focusing on one interview. How do you think that the actions that you have taken, the words that you have used or the stance that you have taken might influence the situation? Do you nod a lot in interviews, or make encouraging noises? Do you show your disapproval? Might this be reinforcing? In what other ways might you be influencing behaviour?

2. Identify a situation from your practice in which you might consider using behaviour modification techniques (or referring someone for this kind of treatment). Write down all the reasons for using such techniques and all the reasons against using them. Are there any situations in which you feel it would be totally inappropriate? Why?

Further reading

Trotter, C. (1999) *Working with Involuntary Clients*. London: Sage. This book describes Trotter's research within the criminal justice system in Australia, but it gives some useful background discussion of the principles of behavioural methods and the approach can be transferred to work with other user groups.

Sheldon, B. (2000) 'Cognitive behavioural methods in social care: a look at the evidence'. In P. Stepney and D. Ford (eds) *Social Work Models, Methods and Theories*. Lyme Regis: Russell House. This chapter argues, on the basis of research evidence, for the use of behavioural methods in social care.

Cigno, K. (2002) 'Cognitive-behavioural practice'. In R. Adams, L. Dominelli and M. Payne (eds) *Social Work: themes, issues and critical debates*. Basingstoke: Palgrave. A useful summary of the use of cognitive behavioural methods in practice.

part **3** | **Contexts of intervention**

Contexts of
intervention

9 | Working with families and children

Introduction

The third part of the text focuses on the contexts in which the various methods and interventions discussed so far may be applied. Work in specific 'contexts' requires consideration either because the setting has implications for the way those methods are used or because there are additional specific methods that have evolved from different settings. Obviously not all settings or contexts are covered. The most obvious omission is working in residential settings, but that is not to say the methods are not relevant here.

The focus of this chapter is on the family as the site of intervention. Working with families and children is dealt with first because it is both a high priority for social services departments, as was reinforced by the introduction of the Children Act of 1989, and a highly contentious area, as is indicated by government consultation on children's services (DfES, 2003). However work with families is not just about working with children. Many direct referrals to social work are to do with families. Sometimes referrals for practical problems turn up difficulties rooted in unsatisfactory family relationships. Assessments for community care require workers to consider family relationships, and the dynamics of these relationships influence the outcomes of such assessments. Care managers or provider agencies who are offering support and oversight of care packages which involve family members in caring for older people or those with mental health problems may well have to become involved in some family work using their understanding of family dynamics and specialist interventions. Workers in the criminal justice system frequently have to assess both the influence of the family on patterns of offending, and the impact of the offending on family dynamics. Families experience loss and bereavement, or they respond to counselling or short-term work.

This chapter however concentrates on developments in policy and practice that have influenced approaches to working with families. Interventions that focus solely on the dynamics of family members include 'family work' or family therapy. The chapter looks in more detail at the skills that are used when the family is specifically the focus of the intervention. In doing this it recognises that childcare policies have been influential in shaping work with families, and therefore makes reference to material based on research and evaluation of practice that is available for further study in the area of working with children.

Understanding families

It is impossible to advise what is a 'conventional family': quoting research from the Family Policy Studies Centre, Jervis (1990) showed that cohabitation, children born outside of marriage, lone parent families, stepfamilies and dual working couples are increasingly becoming the norm. A decade later trends indicate that three in ten of all households have a single person at their head, and households are getting smaller because fewer people are marrying and women are having fewer children (Butler and Roberts, 2004). Also changing demographic patterns mean that there is diversity among families based on differences of class and race. As Allan (2002) reminds us, family organisation is inevitably shaped by wider social and economic formation 'even if ideologically the family is presented as being separate'. It is important to remember that not only is each family different in its composition but also each family differs in the way members communicate their values and their structural relationships. This attention to diversity should be at the heart of work with families.

Diversity

We all have a picture of how families behave and their composition, but this often stems very much from our experiences in our family of origin. Also representations of families in the media tend to subscribe to a hegemonic view of families made up of two heterosexual parents and two children. Such ideologies can be oppressive to families that do not fit into this model, especially when they permeate policies for intervening in families. Those who do not conform are often perceived as deviant and as in some ways in deficit. This of course ignores that fact that those families that do fit the model can be oppressive and destructive, as research into domestic violence and child abuse has illustrated.

There is a danger that, despite acknowledging diversity, when trying to understand family dynamics if we are from the same ethnic group or class we assume we have a lot in common. Trying to replicate our own family style with client families is a trap for the unwary. For example, O'Brian (1990) gives the following account of trying to engage a Bangladeshi family whose 15-year-old daughter had not attended school because her father objected to the school and to the need for her to have any formal education. Being from the same minority ethnic group, O'Brian said, 'Look, Mr M, I know what it is like living in this country and having to accept its rules and regulations. We are both foreigners here and I understand what it is like for you.' Mr M replied, 'Sir, with the greatest respect you are not the same as us.' The girl's father went on to say that it had nothing to do with different religions either – it was that the social worker was in a position of authority.

Another social worker, one of three brothers, was working with a family of the same composition. Despite having many years of experience in family therapy, he began to behave as if he were one of the brothers. In work with families there is danger that workers attempt to recreate a mirror image of their own family's functioning. (Bowen (1978) believed that, before working intensively with other people's families, we should sort out our own!) Thus, it is as well not to generalise but to try to understand: 'How does this family work?'

Lifecycles

Trying to understand a family is like jumping on to a moving bus: you have the disadvantage of being a temporary passenger on their journey through a stage in their life, with people leaving and joining along the way. Like individuals who cope with transitions and life crises, families go through a lifecycle. But it is a much more awkward business, because at each phase in their development the whole group has to reshuffle, while at the same time providing stability and continuity for its members. Gorrell Barnes (1984) deals with this concept of the family lifecycle, explaining what happens when we leave home, achieve independence, become half of a couple, have children, face an 'empty nest', become dependent and so on. Even though families might not now enter into formal relationships so readily, what she is illustrating is that individuals go through processes of engaging and disengaging with others within some form of family unit. As such they become part of a socially constructed unit based on some form of mutuality that is based on 'a relationship of kinship, obligation and intimacy' (White, 2002, p. 147) – a family by another name.

Such processes are made all the more demanding as each member is probably struggling with his or her individual life stages at the same time: a woman who has launched children and achieved independence may be faced with her mother who is having to adjust to dependence, perhaps on this same daughter. All the time, families are losing members and gaining members, making space for maybe competing needs, renegotiating the numerous patterns of relationship between people – this is why referrals often have life-cycle changes at the nub of what is going wrong.

Family patterns

According to Gorrell Barnes (1984), families can be placed at one of three possible points on a spectrum from flexibility, through rigidity to chaos. Jordan (1972) illuminatingly described families that were difficult to break free from as 'integrative', and those whose members were segregated and went their separate ways as 'centrifugal': Minuchin (1974) termed these patterns of closeness and distance 'enmeshed' and 'disengaged'. These ideas may help us to assess if a family can 'bend' with its changing membership and processes (for instance, if there is adaptability of rules when a child enters adolescence). Also, albeit that there are different cultural norms, they enable us to enquire if a family is able to regulate its boundaries and can tolerate closeness and distance, dependence and independence.

Another useful concept that helps in understanding how families act is to see family as a system, a set of interacting parts with a particular purpose. Families may have subsystems that comprise the marital subsystem, the children subsystem, sibling subsystem, mother–daughter and father–son subsystems and so on. The family's relationship to outside, wider systems, that is the suprasystem, is as important to understand as their internal dynamics. O'Brian (1990) points out that the suprasystem cannot be ignored when working with black families – racism affects every aspect of their lives. Remembering our discussion of systems theory in Chapter 3 it helps to think of the family as an open system in transformation, constantly changing in relation to internal and external forces. Occasionally families 'get stuck', maybe as the result of coping with their own internal crises or because the agencies with which they interact overreact (Coulshed and Abdullah-Zadeh, 1985). When this happens, solutions become part of a problem spiral. For example, services are sometimes dependent on someone being given a label, such as 'a violent family'. In one family the education service managed to gain the attention of the social services by labelling an unhappy boy as an 'arsonist', although the actual event was a fire in a wastepaper basket.

Environmental circumstances are a large part of the assessment of family dynamics, if only to ensure that all efforts are not unravelled once a person returns to the context in which difficulties arose. In one agency, every member of a family had received individual programmes of help for over 20 years. Each time anyone returned to the fold, from residential assessment or care, his or her problems returned with him or her.

Understanding the way the wider context of families can impact on them, and the ways that families experience this, is assisted by ways of charting family relationships. Methods used can be part of an assessment, formal or informal, but can also form part of work with families.

Networks

Networks can be relevant to community work, group work and organisational studies (see Chapter 11), but they are particularly useful when working with families. While the study of networks can involve quite wide social fields, the most useful when considering families is the personal social network, one that comprises those with special and emotional significance. Hill (2002), in a useful overview of using networks in social work, points out that it is these networks of relatives, friends and neighbours to whom people with problems often turn. It is part of the social work task in family work to identify how far these networks have contributed to the need or problem.

However an understanding of the structures and processes in a person or family's network also helps in assessing to what extent they can facilitate or hamper resolution of the need or problem. He suggests that there are ways of classifying networks by observing and documenting interactions between network members. These may be members of a family, or could include others with whom family members interact. Hence the factors to consider include:

● content
● degrees of intimacy
● frequency of contact
● directedness
● durability
● intensity
  (Hill, 2002, p. 238)

An important aspect of using these categories is that there are no prior assumptions about how the network should be, but it becomes an important tool to document how things are for particular families. So plotting a network helps avoid stereotyping, for example, of Asian families as being 'close'. It also helps to identify if families are being socially excluded because of systematic racism. In that networks can be inclusive they can also acknowledge pressures and losses that, for example, asylum seekers might experience because they are separated from their families.

The network can be represented in a variety of ways but the most frequent is some form of diagram. The use of a diagram helps workers to process a great deal of information and can also be a tool that is developed interactively with the individual or family. Hill (2002, p. 244) identifies six main types of diagram:

● *The ecomap, ecogram or star diagram* where a key person is put in the centre and others are represented and connected to the key person.
● *Concentric circles* where people are placed at different distances from the central person to represent geographical or emotional closeness.
● *Genogram or family tree* depicts relationship patterns and events over generations. Births, deaths, divorce, crises and other significant life events can be recorded briefly and several pages of social history can be condensed into a diagram.

Typical symbols used in a genogram are shown in Figure 9.1. Figure 9.2 illustrates a family whose eldest son, aged 14 has committed offences. He has been brought up mainly by his mother, who is now widowed. The boy has a brother aged 10 and a sister aged 8. Prior to their father dying, the children's parents were separated. The maternal grandfather died before the grandchildren were born, though his divorced wife, the maternal grandmother, is still alive.

Burnham (1986) gives more examples of less easy to draw family trees, such as those with multiple relationships, step-relationships

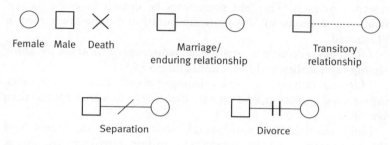

Figure 9.1 Genogram symbols

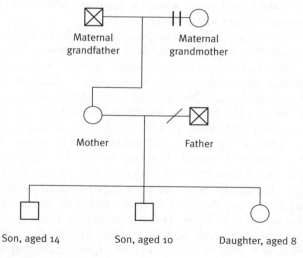

Figure 9.2 Illustrative genograms

and transitory contacts. As with other diagrams, genograms can become a useful talking point for families who, while they are helping the worker to complete them, begin to uncover their family's unwritten rules, myths, secrets and taboos. This map of family relationships can also reveal how patterns might get repeated across generations. Thus, the family represented in Figure 9.2 had marital breakdown, death and children reared single-handedly by their mother as repetitive themes.

Life space representation portrays key locations in an individual's life space with indications of the people and activities relevant to each. This can sometimes be drawn as a life 'snake' where the snake bends at significant points and these are named or illustrated.

Life course changes involve a sequence of houses to show changes in locality and household composition.

Matrices consist of tables listing people, their interactions, importance, function and so on, described in words rather than symbols.

Hill's work (2002) with social work students illustrates how these diagrams can be interactive and/or retrospective, giving opportunities for the individuals and families to personalise them. The ultimate in dynamic diagrams is family sculpting, where one member of the family places others in positions and poses to reflect the closeness of their relationship.

Often the use of such tools helps us to view the family as a small organisation (but with a shared history and future). We may see that it has a hierarchy, communication systems, values, controls, decision-making, conflict resolution, norms of behaviour and ways of coping with change. Just like an organisation, a family has an invisible set of rules for how people interact with each other and how homeostasis (stability) is maintained. In order to protect themselves families develop ways of managing interactions between themselves and with outsiders. Sometimes, as we have said, these sequences and habits get in the way of moving on. They do not mean that the family is ignorant or rigid; indeed, none of us is prepared to accept change unless we know the advantages and disadvantages of this. What used to be termed 'resistance to change' has fortunately been rethought (Carpenter and Treacher, 1989).

Possibly, it is only when we join an organisation that we learn how it really works. The same is true of families. Only if we achieve an alliance (throughout the process, not just at the beginning) together with an attitude that they are 'OK', will we ever have any inkling of what is going on.

This is not the same as saying that we approve of everything they do; in fact, as Dale and his colleagues at the NSPCC propose (Dale *et al.*, 1986) professionals can act dangerously if they trust the family too much or have too much optimism that things will improve. Numerous child abuse enquiries have reminded us of the need to be alert to risk of abuse. There is a tension in practice between providing support when families ask for it and the possibility of compulsory intervention (Waterhouse and McGhee, 2002, p. 273). Often families might be deterred from seeking help if workers are only going to concentrate on possible abuse. Working with families requires taking time to listen to every member's point of view, being courteous, not taking sides and not confronting people with what you see as the 'truth' of their difficulties. This is more likely to encourage discussion and sharing in which the worker is free to engage and disengage when the need arises. However workers should not shirk from their responsibility to protect children, and others, in family situations.

Working with Families

For some years social work with families that focused on the relationship within families was known as 'family casework' (Jordan, 1972). In this model the whole family was seen together and this was intended to better the welfare of one of its members. This approach developed over time and ultimately 'family therapy' became an accepted approach: this is more than doing 'casework with more people in the room', it is used when the whole family is the client and the target for change. When one or more family members are having difficulties this is thought to be a cause and a consequence of interaction. People affect and are affected by one another, and so it is necessary to see how people get along with each other and, more fundamentally, how the family solves its problems. This is an important part of the assessment, giving an indication also how dysfunction might be prevented.

Although there has been dismay at calling these methods of practice 'marital and family therapy', with connotations of clinical

206 | Contexts of intervention

work and learning 'tricks of the trade' (Whan, 1983), they will be referred to as such, merely for convenience. Parading skills or using the family as entertainment, which was the style of a few early 'followers' of this movement, are not appropriate rationales for, or outcomes of, family work. Down-to-earth workers have shown that the ideas can be used practically and in a range of settings (Treacher and Carpenter, 1984). Strategies for change that are employed with humanity and humility (Walrond-Skinner, 1979) can help families and couples to draw on their own problem-solving solutions and strengths. Also there is now evidence that family therapy is a promising treatment approach in particular for many child and adolescent problems (Vetere, 1999, p. 145).

There are many different forms of family therapy, all of which draw on either psychoanalytic practice or systems theory (see earlier chapters for discussion of these) to try to describe the complex relationships between family members. Some try to understand how these dynamics influence the way particular families interact with other systems such as health, education and social services.

Four theoretical viewpoints in family therapy

Based on an understanding of family dynamics, there is a range of interventions, spanning psychoanalytic to behavioural approaches, available to the worker. Although it is unlikely that student and/or beginning social workers will be expected to undertake 'pure' family therapy, it is helpful to understand the different approaches as they give insight into understanding family patterns and dynamics. We shall therefore examine the central tenets of four of these: psychoanalytic, structural, strategic and behavioural.

Psychoanalytic models

Such models (see Box *et al.*, 1981) emphasise historical factors, uncovering unresolved conflicts from the past that continue to attach themselves to individual members of the family and their current situation. Some of the discussion in Chapter 5 is relevant to this approach. Names of therapists associated with this approach include Nathan Ackerman, Robin Skynner and Christopher Dare. The latter, interviewing a family whose son stole his mother's tights and lipsticks whenever she went into hospital, explored the mother's relationship with her father in order to help the whole family gain insight into transgenerational family patterns.

The role of the therapist is to make interpretations of individual and family patterns and focus on how members feel about each other. In addition, there is an attempt to reduce interlocking pathologies; examples of these are when children are drawn in to act as 'marital distance regulators' (Byng-Hall and Campbell, 1981) or when symptoms such as children soiling are part of projected marital conflicts (Mainprice, 1974). Some of the tools used include the genogram and sculpting as discussed above. With one family whose teenage son had taken on his father's role following divorce, a sculpt showed the family how little space was left for the father to fit in again, once the spouses agreed to remarry.

Structural models

These models 'start where the family is', centring on present transactions, although the influence of what habits and role assignments have been learned earlier may be part of the assessment. People associated with this approach include Salavadore Minuchin and, in the UK, Andy Treacher and John Carpenter. Change in the way that members of a family deal with each other 'here and now', in the session, is the focus of the change effort. The worker joins the system to see how it works; to avoid being unable to withdraw from time to time, strategies have been devised to prevent him or her getting too drawn in. These might be having a co-worker in the room or linked by audio/video facilities; physically withdrawing at intervals helps, as does leaving fairly long intervals of two or three weeks between interviews. The goal is to restructure the family's organisation so as to change unhelpful patterns of relating to one another. For instance, films of Minuchin working with families show him asking a child who is carrying parental responsibility to keep out of problem-solving while an overlooked parental figure tries on this role. In his work with another family a child was closer to her mother because her father was either pushed out or pulled himself out of family transactions – the direction given was for mother to encourage father there and then to talk with his daughter for a time. Some of the specific techniques used include:

● working with different sets of subsystems
● changing boundaries (for example, by seating arrangements or task-setting as above)
● 'tracking', which approves of family functioning by mirroring it, commenting on it and sharing information about one's own family; encouraging people to interact and then stage directing them to try a different pattern in the session and at home.

Strategic models

These keep the time focus on the present. The hypothesis is that current problems or symptoms are being maintained by ongoing, repetitive sequences of interaction between family members. Rather than historical events or unconscious conflicts determining behaviour, particular family 'truths', solutions to problems, communication mechanisms and mental constructs are given as explanations for the persistence of difficulties. There is nothing inherently 'wrong' with the family; in their efforts to sort out a solution, they have redoubled their efforts producing a 'more of the same' rut. Theorists associated with this viewpoint are Jay Haley, Mara Selvini-Palazzoli and Milton Erickson. Usually, the methods of helping are active, time-limited, focused on the attempted solution, planned ahead of the session and directed at problem-solving. This might involve a team approach, using techniques such as circular questioning (mentioned in Chapter 4), neutrality and delivery of a prescription, given at the end of a session, on how the family should proceed. Because some of these prescriptions are paradoxical in nature (for instance, suggesting no change in the family in order to get them out of keeping on trying more of the same) some of the techniques have been decried as manipulative and disrespectful.

Families were thought to resist change because the presenting problem was needed by them to serve a function in their system. Thus, a family with a member suffering from schizophrenic illness might unknowingly resist attempts at change, fearing that the removal of the disorder in one person could unbalance family homeostasis. In other words, another relationship sequence more feared might be triggered by the change.

In one family, a 12-year-old girl had become 'paralysed' for some time, despite no organic cause being found. All kinds of systems had been found by the family to cope with this symptom (what are known as 'redundant' behaviour sequences): these might be viewed as metaphors for the family saying that they could not move on through their lifecycle. Interventions might encompass 'reframing', that is, implying that this was a positive solution, for example in bringing them closer together.

Workers in this way are using the family's language – to the above family the paralysis might not be talked of as an illogical feature of family life. However, as we noted earlier, some of the theories about resistance are being rethought. In their clear text, which offers an alternative to the somewhat adversarial strategic approaches, Carpenter and Treacher (1989) note that families who come to our agencies do so because of change, one that has either taken place or is in prospect. What families need is a worker who *expects* change, seeing it not only as possible, but inevitable. Noting strengths and family cooperation is preferred to noting the pathology of resistance. Indeed, we ourselves may be what are producing the resistance, failing to match what the family need with what we have to offer.

Behavioural models

These models again emphasise what is happening in the present, focusing on interpersonal/environmental factors that are 'rewarding', that is, maintaining behaviour patterns. Generally, marital therapists, working with the relationship of a couple, rather than on individual 'failings', favour these methods; thus couples are taught to improve their communication skills, sexual satisfaction, assertiveness and negotiation skills, practising in-between interviews with homework tasks. Behaviour might be viewed as faulty learning or copying from one's own parents. Using techniques described in Chapter 8 work might involve directing a couple to try out different behaviours in the session itself, with the worker operating as a trainer, model or contract negotiator. Therapists such as John Gottman (see Gottman *et al.*, 1977), R. Liberman and Michael Crowe are usually associated with this viewpoint. For some workers common elements from the four 'schools' of thought are integrated: structural and strategic techniques are used to extend therapeutic interventions.

Response to criticisms

Family therapists who base their practice on systemic thinking suggest that while some events can be described in a linear, cause and effect way (that A causes B which has no feedback effect on A), this does not account for complex human interactions. To take one situation, can it be said that a husband drinks because his wife gets depressed without considering that both are involved in the sequence? Another valid explanation could be that his drinking causes the depression. Seeing events in this 'whole' or systems way reveals that each person is part of a circular system of action and reaction, which can begin and end at any point, and therefore there is little point in asking, 'Who started it?' However, one big problem with this circular view of events is that it ignores the unequal distribution of power. Where power is an obvious factor, such as the use of violence in marriage against women in the main, then this idea of complementarity, that behaviours fit together, is questionable (see for example Perelberg and Miller, 1990).

Underpinning all the approaches was an assumption of expertise and the potential to 'cure' or 'solve' family problems. This position has been associated with medical approaches that have been critiqued in social work generally. As was discussed in Chapter 2, constructivist approaches to social work have less emphasis on a simple definition of truth, but try to elicit different understandings and experiences of problems. These approaches are now influencing family therapy, and narrative approaches are being developed to help separate the person from the problem (Vetere, 1999, p. 147) and to help families create positive affirming narratives about themselves that emphasise resilience rather than 'healing' (White, 2002).

Feminist critiques

Feminist critiques of family therapy's systems framework have pointed out that this approach treats the family as an autonomous entity, denying or ignoring the socio-political context (Beecher, 1986). The family is, after all, a subsystem of a much larger system, if we accept this approach. The consequence of a narrow view that focuses on maintaining the family system ignores critiques of the family as a site of oppression. These critiques include:

● The family preserves conventional male and female relationships.

- Women clients are told what to do to be 'good wives and mothers', mirroring society's expectations.
- This pathologises women's emotions or labels them negatively if they do not conform to stereotypical expectations.
- Preoccupation with the nuclear and immediate family ignores the fact that many women receive emotional support from other women.
- It does not address the fact that the family is a primary arena where women suffer injustice because of their sex (which is why so many institutions are required to ensure its continued existence).
- There is a functional assumption that achieving balance in the family system is a common goal for each individual; but for women experiencing domestic violence, there is inherent conflict when one person has more power than another.
- The minutiae of techniques that, as O'Brian (1990) points out in relation to racism, confine work to the family system rather than its links to the social structure.

If Carpenter and Treacher's (1989) analysis is accepted, that in every organisation including families and marriages there are winner and losers, then in general, it is the loser who seeks help to restore his or her position. The winner has the least to gain by seeking help and is therefore a reluctant customer. Interventions that focus on power differentials are therefore crucial. Hence some writers affirm that it is possible to be a family therapist and a feminist (Pilalis and Anderton, 1986). Indeed, it could be an ideal position from which to challenge a family's assumptions and routines. The 'gender lens' gives a different perspective on, for example, the way gender-patterning contributes to the family's problems (White, 2002, p. 151).

Just as those in community work have helped to raise consciousness, social workers in family situations and in marital work, without imposing their values, might address the issue of power, using their advocacy, negotiation and education skills. Arrangements for intervening in families, including male and female coworking which can role model strong female leadership in partnerships, and techniques such as circular questioning which allows different perceptions of the relationship to be articulated, can contribute to the restructuring of oppressive power relationships within families. In this context therapists could facilitate women in establishing their own boundaries within family structures and in response to family demands. In doing so the family's interaction patterns which reflect societal expectations of gender roles could be made more explicit, and therefore more open to challenge.

Feminist approaches to family therapy therefore provide more than a critique, they provide a framework for working with women, and with significant others in their lives, therefore offering perspectives for working with men too. Developments in feminist approaches to social work are explored in texts such as Hanmer and Statham (1988), Featherstone (1997) and Milner (2001). What is significant is that such approaches do not always advocate the same thing, indicating the richness and complexity of feminist analysis in this area. Feminist approaches have encouraged perspectives on working with men developed by women (Cavanagh and Cree, 1996; Orme *et al.*, 2000) and men (Christie, 2001; Scourfield and Coffey, 2002).

Domestic violence

This discussion of power balances within partnerships, and the need to both make overt and challenge stereotypical assumptions about gender roles that may oppress women within family work, raises other issues about the position of women within families. There have been references above to situations of domestic violence, and before going on to discuss the other frameworks for intervening in families, and the techniques that might be employed, it is important to spend time considering the implications of domestic violence for working with families and couples.

In recognising that abuse takes many forms (physical, sexual and emotional), Mullender (1996) is clear that it is physical abuse, or the anticipation of it, that keeps all other forms of abuse in place, and that the aim of such physical abuse is power and control of men over women. When considering contra-indications for working with families, it seems obvious to make links between the position of women and the need to protect children from the various forms of abuse. However, the situation is more complicated than this. Children need to be protected from abuse by men, but they are also subject to abuse by women (see Wise, 1990 and Featherstone, 1997 for discussion of the implications of this for practice). Also, studies have shown that children are witnesses to, or are aware of, the violence between their parents, and this has adverse affects which are manifested in many different ways (Mullender and Morley, 1994). To make these claims is not to blame women for their failure to protect children, but to highlight that before any work with families is contemplated, workers need to be clear that they are not colluding with, or contributing to, abuse of women and/or children. In all work with families and couples, there has to be awareness that symptoms of abuse, or direct revelations of abuse, may be an outcome. Workers should be prepared to face such revelations, and to terminate the family work.

It might seem to be stating the obvious to say that family work and/or work with couples should not be contemplated when abuse is known to be taking place, but in Chapter 7 of *Rethinking Domestic Violence*, Audrey Mullender documents clearly why such statements are necessary. She reiterates and reinforces the guidelines given by Canadian writer Sinclair that marriage counselling is a viable option only after the following conditions have been met:

1. The offender has accepted full responsibility for his violent behaviour and has made concerted efforts to change that behaviour.
2. The victim is clearly able to protect herself, measured by her understanding and willingness to assume responsibility for her protection.
3. The potential for future abuse is minimal (there is never a guarantee).
4. The degree of intimidation and fear felt by the victim is significantly reduced, so as not to interfere with open discussion of marital issues. Make sure she does not think the issues she raises during the session will be used as an excuse by her husband to assault her after the session.
5. The goals of the couple are mutually agreed upon and couple work is entered into freely by both partners. Make sure he has not instructed her to remain silent on contentious issues. (Quoted in Mullender, 1996, p. 179)

This is not to say that all work should be abandoned if there are obvious signals, or even suspicions, that abuse has taken, or is taking, place. The arguments for, and the implications of, working with men have already been referenced. What is being said here is that before working with families and couples it is a prerequisite that consideration should be given to such checklists to ensure the safety of women and children. Only when these conditions can be met should decisions be made about working with families and couples along the lines discussed below.

Case example

Sue, 13, had not been to school for a year. The school social worker had never seen her as Sue refused to come downstairs during home visits. A psychiatric assessment was planned, but the family, which included three older sisters who had all left home, agreed instead to work as a group. Co-workers, one male and one female, from an area social services team saw the family at home in the evenings on four occasions. Prior to contact, the workers hypothesised from the family lifecycle stage and the family tree that Sue might be struggling with adolescent challenges while her parents faced reforming as a couple, preparing for the prospect of their last child leaving home.

The workers knew from the school social worker that father was a long-distance lorry driver, who had never been interviewed, and that mother and daughter were very close. There was some suggestion of marital violence throughout the marriage, plus some strict disciplining of the three other sisters. The workers hypothesised that the women needed to ally themselves against the father's physical power; in family therapy terms, this would cross hierarchical and generational boundaries. Also, when men are temporarily absent from the family and return at intervals from their jobs, this increases strain on the couple, who have continually to renegotiate space, decision-making and roles.

On each visit, timed to coincide with the father's trips home, the workers often had to wait for him to arrive. Though there was some pressure to begin without him this was resisted because this would have been no different from previous problem-solving which had not produced change. The workers had to demonstrate to the family that they were 'with them', but at the same time objectively trying to help them sort out Sue's non-attendance at school. So the meetings were kept informal until father arrived.

Father was a large-built man, quite intimidating to look at but the workers treated him as if he were cooperative, asking him to plug in their audiotape, which he happily complied with. (The reason for this and returning the tapes to the family on completion had been discussed.) Sometimes, just as in network assemblies, the mere bringing together of a whole family is powerful enough to unblock communications or prevent them being diverted through something or someone else. Thus it was with this family; although Sue never spoke, she listened intently as the women bravely confronted her father's over-zealous disciplining. He confessed he was ashamed of once having tipped one of them out of bed, but he had never hit Sue. He looked astonished when his wife said that she intended leaving him once Sue had left school. She indicated that she planned to get a full-time job and establish her independence.

Sue looked young and boyish with jeans and a short haircut. She kept her head bowed throughout most of the meetings. Mother was asked if she would take Sue with her when she left, and she said she had not decided. The workers addressed what seemed to be connected themes of growing up and leaving home, using the co-therapy relationship to model problem-solving and respect for each other's views. Tentatively they suggested 'Perhaps Sue is sacrificing her growing up to save the family from splitting up?'

The use of circular questioning revealed different viewpoints, introducing new information about how each third party saw relationships in the family, in regard to the specific problem but also because the family's reality was that marital conflict was an issue. For example, the workers asked, 'When your mother rows with your father, what does Sue do?' and, 'When your mother leaves home, who will be most, and who will be least, upset?'

In many ways, the sessions provided a channel for the family talking about something that had been simmering for some time but that all were afraid to confront. Since the older girls had ideas about growing up and managing school, it was decided to draw on their expertise. Working with the sibling subsystem on their own for a time in the front room, the social workers set the older sisters tasks to confide in Sue what their teenage years had been like. Their parents agreed that no one would enquire about these get-togethers.

After six weeks, during which the sisters met each other for these talks, which all enjoyed, Sue returned to school where she subsequently did extremely well. The married couple believed that they would carry on sorting out their plans for their relationship; neither wanted help with this, and some time later they are still married.

Working with couples

Before summarising the therapeutic approach we will consider some observations on marital or couples work. The theoretical viewpoints remain the same, in that there are psychoanalytic, structural, strategic and behavioural forms of work, usually based on systems thinking. However social work students and practitioners seem to be reluctant to engage in marital or couple work. Maybe it is 'too close to home'; most of us have experienced marriage at close quarters and some have experienced the trauma of marital breakdown.

For those who have decided to work with marital difficulties, James and Wilson (1986) give a useful breakdown of how to proceed; when to work with the marital system or one partner, whether the goal is enriching the relationship or freeing the couple from it. These authors also have a useful chapter in their book on working with couples from minority ethnic groups, again recommending that we look beyond cultural stereotypes of, for instance, the subordination of South Asian women or the issue of arranged marriages. This is a useful reminder that working with couples can include various arrangements for partnership that do not have to involve either legal or religious marriage ceremonies. It is the dynamic of the couple relationship, and the emotional commitment to being a couple, which are the focus of the intervention.

What one might find in the initial assessment of a couple whose relationship is fundamentally stable is that they have sought help with a transitional crisis: often expectations of marriage or partnership are too high and they are unaware that there is no partnership without conflict. Those in couple relationships sometimes project the unwanted part of themselves on to the other, so that there is a great deal of blaming and attempts to make the social worker an ally of one partner. However, referrals, especially to statutory agencies, often come in the guise of problems with parental roles, attacks from the family of origin, continual threats of separation and eviction that stem from ambivalent marital bonds (see Mattinson and Sinclair, 1979). These are marriages and partnerships characterised by instability, where there is difficulty in trusting each other and making attachments, related to a deepseated longing for love and security. Because of this, there may be a lot of work to be done with the individuals on their own as well as on their relationship.

Incidentally although therapists prefer to work conjointly (with both partners) there is no objection to seeing only one. Carpenter and Treacher (1989) place an empty chair in the room and say something like, 'If John were here what would he say?' as well as giving the participant (usually a woman) support to get the other person to accept help. Also, as was indicated in the discussions about domestic violence, there are some situations when to insist on conjoint work might put the woman and/or the children at risk, and would be totally inappropriate. (For discussion of the implications of, for example, mediation work in cases involving domestic violence see Hester and Radford, 1996.)

Where problems are sexual ones, generally behavioural methods are preferred, although a deeper understanding may be required if these have little effect. For instance, some couples dread differentiation; they keep negative feelings and differences out of their marriage or partnership, thereby frustrating adult sexual roles. (Books by the Institute of Marital Studies, for example, *The Marital Relationship as a Focus for Casework*, are valuable in exploring psychodynamic factors in marriage.) Many of the underlying problems for couples, whatever their composition or legal status, are about intimacy and distance, sameness and difference, or how each person gets their needs met, 'how often each can be allowed to be the baby' (Clulow and Mattinson, 1989, p. 56).

Framework for understanding family and couples work

- *The theoretical base* is systems theory used in combination with psychodynamic, structural, strategic and behavioural ideas. Important concepts include the question of causality, boundaries, hierarchy, homeostasis and interactions inside the family and with the suprasystem, that is, external systems.
- *Problems* are those of family transactions; family problem-solving patterns and communications that become blocked, distorted or displaced through one member. Myths, secrets and taboos carried over from previous generations might also hinder problem-solving. A number of problems arise as a response to lifecycle transitions when there is a need to flexibly adapt and realign relationships. Some solutions could become the problem.

- *Goals* are minimal, often aimed at changing overt behaviour, though some methods aim at insight as well. The family is helped to choose limited, specific goals, usually within a brief timeframe. Workers aim to join the family or couple, inasmuch as they offer support while attempts are made at restructuring relationship patterns and behavioural sequences.
- *The client's role.* In this approach, the couple or the family is the client. They may also be the target for change, and the team that works alongside the therapeutic team to change transactional patterns within or outside their system.
- *The worker's role.* There may be two workers as co-therapists or a therapeutic team who hypothesise how the system of family transactions relate to the problem presented. Work with external systems could be just as important, especially when numerous agencies are involved who unwittingly mirror family dynamics. It is vital to sustain the couple's or the family's attempt at problem-solving; to not take sides or allocate blame; not to perpetuate power inequalities but to raise awareness of these and to offer a positive redefinition of their difficulties to help those who have become stuck trying 'more of the same'.
- *Techniques* are numerous. This is why caution is advised against being bewitched by technique at the expense of helping the family in an authentic, non-adversarial way. Joining and restructuring operations include tracking communications and themes about family life (sticking to detail helps – mundane themes often reveal the typical ways in which people manage each other). Intensity around the specific problem might be necessary in order to break out of 'redundant' problem-solving routines. Observation is as important as listening, so that process and content, how the family behave and what is said, are clues to helping. Finally it is necessary to be careful not to undermine the family's competence but to confirm their strengths. Other methods involve use of the family tree and genogram; creating physical space and shifting relationship boundaries; setting tasks; taking time out of the interview to check with colleagues what is happening, or using 'live' supervision with the supervisor in the room to ensure effectiveness and objectivity. More 'advanced' techniques, aimed at exceptionally chronic difficulties, might be the use of paradoxical prescriptions (advising no change) and the (possibly gifted) use

of metaphor, stories and anecdotes. Self-disclosure, in a self-aware worker, can be used on occasion to talk about one's own family life.

Families and children

So far this chapter has deliberately not concentrated on specific work in families who have abused children, or focused on work with children in families. There is a growing amount of specialist literature that is particularly helpful in these areas. This literature draws on research to evaluate the effectiveness of family work (Hill, 1999); gives overviews and discussion of practice initiatives with families (Bell and Wilson, 2002); and children (Brandon *et al.*, 1998; Colton *et al.*, 2001). Butler and Roberts (2004) provide very practical workbook approaches to working with children and families.

That said, in thinking about family work it is necessary to consider some of the other developments that have taken place in working with families. Although they are not so heavily therapeutic, they draw upon the notion of the family as a system and work with the potential within the family. In doing so they answer some of the above criticisms.

These developments are part of wider changes that have been taking place in work with families and children. Such changes are a reaction to the number of inquiries into the role of social work in cases of child abuse and what was seen as an increasing focus on the 'deficit' notion of families. As has been said, intervention in families has to balance the needs of families with protection of children. However in 1995 the Department of Health report *Child Protection: messages from research* undertook an overview of 20 pieces of research. It concluded that overall when child protection investigations take place little account is taken of the context; parents were generally left feeling alienated and angered; and a disproportionate amount of resources were being taken up in investigation, which took away resources from prevention and support. Overall the principles of partnership that had been enshrined in the 1989 Children Act were not operating (Frost *et al.*, 2003, p. 26). Calls for refocusing (DoH, 1996) were supported by organisations such as family rights groups which argued for involvement and empowerment of families in the decision-making processes. However these two things are not synonymous. Research into child protection procedures had indicated that a procedural approach to involving families in formal meetings could be just as exclusionary as no involvement at all. Two different initiatives highlight the changing approach to families within statutory services and attempts to ensure families were both empowered and supported.

Family group conferences

The introduction of pilot projects in England of 'family group conferences' was an attempt to involve families in decision-making. Based on projects in New Zealand that had been initiated by Maori groups, the conferences were an attempt to reduce the role of the state and re-emphasise the responsibilities of families and the wider community for care of their children (Lupton, 1998). The model, which was used in child welfare and youth justice, gave families support for their decision-making. There was collaboration with families rather than direction. The principles were that the social worker attended a family group conference at the beginning stages to give information, but then withdrew to allow the family to discuss their 'problems' in private and develop a family plan. The conference itself is convened by an independent coordinator, and in the third stage the coordinator joins the family to be informed of the plan. Lupton's research (1998) is cautious in concluding exactly how empowering such an approach can be. For example, it is the social worker and not the family who decides there should be a conference, and there is no guarantee that resources will be made available.

However such initiatives do indicate a willingness to try to think differently about ways of working with families, based on principles of partnership rather than treatment.

Family support

Another initiative that attempts to move the focus from child protection practice to more supportive interventions is 'family support'. Initially defined as 'any activity or facility ... aimed at providing advice and support to parents to help them bringing up their children' (Audit Report Commission, 1994, p. 39), family support should involve support that has no stigma attached for all families. This should be available across the board and accessible to all who need it (Frost et al., 2003, p. 5). A framework gives indications of the levels of support involved. The four levels indicate the gradation of services that should be available to all.

Level One: Projects and services such as SureStart.

Level Two: Targeted services addressing expressed need that is individually family-focused and might include casework or family therapy.

Level Three: Where there are more severe problems of child care/child protection more intense services might be made available, for example support for families where parents have drug and/or alcohol problems.

Level Four: Rehabilitation back into families of those who have been looked after.

Frost *et al.* (2003) attempt to give an overview and an introduction to these notions of support. However reviews of approaches to work with children and families are proposing a far more radical agenda. What is uncertain is the direction this agenda will take. Bob Holman, whose work with families has been community-based, has argued for a revision of the organisation of services that would be family-focused, involving both a neighbourhood approach and a 'facility' approach – that is, day care and family centres should be provided (Holman, 1998). Waterhouse and McGhee (2002) suggest that partnerships need to be developed at a variety of levels: with other professions, with parents and children, and with residential care.

Such approaches have to be considered in the context of the official agenda. In a set of recommendations that oscillate between facilitating and punishing, the consultation paper *Every Child Matters* (DfES, 2003) states that the government intends to put supporting parents and carers at the heart of its approach to improving children's lives, where support is needed by providing:

- *universal services* such as schools, health and social services and childcare, providing information and advice and engaging parents to support their child's development
- *targeted and specialist support* to parents of children requiring additional support
- *compulsory action* through Parenting Orders as a last resort where parents are condoning a child's truancy, anti-social behaviour or offending.

But in doing so it will establish a Children's Workforce Unit, based in the Department for Education and Skills. Hence the focus of the work, while espousing support for families will be firmly focused on children.

Conclusion

This chapter has given an overview of approaches to working with families. It has highlighted that this is an enormous area and one that is becoming an ever more important concern of practitioners, policy-makers and members of the public, mainly because of the focus on child protection.

While acknowledging this as an important area the chapter has sought to highlight that work with families is relevant in every aspect of social work practice and that techniques and skills can be drawn upon when working with families in the provision of community care services. The chapter also draws attention to important changes in policy and practice relating to children and families. Significantly this moves away from a therapeutic approach to a more holistic approach that makes links with community development work rather than with counselling.

---

putting it into practice

This chapter has indicated that there are many ways of working with families and many tools to help that work. It is useful to practise some of these before using them with families in distress.

1. Drawing a family. Think of a family with whom you have been working for some time. In the first instance practise using the symbols to denote the different people in the 'family'. If you have not yet started working with families you could think about the people and relationships in your own family.

2. Drawing a network. Choose one of the methods for depicting families described in this chapter. Now draw a diagram representation of this family as you see their relationships. Think about why you are putting different people in different places – on what basis are you doing this? What does this say about the way you see the family 'functioning'?

3. Getting feedback. If you have chosen a family with whom you are working it might be appropriate to think about using this technique with the family (or one member of the family) to help understand their perception. It is important that you only do this if it makes sense in the context of the work you are doing. It is not appropriate to practise on families just for the sake of it. If you are able to use the exercise with a family, or family member, then compare what they have drawn with your own drawing and look at the points of difference, and how this might help you understand better what is happening in the family.

Further reading

Hill, M. (1999) *Effective Ways of Working with Children and their Families*. London: Jessica Kingsley. A useful edited text that draws together results from research to describe effective ways of working with children and families.

Allan, G. and Crow, G. (2001) *Families, Households and Society*. Basingstoke: Palgrave. This is basically a sociology text but it gives an analysis of different organisations of families and households which helps to move away from stereotypical thinking about families.

Butler, I. and Roberts, G. (2004) *Social Work with Children and Families*. London: Jessica Kingsley. This text is focused on the practicalities of working with families, but with exercises and activities to help think more widely about the implications of working with children and families.

Featherstone, B. (2004) *Family Life and Support: a feminist analysis*. Basingstoke: Palgrave. Using a feminist analysis, this text looks at family roles and relationships and the meaning of family support.

10 | Working with adults

Introduction

A separate chapter on working with adults takes us back to issues raised in the Introduction: how best to organise writing about social work practice. Adults experience crisis and bereavement, they form the major part of user groups who would benefit from counselling and task-centred work, and might respond to behavioural approaches. Equally adults are members of families, groups and communities. Recognising this, this chapter will describe working with adults by drawing attention to the organisation of services for adults.

This however raises another set of issues because adults do not constitute a single group. Those who come into contact with social work agencies, who require services, are variously described as older people, people with physical or learning disabilities or those who are involved with health and/or mental health services. In Scotland adults in the criminal justice system qualify for social work services, while in England they are now dealt with in a separate criminal justice agency, which may or may not use social work interventions in its work. Social workers also come into contact with adults who provide care for others. However categorising or labelling people by their problems or roles is problematic because it denies the different issues that those who require services experience because of, for example, their gender (Orme, 2001a) or their colour or ethnic background (Ahmad and Atkins, 1996). This will be borne in mind throughout this chapter.

Over the last decade significant changes have been introduced in the way that social work is organised to work with adults. The introduction of community care and care management was both radical and controversial. It sought to introduce different philosophies for the provision of services, and required different practices for those involved in delivering those services. This chapter will discuss arrangements for community care, and care management within these. Criminal justice social work was excluded from these arrangements, and there is a continuing debate about whether offenders should be part of a social work service. This constitutes a major topic in its own right which will not be part of this chapter, although at other points in the book reference has been made to the use of social work methods in criminal justice settings.

In looking at the implications of community care for working with adults, the chapter links with other chapters, but also discusses approaches that have not been dealt with in detail elsewhere. Importantly this includes thinking about service provision in a particular way, one that respects the diversity of adults receiving and providing care.

Community care and care management

The legislation that introduced care management, the National Health Service and Community Care Act (1990), was the culmination of policies of community care that had been developed over many decades, but which gathered momentum in the 1980s. The key components of community care, as interpreted by the policy initiatives, are:

- services that respond flexibly and sensitively to the needs of individuals and their carers
- services that allow a range of options for consumers
- services that intervene no more than is necessary to foster independence
- services that concentrate on those with the greatest need. (DoH, 1989a, para. 1.10, p. 5)

Delivery of social services for adults has always been complex, and practitioners have been required to organise and coordinate services across a range of field, day and residential settings, drawing on family, voluntary, private and statutory sources of help. In order to meet the requirements of community care the legislation requires that an individual worker be assigned to provide an overview of the arrangements made: 'a "case manager" to take responsibility for ensuring that individuals' needs are regularly reviewed, resources are managed effectively and that each service user has a single point of contact' (DoH,1989a, para. 3.3.2 p. 21).

This requirement introduced the role of 'care manager', and the title is now used interchangeably with 'social worker'. Its usage begs many questions. Is the work of a care manager and a social worker synonymous? What does care management involve? If, as the guidelines that accompanied the legislation suggested, it is not necessary to be a qualified social worker to be a care manager, how can social work and care management be the same task? Some commentators argued that care management, as a way of organising services, requires the knowledge, values and skills provided by professional education and training for social work (Orme and Glastonbury, 1993). To date this has not necessarily been the practice of social work agencies and workers who are not qualified as social workers have undertaken the tasks of care management.

The relationship between care management and social work may be resolved by other factors. The requirement that social workers be registered was introduced in 2003 as a result of the Labour government's policies to modernise social services. From 2005 only those who are registered will be able to use the title 'social worker'; it will become a protected title. Registration as a social worker requires that the person has a professional social work qualification. Hence only those who have a social work qualification will be able to use the title of social worker. However this protection of the title 'social worker' demands that the functions that require a social worker be defined, and it will be in this definition that the distinctions between social work and care management will become clear.

Care management

The care management process aims to achieve planned goals using what are familiar and central tasks in social work, namely data collection, analysis and planned intervention. These could be equated to early social work processes, modelled on medicine, namely study, diagnosis and treatment. Similarly the requirement that care management involves 'The process of tailoring services to individual needs' (para. 7, *Summary of Practice Guidance*, 1991) suggests that care managers require practice skills such as interviewing, communicating, assessing, recording, counselling and mobilising resources. It might also be seen to draw on the values of individualisation and respect for persons (see Orme and Glastonbury, 1993, for a discussion). Significantly the term 'care' management was used in the UK in preference to the North American term 'case'. The change indicated a move away from the individualised approach to service delivery which had been the focus of casework, and emphasised that it was the care that was to be managed and not the case or person.

Discussions accompanied the introduction of care management around the distinction between care management as a system and as a practice (O'Connor, 1988) or between care management as a method of organising service delivery or a method of intervention (Orme and Glastonbury, 1993). Community care packages could be seen as examples of systems, or methods of organising service delivery, where agencies have devised policies and programmes, designed jobs, organised staff training and made arrangements with other organisations in order to bring about the delivery of services to the individual. Care management is a practice or set of practices that involves individual workers mediating those arrangements and services for individuals in need. As such care management draws directly on systems theory, described in Chapter 3.

Another way of describing social work with adults is systematic practice (Thompson, 2002). By this it is suggested that good practice requires clear planning, defined goals and a holistic assessment. Again this could be seen to be a shorthand way of describing the processes of care management.

Purchaser/provider split

One of the most significant changes brought about by the introduction of care management was that care managers were given responsibility for allocating and managing resources, including finance. Social work has always had a gatekeeping function, but budgetary devolution, introduced with the community care legislation, requires skills in accountancy to assess the cost of the services required. The policies also require the separation of assessment of need from determination of the service response based on the resources that are available. Now translated into a shorthand version, 'purchaser/provider split', this requirement was introduced to ensure the development of a mixed economy of welfare, with a greater involvement of voluntary and independent sector agencies in the provision of facilities in the community. The aim was to provide more choice for users and carers, and to find more flexible ways of maintaining people in the community.

The purchaser/provider split has had a major impact on the way that workers in the statutory sector carry out their role and tasks. One consequence is that it is often assumed that care management equates solely with the process of assessment for the purposes of community care. However, care management is more than this. At its simplest level it can be described as a circular process of case finding and screening – assessment – planning, monitoring and review – (and eventual closure). A more detailed description of these stages (listed below) is found in guidelines produced by the Social Services Inspectorate (SSI) to accompany the legislation, *Care Management and Assessment: practitioners' guide* (SSI/SWG, 1991). These provide a useful 'action checklist' for practitioners and identify seven core tasks in arranging care for someone in need.

Stages of care management

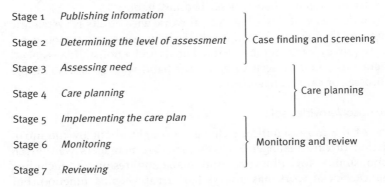

Stage 1 *Publishing information*

Stage 2 *Determining the level of assessment* } Case finding and screening

Stage 3 *Assessing need*

Stage 4 *Care planning* } Care planning

Stage 5 *Implementing the care plan*

Stage 6 *Monitoring* } Monitoring and review

Stage 7 *Reviewing*

Figure 10.1 Stages of care management

Case finding and screening includes publishing information and determining the level of assessment, while assessment of need involves both assessment and the beginning of the planning process. Care planning includes the implementation of the care plan or 'package of care', but this can only be achieved if services have been commissioned and the voluntary and independent sector stimulated to ensure that the range of needs identified have appropriate services in place to meet them. Finally monitoring and review includes ongoing assessment, as well as methods of quality assurance designed to ensure that the services are being provided in an appropriate manner, and to the required standard (DoH, 1994).

Stages 3 onwards reflect the circular process of much social work intervention that preceded care management, and which is recognised as good practice in other areas such as childcare and working with offenders. As such it could be said that care management is a codification of the social work process, and that performance of all these tasks remains dependent upon core social work skills that include interviewing, assessment, negotiation, consultation and counselling. Seemingly new processes such as advocacy and working in partnership (discussed in Chapter 3) draw on many of the basic skills, but are often employed in different circumstances, or with people other than those traditionally defined as clients of the social work agencies. For example, negotiating skills may be used with line managers in order to secure resources for particular users' needs, or with representatives of a voluntary agency in order to ensure that a particular need is provided for.

The various tasks and skills also differ according to the role held in the organisation. For example, programme development and service commissioning might be the main feature of a middle manger's role and involve liaison with managers in, for example, health authorities. Front-line workers (care managers) might rely more on direct skills such as those written about here. Another way of analysing or dividing functions of care management is to draw a distinction between skills that are used in planning, commissioning or purchasing, and those required for providing services in community care. Such distinctions are always arbitrary, because in both sets of activities the elements of communication encompassed in interviewing skills are necessary and fundamental.

Critique of care management

A decade after the introduction of care management there is an emerging critique of the implications for social work practice with adults. In general care management is described as a system for organising services to vulnerable people. Significantly Horder (2002) suggests it is a system pre-eminently designed to provide rational and fair allocation of public resources for older people because they are numerically the largest adult group in need of care. The original research that led to the development of care management in the UK was undertaken with older people (Challis *et al.*, 1990) and subsequent research evaluating its implementation (see for example Gorman and Postle, 2003) also relates to the experiences of older people, or those who work with them. A well-developed system of care management for people requiring mental health services is the Care Programme Approach (CPA). This tends to be distinguished from care management because it is led by health services, as opposed to social work or social care services. It focuses on the whole programme of intervention, including the management of medication. However both CPA and care management require multi-disciplinary work or inter-agency work to ensure that a range of services is accessed to provide a holistic approach to meeting the needs of service users.

As has been indicated, when care management was introduced there was concern that this would radically change not only the organisation of service delivery, but also the role and tasks of social workers. It was not that social workers were against care in the community. Quite the opposite, the notion of user choice and the impetus to maintain people in their own homes, if that was their choice, clearly embodied social work values. The concern was that the demands of community care, and in particular the need for social service departments to be both purchasers and providers of services, would either de-skill social workers, or require different skills: for example, accountancy.

The impact of community care policy and practice is therefore controversial. Those who are positive about its introduction suggest that it has given increased prominence to adult care, acknowledging that this had previously been a low priority for personal social services (Horder, 2002). Prior to the introduction of care management the criticism of services for adults was that they involved slotting people into limited inflexible services.

Gorman and Postle acknowledge that there should not be unrealistic harking back to a 'golden age' of social work practice, but they argue that the philosophy of community care has not necessarily been translated into practice. They suggest that 'the rhetoric of community care has been distorted to become the reality of care management' (Gorman and Postle, 2003, p. 7). Drawing on research that asked social workers what they thought about care management, they argue that care management has become the administrative and operational envelope for the operationalisation of community care. By this they mean that notions of consumer choice and individualised packages of care have been curtailed by controls such as eligibility criteria and restricted resources. To illustrate this they, like many other commentators on community care and care management, reference case law such as *R-v-Gloucestershire ex parte Barry* (1997), which allowed social workers to take into account resources when identifying need (Gorman and Postle, 2003, p. 21).

While part of the problem is the lack of resources available to fund 'packages of care', there are other factors. For example voluntary and independent sector organisations have to be prepared to contract to provide innovative services in the community. While the annual Community Care Awards are testament to the enthusiasm and innovation of the voluntary sector and independent sector in small-scale projects, market forces mean that provision of services in the community is not attractive to private organisations. Therefore resource limitations, the existence of eligibility criteria and the lack of provision in the independent and voluntary sector mean that assessments are not totally needs-led, and consumers do not have unlimited choice. As has been suggested, this influences how the principles of care management operate: 'there is little point in having user-centred care managers if all they have to purchase is a limited set of services from a set list' (Means and Smith, 1998, p. 123).

Just as controversial is the continuing question of whether care management is a social work method. Horder (2002) suggests that in that it defines what social workers should do and how they should go about their work it is a social work method. Gorman and Postle (2003) argue that the 'reality' of care management is that it has turned social workers into brokers of services, and involves individual workers in bureaucracy, paperwork and the use of computer software to undertake detailed financial assessments and issue contracts. Their research found that social workers felt deskilled because the emphasis was on management, and particularly management of risk, rather than on care. This is accompanied by a sense that 'real' social work, often described as counselling or face-to-face work, is disappearing (Postle, 2001). This is not just about social workers wanting to 'hang on' to old ways of working but a sense that their work has changed and they are not as effective.

However there is other evidence that suggests social workers, operating as care managers, have about the same level of face-to-face contact as they did prior to the introduction of care management. Weinberg et al. (2003) undertook one of the few comparisons based on the actual time social workers spend with users. They found that there was in fact little change in the balance of activities between, for example, direct work with service users and paperwork or administration. In particular they found that social workers have a great deal of input into answering the needs of service users and their families (Weinberg et al., 2003). This is sometimes called direct work, and involves finding practical solutions to problems, a service that is valued by service users.

However, need is not always alleviated just by the provision of practical help (Means and Smith, 1998). The sense that workers had of having less contact might be because the content and quality of direct work had changed. So, while those undertaking care management tasks might have contact with individual service users, this might be focused on highly complex assessment forms and testing out eligibility criteria. As was discussed in Chapter 2, the process of undertaking an assessment is just as important as the content, and assessment schedules can sometimes interfere with that process. Also the study was looking at actual time spent with service users, but it might be that because of a focus on assessment and meeting targets, the time was spent with a number of different service users, rather than ongoing contact with the same service user and his/her family.

Users as care managers

The introduction of direct payments (Community Care (Direct Payments) Act (1997)) had a significant effect on the arrangements for care management. As was said in Chapter 3, there was a clear sense from some user groups that it is only when service users are given control over their own care that they can be empowered. This has sometimes been discussed rather negatively as the 'commodifica-tion' of care, where care services are purchased as a commodity, like furniture or food, and that there is no need for social work input. This has complicated implications for workers. The positive consequence is that direct payments allow the service user to become her/his own care manager. However there is still a role for workers to be involved, even at a distance, because arrangements for care break down and service users' situations change and deteriorate.

Lloyd (2000) develops the notion of users as care managers from a different perspective. Writing about older people who have specific problems, that is, those who suffer from Parkinson's disease, she found they were poorly served by care management. They were older people who because of the nature of their illness, which was episodic and progressive, would benefit from an individualised care package approach. These illness characteristics also meant they were involved with many professionals, but had most contact with highly specialised medical services. Lloyd found that this meant that they were rarely offered a care management assessment, there was little joined-up practice that would meet both their health needs and their practical needs. She suggests that one of the weaknesses of the care management approach was that it required a professional to be involved. She suggests that a true care management approach should take seriously the largely untapped resources of service users as care managers. In the case of Parkinson sufferers they were the people who knew about their contact with the different professionals and the level of service they were receiving. Lloyd acknowledges that each individual would need to be supported by professional knowledge, expertise and resources in order to manage his/her situation (Lloyd, 2000, p. 752), but argues that this could be developed in partnership. Such an approach resonates with the exchange model of assessment discussed in Chapter 2, and also draws on a person-centred approach to social work (discussed below). It also highlights that when a number of services are involved a single shared assessment is beneficial, as is multi-professional working.

Single shared assessment

Central to community care arrangements is the creation of individualised, flexible packages of care, requiring workers to arrange and provide services from independent, voluntary and statutory groupings. Often such packages of care involve a number of different services/agencies, and a key responsibility of a care manager is collaboration with medical, nursing and other caring agencies

(DoH, 1989a). Ideally the care manager is the person who facilitates and coordinates multi-disciplinary activity designed to provide a holistic assessment. In the case of health assessments of older people, these can take place at home, in a day or residential centre or in a hospital setting. Various professionals (for instance, health visitors, occupational therapists, physiotherapists, general practitioners, district nurses and social workers) work together in shared assessment of older people.

Such assessments might be seen to be good practice, and it might be assumed that professionals would agree about categories for assessment, but research carried out by Runciman (1989) revealed differences in perspectives. Difficulties in rising from a chair, for example, might be assessed by a GP as arthritic hips, by a health visitor as a low chair or by a physiotherapist as poor hand function. Similarly, interesting differences in starting points or foci for assessment were noted, the social workers homing in on attitudes and feelings, or practical problems such as housing; occupational therapists, not surprisingly, starting with mobility. The groups differed over whether or not they carried a framework for assessment in their head; where a particular theoretical framework had been adopted, for example among district nurses, this proved to be a barrier to more detailed considerations of need. Different frameworks can also lead to poor communication between professionals.

Because of differences in approach to assessment, policy guidance has been issued to require effective joint working. The Joint Future Group of the Scottish Executive (2000) has made single shared assessment a requirement for working with older people from October 2001. This was mirrored in England in the NHS Plan (DoH, 2000b) and a National Service framework for older people (DoH, 2001). Such directives recognise that social work assessments frequently ignored or minimised health needs, and health assessments did not address social issues. They are therefore designed to avoid concentrating on a single aspect of a person's situation, and to reduce the number of assessment 'events' service users and their carers have to undergo. A single shared assessment is expected to:

- be person-centred and needs-led
- relate to level of need
- be a process not an event.

To achieve this agencies (including local authorities, NHS services and housing departments) are required to have joint protocols and joint training. This means that a lead professional from any agency can co-ordinate documents, share appropriate information, co-ordinate all contributions and produce a single summary assessment of needs in ways that are acceptable to all professionals involved, whatever their professional setting. To help achieve this, the Scottish Executive is also planned to produce assessment tools to help co-ordinate assessments.

The single shared assessment will not decrease the number of professionals involved; the expertise from each is still required. In fact the Department of Health guidance (DoH, 2002) in England recognised that best practice should include local stake-holders in the assessment, including older people, service users, carers and providers. A single shared assessment should avoid the duplication of information provided by the service user and carer and ensure that no significant factors are overlooked. The difference in practice will occur in sharing information and agreement about how to respond to the needs of the individual. Also the service user and his/her carer will be aware of the assessment process and its results. Hopefully this will avoid the situations found by Baldock and Ungerson (1994) in their research, where people in hospital received visits from profes-sionals, but were not sure who they were and for what purpose they had visited.

The guidance for local implementation of single shared assess-ment summarised by Parker and Bradley (2003) covers two main aspects of assessment:

● Processes for preparing for and initiating assessment. To include agreement on language, purpose and culture of the assessment.
● Processes of undertaking the assessment. To include stages for gathering and collating information and developing tools to assist this.
(Parker and Bradley 2003, p. 30)

Both of these require those involved to develop shared values and joint training, and have major implications for multi-professional working, sometimes called multi-disciplinary teamwork.

Multi-disciplinary teamwork

Multi-disciplinary teamwork is crucial whenever we attempt to put together a rounded picture of someone's circumstances. Multi-disciplinary teams consist of a number of different disciplines sharing their knowledge and expertise about a specific client with the objective of identifying and using those services that most effectively meet assessed needs (see DoH, 1989a). As Petch (2002) points out, community mental health teams and community disability teams provide examples of multi-disciplinary work because they consist of workers from different disciplines or professions. However she sees a key distinction between whether the team is single agency, for example in social services but consisting of different professionals, or whether it is multi-agency and multi-professional, bringing together, for example, social workers, social work assistants, home care workers, community nurses, occupational therapists and housing and welfare rights specialists (Petch, 2002, p. 222). The role of the social worker in such a team would require the following skills:

- *Partnership*, the ability to engage with colleagues, allocate tasks and give feedback.
- *Negotiation*, making clear what outcomes for self and others are desired; compromise and confrontation.
- *Networking*, gathering and disseminating information, linking people and establishing mutual support groups.
- *Communicating*, writing effective reports, speaking and writing in a non-jargonised way.
- *Reframing*, offering different perspectives by placing the problem in a wider frame of reference and discussing alternative ways of seeing the problem.
- *Confronting*, assertively challenging a dominant view.
- *Flexibility*, learning from the skills of others.
- *Monitoring and evaluation*, measuring outcome and modifying methods or goals accordingly.
  (CCETSW/IAMHW, 1989)

All workers who wish to be equipped for this kind of work require respect, openness and client-centredness if they are to make a distinctive contribution to the team. Otherwise individual workers could become either hostile or marginal figures or, chameleon-like, opt to fit in with the view of the rest. While consensus is not the goal of multi-disciplinary working, honest dialogue can expand everyone's skills and horizons. However there has to be acceptance of the final assessment.

As Petch (2002) points out, management structures are vital. Managers have to have the respect of the team, and workers have to accept different management structures. Many of the tensions that arise amongst interdisciplinary team members relate to the myths and stereotypes that we hold about other professions. Stereotyping can be overcome via joint training, working and peer supervision activities in multi-disciplinary teams.

Case example

Mrs Short is an 89-year-old woman living in her own home in a middle-class district of a northern town. She has been widowed for over 20 years and has two sons. One lives in a nearby town and the other lives some distance away. She is fiercely independent and house-proud but has recently had an operation for a thrombosis in her arm. Just prior to being hospitalised she called out her GP because she experienced chest pains. Her husband had died of a heart attack and she was obviously very frightened by her symptoms. However the GP, who had known the family for many years, was convinced they were probably caused by indigestion. On the visits he noticed that Mrs Short was having problems with her short-term memory and was becoming confused. Also the house was not as clean and organised at it usually was.

At the point of her discharge from hospital Mrs Short was assessed for both her immediate needs and her longer-term needs. The social worker in the area team with responsibility for older people in the area was contacted by the hospital and informed of the imminent discharge. She in turn contacted the GP for information and was put in touch with the practice nurse who would be visiting Mrs Short to change her dressings when she returned home. The nurse was aware of the GP's concerns and conveyed these to the social workers. She informed the social worker that the GP was making a referral to the psychogeriatrician. The practice nurse also suggested that a physiotherapy assessment might be useful. She agreed to action this from the surgery.

The area had a computerised single assessment document, and all workers involved with the system had had joint training days. The social worker began to input the information into the system. The information that she received alerted her to the possible need for a home care assessment. She was therefore able to visit Mrs Short knowing what potential health problems she was experiencing, and aware that she could get expert information about these and possible responses. During the visit she discussed with Mrs Short events that had happened and sought Mrs Short's views about these.

Throughout the interview Mrs Short was adamant that she did not want to leave her own home. She had been unhappy in hospital, and said she could manage with the help of her son, who visited weekly, and her next-door neighbour, who did her heavy shopping for her. However she did agree to a visit from the home care organiser, but expressed concern both about the cost of any services and about having no choice who came into her home. The social worker also reminded Mrs Short that she would be having a visit from the physiotherapist. Mrs Short did not seem to have a problem with this as it was seen to be 'medical'.

After the various visits had taken place the social worker received information from all those involved and completed the computerised assessment document. She made this, and her conclusions, available to the other workers, and a case meeting was held at the hospital. Mrs Short was invited to this meeting. She was accompanied by her son. They were given a 'user friendly' version of the computerised assessment, but the social worker also ensured that Mrs Short understood what it was recommending.

The conclusions had been that Mrs Short was suffering early stages of vascular dementia and that she had circulatory problems which meant there was the possibility of further thrombosis. It was agreed that she would be able to stay in her own home but would need help with domestic chores, and would also benefit from daily meals being delivered. Lack of food and drink and long periods of loneliness were thought to contribute to her digestive problems and her increasing confusion. Once Mrs Short's wound had healed the practice nurse would stop visiting, and a care assistant would visit to ensure that she was taking her medication and was functioning generally. While Mrs Short expressed some reluctance at all these strangers coming into her home, she accepted that this would enable her to continue living at home.

It was also suggested that Mrs Short might attend a day centre once or twice a week for company. At first she was resistant to this, but her son had reminded her how much she used to enjoy her social activities, and in a small town, she knew some of the people who were attending the centre. She agreed on the basis that she would be able to help others who were there.

Part of the assessment had to consider long-term possibilities, and the social worker was clear that the aim was to enable Mrs Short to live in her home for as long as she could – but that in the future they might have to think about residential care. Mrs Short was adamant that she would not consider this. While this seems to present an impasse it was important that Mrs Short was aware of what the long-term arrangements might be, and that her feelings about this be communicated to all involved.

It was agreed that all involved in Mrs Short's case would keep the social worker (operating as the care manager) informed, and that she would call a review meeting in six months, or earlier if the situation demanded it.

Person-centred planning

The above case describes the multi-professional collaboration involved in developing and delivering a care package. It also has elements of person-centred planning. Person-centred planning was developed initially among service users with physical disabilities, and represents a move against the notion of counselling associated with medical and tragedy models of disability (see Oliver, 1996, for discussions of models of disability). Hence while there may seem to be similarities between person-centred planning and person-centred counselling (see Chapter 5), the similarities are predominantly in the title. The medical and tragedy models of disability assumed that because individuals had an impairment they were either ill, or were grieving for the loss of not being 'able-bodied'. Such attitudes deny the personhood of people with disabilities because they focus only on their needs and ignore the strengths that people bring to their situation.

Person-centred planning can be used with many adult users of social services. It is usually associated with needs-led assessments, but in fact should inform good practice throughout contact with adult users, including long-term contact, service provision and review.

Petch (2002, p. 226) identifies 17 aspects of person-centred planning, but these can be summarised as follows:

- Focus on the individual as unique and special, the person in his/her situation.
- At the same time recognise that some needs are universal, common to all.
- Facilitate communication and participation throughout all the processes.
- Operate in a culture of rights and entitlements.
- Make plans for monitoring and review to inform long-term goals.

This approach becomes crucial in shared assessments and multi-disciplinary work because the person can very easily become a 'case' defined by his/her problem or illness. It is vital in organisation for community care to counteract bureaucratic tendencies to categorise individuals. It is only by recognising and responding to the circumstances of individual users that the principles of justice can be reflected in service delivery. Person-centred planning draws more on the principles of justice than it does on problematic understandings of care (Orme, 2002).

'Just' practice

Driven by the need to provide 'care' and to ensure that they are meeting managerial targets for time taken to provide assessments, workers can often stereotype older people and other service users by assuming they all share the same characteristics. As was said in the introduction to the chapter, work has been done on how issues of gender (Orme, 2001a) or race (Ahmad and Atkins, 1996) influence assessments and service provision in community care. This work highlights the fact that two phenomena occur. With one, workers operate according to categories that have been developed for bureaucratic convenience, such as older people, people with disabilities or people with mental health problems. The worst representation of this is in oppressive language such as 'the disabled', 'the elderly' or 'the mentally ill'. Alternatively they recognise some differences, some aspects of a person's identity, and make certain assumptions and act in a particular way 'because she is a woman' or 'because he is black'.

Both of these approaches have limitations. The first, as been said, denies the personhood of the service user – and even that catch-all term is problematic. One woman in a group discussion in a mental health hostel about users' rights stated that she did not want to be seen as someone who 'used' other people – she wanted to be called a patient. The categories acknowledge only one aspect of a person's identity and experience, and at any one time this might not be the most important aspect for them, or the one that is contributing to their needs. Using such categories might mean that the worker focuses only on this aspect of the situation.

Increasingly awareness of anti-oppressive and anti-discriminatory practice (Thompson, 1993; Dominelli, 2002) alerts social work practitioners to recognise other aspects of a person's experience. Most frequently this involves recognising that being a woman and/or being black significantly affects people's life experience and the way that they have been treated by health and social care services. However this sometimes happens in simplistic ways and leads to unhelpful stereotyping or unjust practices. Ahmad and Atkins (1996) for example highlight that social workers, in recognising cultural differences, make assumptions that Asian communities look after their own and therefore packages of care are not necessary. This not only denies individuals and families services, which is unjust, it also assumes that all Asian people are the same. While it is important to respect cultural diversity it is also important to recognise the complexity of black perspectives which, according to Prevatt Goldstein (2002), consist of different interlocking experiences of each individual and have multiple expressions.

In the case of women, assumptions about women's caring capacities have locked them into caring roles, or denied them services. Just as importantly, focusing solely on women has meant that the needs of men, and the contributions that they can make to caring, have been ignored (Orme, 2001a). There are many aspects of a person's experience that should be acknowledged in assessing his/her needs and developing a package of care; for example his/her class, sexual orientation and/or religion.

Good practice demands that we try to understand the multiple aspects of service users' experience without creating a hierarchy of disadvantage. To do this it is necessary to recognise what is significant and different about these experiences, but also what is common. Most importantly we should allow the person to express how he/she experiences the situation and what he/she wants changed. In many ways this constitutes what is known as empathy in social work – understanding the person in his/her situation.

However empathy has been criticised for being associated with professional distance and the interpretative methods of a psychodynamic approach (see Chapter 4). An alternative way is to think of working at borderlands (Orme, 2001a) between the person and the world as he/she experiences and interprets it. This requires that we can communicate with the individual effectively, but also that we understand the discriminatory and oppressive practices and processes that he/she may be experiencing – this may be as a disabled woman, or as an older Asian man.

The notion of 'just' practice (Orme, 2002) is associated with a person-centred approach because it avoids assumptions that a person has to be cared for, in the sense of being disempowered and/or pitied, because he/she has a set of needs. Critiques of 'care' have suggested that it can be overwhelming if it is assumed that in some ways having needs means such people are not able to think and act on their own behalf (see Orme, 2002 for a discussion of these critiques). Nor does just practice make any assumptions about whose needs are greater, or who is more deserving. It argues that all those who come to the attention of social services have the rights to express their needs, to have these dealt with in a fair and appropriate manner, and to have equal access to resources.

Working with carers

The notion of 'just' practice is particularly important in community care because the provision of care often raises issues of competing needs between those who require care and those who provide it. The legislation introducing community care highlighted the need for carers to be recruited from a variety of sources, but assumed that informal carers would be predominantly family, friends and/or neighbours. There have been many criticisms of the subsidising of statutory services by informal and unpaid labour. There are also many debates about community care as 'women care' (see Orme, 2001a for a discussion of this).

While the introduction of direct payments has brought about some changes in the way that care is purchased and provided, there is still a huge army of informal carers. That care is a 'burden' is now recognised by the existence of a charter for carers and many support mechanisms. However to express care in this way is problematic because it means that those who require care could be seen to be the burden (Morris, 1993). Nevertheless it has to be acknowledged that informal carers are undertaking responsibilities that could/should be provided by statutory services either directly or by commissioning and paying for them from voluntary and independent sector agencies. Undertaking these responsibilities creates stress, and can also mean that those who provide that care are denied their own identity; they are seen only as the carer (Barton, 2002).

The complexities and demands of being a carer were recognised by the introduction of the Carers (Recognition and Services) Act (1995), which gave carers the right to an assessment. The implementation was patchy and even if care managers were spending time with individuals, research found that relatively small amounts of time was spent with carers (Weinberg *et al.*, 2002; Carpenter and Schneider, 2004). The Carers and Disabled Children Act (2001) enables:

- assessment of the carer where the cared-for person refuses an assessment
- innovative and creative services for carers based on outcomes that they value
- the extension of direct payments.
  (DoH, 2000b, p. 2)

These principles represent rights for carers, but fulfilling these rights is not straightforward. While it might be true that the traditional role of the social worker as the link person with the family is being fulfilled by care management (Carpenter and Schneider, 2004, p. 381), that traditional role has also been criticised for pathologising individuals and for drawing people into the welfare net unnecessarily. While there is an imperative to recognise 'service users and their carers' it has to be remembered that carers are not necessarily service users (although of course they might be: service users can also provide care), they are service providers. Because of this there is an obvious imperative that social workers when working with carers have to operate according to the principles of just practice. This will include:

- treading a fine line between being responsive to carers' needs and recognising the stress of caring, but not assuming that the

person who is providing care either has problems or is a problem
- recognising that, like service users, carers are not a unified group
- responding to carers as service providers
- balancing the rights and needs of carers with the rights and needs of service users.

Conclusion

This chapter has focused on social work with adults, recognising that many of the skills and methods described elsewhere in the book might be appropriate in work with adults. Because of this it has concentrated on the impact of arrangements for care management in community care. Examining the processes of care management and research into these processes led to a discussion of person-centred planning and how this requires social workers to work with the principles of just practice when responding to the needs of service users. These principles also apply to a group of adults with whom social workers work, but in an entirely different capacity, those who provide care.

---

putting it into practice

Read the case of Mrs Short again, then identify a case situation of an adult who requires care. This may be a case that you have worked with, or it may be a friend or relative.

1. Identify all the services and resources that the person needs to enable him/her to continue to live in the community, and to continue living with his/her quality of life.
2. Now think about what resources are available to help meet these needs. You might want to list these according to the sources, for example:
   - the individual
   - family
   - friends, neighbours and other individuals in the community
   - voluntary, independent agencies
   - statutory services, e.g. health and social services.

3. List the resources against the person's needs. Is there a mismatch? What needs are not met? Why not? Are these practical or emotional (for example, is the person lonely)? How can they be met?

4. It is useful to access the website for carers: www.carers.gov.uk on a regular basis to find out about what is available to support carers.

Further reading

Gorman, H. and Postle, K. (2003) *Transforming Community Care: a distorted vision?* Birmingham: Venture Press. A useful discussion of how practitioners have experienced care management, based on research.

Sharkey, P. (2000) *Essentials of Community Care.* Basingstoke: Palgrave. This text discusses community care from a variety of perspectives, and gives a useful description of the policy and practice developments.

11 | Working with groups

Introduction

Groups can be used when undertaking assessments, to give people support or bring about behaviour change, and in processes such as consulting with users and carers. It might therefore be assumed that groupwork is any method of intervention, but with more than two people.

Groupwork is more than this, and theories of groupwork drawing on social psychology demonstrate that bringing people together in groups precipitates particular processes. Handled carefully, these processes can be powerful forces for positive change. This chapter explores some of the theories that support the notion that groupwork is a separate, and some argue more effective, method of intervention than individual work. It describes different stages of groupwork intervention, and considers some of the types and purposes of groups. In doing this it analyses the tasks for the worker and discusses how to handle particular difficulties.

What is different about groupwork?

One definition of a group is that it is a collection of people who spend some time together, who see themselves as members and who are identified by outsiders as members of a group (Preston-Shoot, 1987). However, group membership extends beyond the time that the members spend together: it involves a commitment and loyalty which arises out of the individual's interaction with group members and the group leader(s)/group facilitator. Also, in an age of electronic communication, especially through Internet 'chat rooms' and similar facilities, people might consider themselves to be members of a group that is made up of people they have not physically met.

It is an interesting exercise to list the number of groups of which you are or have been a member. Such an exercise helps to clarify what we think we mean by a group, but also illustrates the number of different groups any one person belongs to. Both of these points are important for some of the basic theories of group-work. For example, when we join a new work team we might not immediately feel part of the group, indeed we might feel quite excluded. What is it that eventually makes us feel that we are a member, that we have 'arrived', and why is it that some people never feel accepted – they experience exclusion? Being part of many groups causes conflicts of loyalties and confusions about behaviour. When we join a new work team we discover that tasks are done differently: systems might be better, or worse. Part of being accepted involves negotiating that fine line between holding on to the positives of our past experiences and working practices while accepting that there are things to be learned in the new situation.

These experiences help us to begin to understand the complexity of group dynamics, and give some indication why we need to consider the literature and gain experience before undertaking groupwork. Leadership in groups involves a set of skills that may only be learned by doing. The best way to do this is to act as co-worker with an experienced groupworker, or to be a participant observer. There is a growing body of literature, including some skills manuals that involve groupwork exercises (see, for example, Doel and Sawdon, 1999), to help students of groupwork.

Groups and change

At the core of groupwork theory is the capacity of groups to bring about change. Peter Smith (1980) considers processes of social influence to demonstrate that groups bring about more lasting change than individual work because groups provide influence by giving feedback and by providing access to coping skills. These processes are similar to Trotter's (1999) principles of pro social modelling discussed in Chapter 8, and are therefore a form of behaviour modification. However Smith argues that because the range of participants in a group includes those who have similar experiences, difficulties or goals, this increases the repertoire of alternative behaviours available to the individual. Three types of social influence are significant for groupwork:

- *Compliance* occurs when a group member behaves in a way that s/he thinks is acceptable to, or desired by the group. Such change might be relatively minor and short-lived. It can also occur in individual interviews, especially as compliance occurs when one person is seen to have more control over another. In groups individuals are often initially compliant to the leader's wishes.
- *Identification* occurs when one person is attractive to another, and the second adopts the behaviour and attitudes of the first in order to sustain a positive relationship. In that groups involve a number of participants, they provide more opportunities for identification to occur. (There are risks here, as those working with offenders are aware. If the attractive person displays anti-social or criminal behaviour then the risk of 'contagion' occurs.)
- *Internalisation* is seen as the most important element in group learning, and occurs when a group member makes changes because he or she observes the behaviour of someone who is attractive to him or her, and the behaviour works for him or her in his/her own situation. Again groups provide a number of opportunities to observe and test out different coping strategies.

Disclosure and feedback

The process of modelling is not the only process that is enhanced by participation in a group, rather than individual work. In all interactions we reveal something of ourselves, and as we get to know people we reveal more of ourselves. This process of disclosure happens in individual interactions, but obviously is multiplied in groups where we reveal different aspects of ourselves to different people, and in different circumstances. When we disclose aspects of ourselves, we receive feedback from others. Sometimes that is direct feedback: people tell us they agree or disagree, or indirectly by their behaviour and attitudes we discern that they do or do not like what we say or do. When we receive feedback from individuals we can ignore it, or perceive it as a difficulty (or a benefit!) of our relationship with that individual. In groups, feedback that is received from more than one source is more difficult to ignore. Also, as group participants, individuals are more likely to give feedback in the knowledge that their views or perceptions will be supported by other group members.

The Johari window (Figure 11.1) devised by Joseph Luft and Harry Blumberg (Golembiewski and Blumberg, 1970) illustrates how this interaction of feedback and disclosure contributes to an understanding of ourselves. Either through defensiveness, lack of insight or not having been in situations before, there are aspects of our behaviour that are not apparent to us. The process of feedback, handled appropriately, helps us to understand how our behaviour impacts on others, and group situations give us the opportunity to test out how much that is a particular response from one individual, or is a more general response to our own behaviour. The experience of being in a group, of disclosing parts of ourselves and receiving feedback, is therefore likely to reduce the unknown or unconscious area and contribute to insight.

Smith's notion of social influence and the processes of feedback/disclosure in the Johari window both involve change. This change is brought about by challenge and confrontation, not in the sense of open argument and disagreement, but by individuals becoming aware of aspects of their behaviour and that of others and having

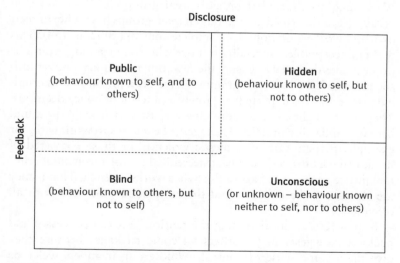

Figure 11.1 Johari window

to deal with it. It is the potential for change that makes groups both an effective method of intervention and a source of anxiety for both participants and groupworkers. This potential is present whatever the focus or purpose of the group, because it is the interaction between a number of different participants which provides the opportunities for feedback and insight.

As Mullender and Ward (1991) point out, even in their model of self-directed groupwork, which sets out with the prime aim of raising awareness and assisting users to set their own agendas for change, personal change occurred within the members of the groups. This was mostly positive in that it enabled members to be more confident and take on more public roles.

Programmes

What is of concern however are developments in the use of groups that proceed on the basis of one-to-one work in groups, with the rest of the group acting as bystanders (Ward, 2002). Here the emphasis is on changing behaviour by using behavioural approaches outlined in Chapter 8 to bring about conformity. In these approaches the emphasis is on the use of the group (its members and the process) not as the instrument or medium for change, but merely as the context. Ward suggests that what he calls 'real groupwork' was rejected because, as is described later in this chapter, groups have a life of their own and workers do not have complete control (2002, p. 154). This was not acceptable, especially to those who were running groups as programmes designed to ensure the cessation of criminal and/or anti-social behaviour. These programmes have been introduced in criminal justice services in particular largely as a result of policy decisions. They are thought to be a more effective use of workers' time, and help to standardise practice. Packages (of exercises to work with, for example, perpetrators of domestic violence, or those convicted of drink-driving offences) have been accredited for use throughout criminal justice agencies as part of the 'what works' agenda. That is they are thought to be effective and therefore should be used with all offenders.

Brown (2002), in discussing the tension between processes and packages, suggests that workers welcome packages because they give them some sense of control, while group members welcome this approach because it takes away the sense of responsibility that they might have to participate. However working unreflectively with these packages can mean that at best opportunities for effective intervention can be lost. At worst the group might become totally disruptive, with negative effects on its members.

Despite Ward's pessimism a survey in the UK (Doel and Sawdon, 2001) found a commitment to using groupwork. Although a high proportion of respondents were workers in criminal justice agencies, who might be involved in delivering packages or accredited groupwork programmes, Doel and Sawdon conclude that they found evidence that there is immense complexity of groups and groupwork. This is supported by edited texts that describe a range of groupwork approaches in a variety of contexts (Cohen and Mullender, 2003).

Types and purposes of groups

Now that we have been critical of a programmatic approach to groupwork it is necessary to explore what Ward (2002) means by 'real' groupwork. In the first instance this involves looking at different kinds of groups, and their purposes. It helps to understand that group aims usually prescribe the type and methods to use. Different purposes of groups are those broadly categorised by Papell and Rothman (1966) – remedial, reciprocal and social goals models. Preston-Shoot (1987) uses more detailed categories and distinguishes between social or recreational groups, group psychotherapy, group counselling, educational groups, social treatment groups (for example, sex offender groups), discussion groups, self-help groups, social action groups (for example, welfare rights), and self-directed groups (for example, campaigning or other objectives decided by the members).

The reason why groups fail to 'get going' might be related to how they are formed, composed and led, but also a failure to be clear about purposes. During its lifetime a group may change its purposes, for instance from discussion to campaigning. Unless it is openly stated at the outset what the purposes are, groups can 'lose their way' and become very puzzling for their members. One group, supposedly a recreational one for single-parent mothers, had a hidden agenda aimed at getting the women to improve their parenting skills, so it was doomed from the start. Whitaker (1975) gives four conditions for successful groupwork:

- Success is more likely if other people in the agency support the group purpose and procedures. Sabotage is also less likely.
- A group is more likely to be effective if a consensus can be established within the group about aims and methods.
- Structural factors such as size, duration, composition, constancy of membership and ratio of staff to members influence effectiveness.
- A group that has lost its purpose should be reconstituted with a different mandate or terminated.

This underlines the need for commitment to groupwork by the individual worker and the agency. The only reason for using group-work, as opposed to any other practice method, is that it is the best way of helping the people concerned, not because the workers want to try it or because it is an economical way of offering a service.

Groups have their disadvantages, not least that some individuals are frightened of them. This fear is linked to a sense of ambivalence; of wanting to belong to the group but being afraid that the group might demand giving up autonomy, asking members to do or think something with which they do not agree. On the other hand, groups provide what Yalom (1970) terms 'curative factors' not available through individual approaches. They can be a source of power for clients pressing for social change; mutual support, exchange of information and motivating hope also stem from group processes. The use of groups in criminal justice services also demonstrates how groups can be used for education (for example alcohol awareness and impaired drivers courses), or confronting unacceptable behaviour (for example anger management and offending behaviour groups). Groups therefore offer the opportunity to learn and test interpersonal and other social skills; they offer a sense of belonging and 'being in the same boat' which is reassuring. There is scope to use the leader or other members as role models and to get feedback about coping attempts. Perhaps, most significantly, there is a chance to help as well as be helped.

Planning the group

Once the type and broad aims of the group have been decided on, a major task is planning and preparation. Questions to be answered in the planning process include:

- *Who?* The composition of a group may already be determined, such as those in hospital wards, residential and day centres and neighbourhoods. Where the group can be selected, an ideal balance suggested by Redl (1951) is 'homogeneous enough to ensure stability and heterogeneous to ensure vitality'. Racial homogeneity might be necessary where this is preferred by minority ethnic groups (see Sheik, 1986); similarly, sameness of gender may best meet the purposes of the group (see Reed and Garvin, 1983; Cohen and Mullender, 2003). While, overall, perhaps the best guide is commonality of needs, it is necessary to be aware of balance of composition. So, for example, it would not be helpful to have only one black person, one woman or one man in a group.

- *How many?* The question of group size depends on the aims of the group, but usually there needs to be more than three and less than 14 people, what Brown (1992) suggests is 'large enough for stimulation, small enough for participation and recognition'.

- *How long?* Open-ended or time limited, this question also needs to incorporate a decision whether or not to have open or closed membership. Open groups are those that can be joined at any time. Closed groups have a selected membership at the outset, are time-limited and do not allow people to join during the lifetime of the group. In settings such as hospitals or prisons there is often little choice, as the movement of patients, prisoners and staff on shift systems dictates membership. The length of each session needs to be considered too, for instance work with children, older people and those who are frail requires short sessions with rest breaks.

- *Which methods?* The methods must suit the members, skills of the leader(s) and the stated aims. It may be that it is only when the group has met that final decisions can be taken. Methods include a variety of games, discussions, activities, experiential exercises and entertainments, depending on resources available. Methods might also be dictated by agency policy, or by the specification of the court, as in the case of a violent offender who receives a community supervision sentence that involves attending an anger management group.

- *What resources?* There are a number of practical issues to be addressed such as is there a meeting place? Is transport available if necessary? Will refreshments be provided? What equipment is needed, and so on? For groups with special needs appropriate accommodation and support systems will be required. For example, some people with disabilities are accompanied by personal care attendants who will assist with practical tasks; older people with hearing difficulties may need someone to sit with them to ensure they hear all that is going on. Resources have to be mediated with the agency. This may include providing a breakdown of costs in terms of time spent, staffing by one leader or two, if an outside consultant is to be used, what recording systems will be used and if workers in the whole team can make referrals, for instance from their current workloads.

Groupworkers can draw on a variety of theories to help them in their approach. Theories of behaviourism focus on individual group members. However most groupworkers draw on theories of social psychology to help make decisions about size, composition, leadership and power and influence. Social psychology also informs understandings of stages of group development.

Stages of group development and the worker's tasks

Groups evolve through stages during which the behaviour of the members, the leader's interventions and the accomplishment of tasks or activities can be affected. Following individual 'screening' (for group members and workers) a groupworker has to follow the energy of the group through trust, challenge, openness, interdependence and finally independence. At different stages, the worker has to be central, pivotal, peripheral and central once again. Accordingly, the worker is in tune with the stages of group development known as forming, storming, norming, performing and adjourning (Tuckman and Jensen, 1977).

Other groupwork theorists name these stages differently, but all agree the phenomena to be observed at each: Yalom (1970) describes orientation, conflict then cohesiveness; Schutz (1966) outlines cycles when the group is concerned with inclusion, control and affection, while Whitaker (1985) talks about formative, established and termination phases.

Forming

In the forming stages, members move quickly from orientation and exploration, in which there is parallel communication aimed at the worker, to more communications with each other. The group and the worker are tested to see if trust can be established. The tasks for the practitioner are to help people to get involved, to link people and their common concerns, and to encourage the development of a group bond. When any people join a group they want to know if the sacrifice of their individual wants will be compensated by the benefits of joining the group. The worker takes any opportunity to point out how members, sharing similar interests and problems, are in a position to understand and thereby help one another. To summarise the skills and tasks of the leader in the early meetings:

- Give a short presentation of yourself.
- Ask members to do the same.
- Review information given to members prior to joining.
- Amend any aims and agreements.
- Acknowledge initial uncertainties.
- Get each person to say what he or she hopes to get out of the group.
- Summarise issues as presented.
- Establish norms for listening and accepting.
- Facilitate interaction: 'Does anybody else feel the same?'
- Play the absent member role, putting into words what people may want to say but are not yet ready to risk.
- Show concern for each individual.
- Balance answering questions with 'Does anyone else know the answer to that?'
(Northen, 1969; Heap, 1985)

Storming

During the storming stage, subgroups and pairings may have formed (later, these relationships extend to include the whole group). It is a stage characterised by the replacement of 'Do I belong?' with 'Do I have any influence?' Struggles for power and control underlie communications, and there is a tendency for members to polarise around certain issues. Further exploring and testing takes place: the group is quite fragile and may not continue if the leadership does not provide enough security while individuals question if they are going to get what they came for. This stage can be draining. Some skills and tasks are:

- Keep calm in the face of member–member, member–leader conflicts.
- Do not retaliate when your authority is challenged; it may stem from ambivalence about membership or a transference reaction.
- Model acceptance and openly recognise that people are different.
- Do not pick out isolated or difficult members for attention.
- Try to pace and time when to facilitate and when to be quiet.
- Begin to release responsibilities to the membership.

Norming

The norming stage indicates that group cohesion is established; members may express intimate and personal opinions to each other. People start to look for 'affection', that is, signs that the wider group accepts them. Cooperation, sharing information and decision-making by consensus promote synergistic (the extra power of combined action) outcomes. People identify with the group and its future: a 'we' feeling develops, a growing *esprit de corps*. A norm of high attendance, ritual ownership of seats and some exclusivity is likely to make it difficult for new members to join. A lack of conformity to group norms can lead to scapegoating or group pressure to conform. New leadership from within the group may result in altering basic group norms. For the worker, the tasks are to:

- Let people help each other by stepping out of a directing role into a listening, following one.
- Be pivotal when observing and commenting on what seems to be happening, asking the group what their perceptions are as well as offering ideas of your own.
- Be more aware of process as well as content. It helps to ask oneself (and perhaps the group), 'What is going on here? What is this issue really all about?' in order to help people to express feelings and challenge comments.

Performing

When performing occurs, this means that the group has developed a culture of acting together to solve problems: it is no longer the leader's group, rather the workers become peripheral as the members perceive that 'This is our group.' Individual and group goals are tackled, meaning that members model coping mechanisms and values for each other. A high-status or charismatic member may further enhance a group's willingness to let individuals 'try on' different roles, thus preparing for eventual differentiation and independence from the group. In one group a member who could be relied on as 'competent and responsible' acted as a facilitator for the rest, and bravely pointed out that sometimes he did not feel confident and would prefer sometimes to take a break from feeling responsible. The worker:

● Observes how the group handle each other and the tasks.
● Gives ideas when these are sought.
● Shows interest and expresses praise and appreciation of efforts.
● Continues to model in relation to confidence, attitudes and problem-solving.

Adjourning

The adjourning or ending stage usually follows the achievement of the task, and requires disengagement from relationships. All groups have to end some time, otherwise they risk stagnation or low productivity. Imposed time limits can prevent the worker from hanging on to a group merely because he/she feels guilty or uncertain about 'letting go'. There will be a sense of loss and maybe rejection and attempts to continue the group, despite agreed parameters, but, with good leadership, ultimately acceptance and a sense of achievement. The worker, more active again, can do these things:

● Set goals for the time left in partnership with the group.
● Review experiences, emphasising gains as well as feelings of loss.
● Reinforce interests outside the group.
● Help the group to return to the planning stage if they want to continue but with some other purpose.
● Evaluate the sessions and ask for feedback.

Handling difficulties in groups

Describing group development through the above phases might suggest that all is straightforward and predictable when, in reality, stages only represent tendencies from which any group can veer. Also it is interesting to note that each time a group meets it goes through some version of these stages, in that each meeting brings people together, and requires them to negotiate the tasks and then prepare to end.

Understanding these processes has to be accompanied by recognition of what Heap (1985) calls 'latent' communication in groups. Often, there are recurring themes, for instance, when a group seems preoccupied with a particular, apparently irrelevant topic. This might mistakenly be ignored instead of associated with something people cannot talk about directly. Literature on groupwork refers to this as a common group tension or focal conflict. Recognising the deeper meaning of content and managing the processes around focal conflicts takes sensitivity and advanced skills.

Beyond symbolic communication difficulties, workers fantasise about the possibility that a group will simply take no notice of the leader or that strong emotions will result in chaos and damaged individuals. Books that suggest techniques, such as that by Doel and Sawdon (1999), can inspire some confidence until more experience is gained. But even experienced workers are anxious when a group member is isolated, scapegoated, speaks too much or too little. Generally, many of these difficulties can be put back to the group for their resolution; otherwise individual counselling might help, or it may be that the behaviour is needed by the group for some reason and should be explored.

Roles in groups

In addressing the *scapegoat* phenomenon, for instance, Shulman (1979) suggests that the worker first observes the pattern, tunes into her/his own feelings about this, avoids siding with or against the scapegoat, and asks the group to comment on what is happening. Then, if the scapegoat does not need protection or mediation, the worker attempts to reduce guilt, fear or whatever feelings the group are suppressing and projecting on to one member by talking about such feelings in a general way. For example, in student groups one person may be aggressive and outspoken; the rest hide their feelings so as not to be different or unpopular. It is possible to point out that what the outspoken student is saying is felt by a lot of people even though they may not admit it. Then one can go on to reflect on how social workers may fear conflict and yet it is an issue every day in practice; having the courage to confront it is what matters.

If the leader does not handle the *monopoliser* in the group, Yalom (1970) warns that members will start to be absent or explode! The problem with allowing someone to dominate a group is that this stops others with useful things to say from contributing. So intervention has to take place early on to prevent group structure hardening, and while the leader still has patience. For example, in a group of carers, one man went on at length about his experience. As this was the first meeting, he might have over-whelmed other participants with his knowledge and so, having thanked him for prompting the group to explore a range of ideas, the worker indicated clearly that she would like to hear everyone's point of view.

Stimulating *silent members* counteracts monopolisers as well as making the group structure a more functional one. If a person stays silent, some groups resent this, believing that the person is quietly judging them or not sharing. Teasing silent members or saying 'We haven't heard from you, Mrs Smith,' is not helpful, while a more positive intervention is something like, 'I remember you said some-thing about this once, Mrs Smith. Could you remind us about your suggestion as I think it would help.' Conveying an interest in hearing from people and modelling respect can also be done non-verbally with a touch, gesture or eye contact – swivelling one's eyes around a student group will usually catch a reticent person who might speak if encouraged with a nod.

Obviously, there cannot be prescriptions for handling all the problems that arise, and it is important to use supervision and 'wash-up' sessions (that is, sessions held immediately after the group to reflect on what has gone on) to identify what has worked, and what has not.

Co-leadership

Problems are also easier to handle if there is co-leadership of the group. Arguments for co-leading or co-facilitating include:

handling large groups; continuity when one leader is absent; managing when members get out of control or express strong emotions; and when work is to be done in subgroups (Preston-Shoot, 1987). Planning, selecting and presenting a co-leader to the group should include consideration of gender and race combinations. Groupwork is demanding, and few of us are able to concentrate all the time. Co-working allows the responsibility for taking the initiative to be shared. On these occasions the other person can observe and reflect on the group processes as they occur. This dynamic can provide valuable feedback to the group itself while it is in process, and to the co-worker in the post-group discussions or 'wash-up'. There could be disadvantages when the co-workers hold widely differing views on goals and styles, and when the sole worker already has the resources required. These can be overcome by careful selection of co-workers, and can be dealt with in supervision.

Recording

Just a few final words on recording group sessions are needed before we proceed to the case example. In relation to recording, some groupworkers keep a register showing standard information such as date, session number, members and leaders present/absent, plan for the session, diagram of seating arrangements, what happened (that is, content and process), and an evaluation of what went well and what did not (Brown, 1992). Others draw a series of circles representing each member: the circles are divided into three portions indicating the beginning, middle and end of the session, noting atmosphere, influence, participation, tasks and decision-making at each time stage in the 'interaction chronogram'. These methods give an account of the group process and are useful for the worker and co-worker to reflect on the session, prepare for the next and make appropriate interventions related to specific group members.

However, where groups involve members who are on the caseloads of other workers, systems have to be agreed for giving feedback to colleagues, which do not breach any confidentiality agreements the group may have agreed. Also, there should be agreement in advance what arrangements there will be for contacting individuals who have indicated specific problems that have not been, or cannot be, dealt with in the group.

Finally groups that operate to enable members to fulfil the requirements of court orders have to develop agreed recording methods that both respect the members of the group, and fulfil the requirements of the court.

Case example: domestic violence group

A criminal justice team set up a group for men who had been sentenced for offences of domestic violence. A team of workers operated in pairs (one male and one female worker) to offer different modules of a programme that had been approved by the Home Office. It was based on a particular approach to challenging domestic violence that had been evaluated as being effective in influencing the behaviour of perpetrators of domestic abuse. The programme consisted of six modules each of five weeks' duration. Men referred to the group by the courts were expected to attend all the sessions as part of their supervision order. Failure to attend the group could lead to a man being taken back to the court and sentenced for the original offence, which might entail a custodial sentence. Each of the modules had a predefined set of tasks and exercises relating to particular themes. The format also required that the men acknowledged their violence, and the group opened each week with the members having to indicate if they had had violent feelings. Group leaders were expected to challenge any behaviour and attitudes that might demean or threaten women.

Part way through the second module of the programme a particular session was extremely difficult for the group leaders to manage. The men were initially silent, refusing to participate in the exercises arranged by the group leaders. When challenged by the leaders for their non-compliance the men became vociferous and argumentative. They said that they felt the group leaders were abusing their power, and that this was ironic when the men themselves were being asked to reflect on their own use of power and control. They also complained that they were being asked to reveal in public (in front of other members of the group) things that they considered personal and confidential.

It emerged during the session that most of the members had met up in the pub before this particular session. They were not drunk, but had spent some time talking about their feelings about the group and deciding what to do. The group leaders had to abandon the exercises planned for that evening, and had to try to resolve some of the strong feelings. It became apparent that not all the men had wanted to take this course of action but that some particularly strong members had suggested it and others felt that they had to comply.

In supervision after this session the group leaders, who were both qualified social workers, were able to acknowledge that in running this 'course' they had ignored the fact that they were in fact running a 'group'. From their training the workers were aware of the theory and practice of group processes, but they had not applied them to this particular aspect of their work. In fact they felt they had been deterred from thinking about groupwork theory because it was associated with 'therapy' and they were not running a therapeutic group. However the fact that the same group of men were meeting together on a regular basis for a particular purpose meant that they were a closed group, and group processes had been operating, but had not been considered by the group leaders. Classic roles had been undertaken by the men, and by not observing these or the processes of influence, the group leaders had not anticipated how the dynamics of the group had developed and were getting in the way of the purpose of the group.

After this supervision session all workers involved in the programme agreed that they needed to be alert to the dynamics of the group processes and to address these, as well as offering the particular tasks and exercises prescribed by the manual. In doing this, the groupworkers became more effective in channelling the more subtle ways that power and influence were being played out in the group, and gained greater insight into the behaviour and attitudes of the group members.

Conclusion

This chapter has set out the theory that informs the practice of running groups. This has implications for the purpose, organisation, membership, and leadership of groups. It has been suggested that whatever the focus of a particular group, there are certain dynamics that occur which should be incorporated into the work with the group. To do this means that the group itself becomes an important and effective medium for bringing about change. If such dynamics are ignored, this does not just constitute lost opportunities, it means that sometimes the intended outcomes of the work will not be achieved. It will be counter-productive.

---

putting it into practice

We are all members of different groups at different times in our lives. We can therefore learn about groups from observing and reflecting on our own experiences.

1. List some of the groups that you have been a member of (see if you can think of about six different groups). Some might be formal ones such as work teams or sports groups; others might be informal such as friendship groups. Then there are 'natural' groups such as families.

2. Now try to identify what was significant about each of these groups. Was it the membership? The purpose? How do you think this group influenced you? Why do you think this happened? When you are working with groups, remember to think about this from the perspective of all participants – do they not come to groups as isolated individuals?

3. Choose a meeting or group session that you are going to participate in. This might be a team meeting at work, a seminar on your course, or a committee meeting. Make a point of observing the processes that the meeting or group goes through. Identify what roles people take on and how that facilitates or blocks the processes. Don't forget to observe your own role. Having an observer can influence the group dynamics, even if the members do not know they are being observed.

Further reading

Doel, M. and Sawdon, C. (1999) *The Essential Groupwork: teaching and learning creative groupwork*. London: Jessica Kingsley. A very useful text that incorporates exercises as well as explaining the theory of groupwork.

Cohen, M. and Mullender, A. (eds) (2003) *Gender and Groupwork*. London: Routledge. This text describes groupwork with women in a number of different contexts.

12 | Working with communities

Introduction

Debates about the relationship between social work and community work have been a common feature of social work textbooks. Some see community work as part of a 'holy trinity' with individual work and groupwork. They argue that community work should be regarded as a distinct form of practice, which calls upon a theoretical and knowledge base that is more sociological and less psychological than individual work and groupwork (Payne, 1991). Radical approaches to social work recognised the importance of using community approaches as part of social work, and welcomed the change of emphasis that community work represented. Working with individuals within their (geographical) context showed problems to have many dimensions, and responses could be more flexible.

There are some who ague that social workers do not 'do' community work. In some ways this reflects the history of community work, which, as we will see, developed outside statutory social work agencies. However the introduction of community care has provided quite a challenge, and the language of *community* care suggests social workers should engage with communities. Also, the policy agendas of social inclusion suggest that even if social workers are working with individuals and families they need to be alert to both the pressures and the opportunities that work with communities offers. Even if social workers do not 'do' community work, they have to work with community workers to ensure that service users are not excluded from communities. In doing so they might even be able to prevent some people becoming users of social work services.

This chapter will therefore explore the context of working with communities. Because definitions, understandings and uses of terms are complex, and sometimes contradictory, these will be examined in the process. Developments that have led to distinctions between community work, community social work and community development will be outlined. In doing this we shall consider the implications for practice and the necessary skills.

Context

As has been said, work with communities has had an interesting place in social work practice. The fact that there has been little emphasis on communities in statutory work has led to suggestions that community work is not part of social work. However, some writers have tried to clarify the connections. For example Howe (1992) identifies collective action as forming part of the methods of socialist welfare work (alongside fighting for rights and entitlements and arguing that social problems are the consequences of a capitalist economy). Feminist writers, while critiquing developments in community work, point out that mobilising strengths and resources in collectives arose out of the women's movement (Dominelli and McLeod, 1989). The dilemma has been to recognise and respond to individual need but also to see personal problems as political issues.

Community development projects (CDP)

The period that marks the most active phase in terms of relationships between social work and community work was the 1960s. The national community development projects (CDP) were set up by the Home Office Children's Departments, and community development workers were employed who were independent of the newly created social services departments. Workers were to be active mobilising resources within the community. The focus was on organising local communities and improving co-ordination between welfare agencies. The work undertaken included:

- individual welfare rights
- advocacy
- surveys
- campaigning
- community self-help projects (for example, advice centres, adventure playgrounds, women's refuges).

These tasks were often called community action. They involved workers working with community groups and finding collective approaches to resolving problems, even if the problems were being experienced primarily by individuals. Those engaged in various forms of community work were 'concerned with affecting the course of social change through the two processes of analysing social situation and forming relationships with different groups to bring about desirable change' (Calouste Gulbenkian Foundation, 1968, p. 4).

This approach to community work has been described as the process of assisting ordinary people to improve their own communities by collective action (Mayo, 2002). In doing this community workers attempt to understand situations in terms of not only who holds the power, but also whose interests are served by particular policies and practices. Although focusing on the community rather than the individual was seen to be a positive move away from casework approaches which had been criticised, there was a danger that a community could be pathologised, and experienced as the problem (Loney, 1983). The notion in the 1990s of 'sink estates' shows how areas that are seen as having numerous problems can be labelled negatively. Other dangers were that community work would be employed as a palliative when the substantial resources needed to overcome major injustices were not forthcoming (Popple, 1995, p. 27). This is a particular risk if community work focuses on communities 'making do' rather than advocating, for example, better housing, local health and education resources.

These dangers highlight competing perspectives on, or traditions in, the role of community work. These are alternatively defined as the differences between the (political) left and right (Mayo, 2002), or the differences between top-down and bottom-up community action (Popple, 2002). An alternative distinction is:

● The liberal approach to community work, which is about promoting self-help and improving services delivery within the existing frameworks. This approach has also been labelled as a professional or technicist approach.
● The radical, or transformational, approach to community work, which tries to shift the balance of social relations by empowering the powerless to question the causes of their deprivation and challenge the sources of their oppression. (Mayo, 2002, p. 165)

As we shall see on the section on 'tasks and skills' (below) these distinctions, often highlighted by the different focus and locus of activity, become significant in the way that community work is undertaken.

The different approaches also have repercussions for those undertaking the work. The 'professionals' had an uneasy relationship with statutory employers if they were inciting communities to overturn arrangements for service delivery. Community action approaches involved emerging voluntary groups who worked with local community groups, particularly in working-class areas, to fight local causes. Definitional distinctions therefore emerged that separated community work, which was undertaken by those paid to do it, and community action, which was undertaken by those in conflict with authority. These distinctions led to debate in the 1970s about whether community workers should become a separate profession, and whether there was scope for radical activities by those undertaking community work in statutory agencies, including social work agencies.

Hence we can see that community work operates in a number of different ways. As well as being a form of intervention it is:

- an *attitude* that defines a more participative and egalitarian set of relations
- associated with a *critique* of existing power and resources
- a *principle* of service delivery, making services local relevant, accessible and accountable to their users
- a *frame of reference* and identification of like-minded people
- a *work site* for those professionals who do their job 'in' the community (as opposed to an office).

(Thomas, 1983)

Tasks and skills

Popple (2002) argues that a generic definition of community work is working with people using skills, information and strategies in ways that encourage them to do things for themselves. However historically the identification of tasks and skills tends to reflect the tension between the liberal/radical and the top-down/bottom-up approaches.

For example early models of community organisation and intervention (Rothman, 1968) included social planning, locality development and social action. Social action was about direct work with people, particularly those identified as having, or joining together because of, mutual interests or oppressions. The power structure is assumed to lie outside the client system, and is therefore an external target of action, but the intervention is top-down.

York (1984) developed a different framework for theorising community work, or community social work, as he calls it. He focuses on the differences between *directive and non-directive intervention*. The notion of directive and non-directive reflects the primary goals of the workers, what they want to achieve, rather than roles that they adopt at any one time in their work. These echo top-down/bottom-up distinctions:

● *Directive intervention*: involves the agency deciding, more or less specifically, what it thinks the clients need, what they ought to value or what they ought to do, and even at times how they ought to behave.

● *Non-directive intervention*: the worker does not attempt to decide for people, or to lead, guide or persuade them to accept her/his specific conclusions about what is good for them, but works to get them to decide for themselves what their needs are. The worker's role is to provide favourable conditions for successful action by strengthening and stimulating incentive, providing information, helping community members to analyse problems systematically.

An example of how different approaches would be viewed in this model is given below, although York (1984) emphasises that this is a continuum of activity, rather than a set of opposites:

Directive intervention	*Non-directive intervention*
Task approach	Problem approach
Initiating roles	Enabling roles
Treatment	Reform

Another way of analysing community work intervention draws on understandings of systems (see Chapter 3) and involves identifying the different arenas in which community workers are involved, and in which they might use the methods discussed above. These arenas involve negotiations with different people and it is these negotiations that provide the focus for activity. For Henderson and Thomas (1981) these arenas include:

1. Transactions with local people, either as individuals or in group situations. These might be tenants, parents, health care users or residents of a particular street.
2. Transactions between the group and other systems in its environment. These other systems are difficult to predict and might involve other local residents, representatives of official bodies, such as the housing authority, or politicians.
3. Transactions about the group within the worker's own agencies. Recognising that, for example, social work services might need to change, the worker has to be advocate as well as change agent.

Drawing on group processes, Henderson and Thomas (1981) identify seven types of interventions/discussions that exemplify non-directive approaches in community work. Although the functions need to be performed in community work with local people (or neighbourhood work), they do not all have to be undertaken by the same person. While others can undertake the tasks/interventions the community worker needs to ensure that the relevant processes occur. They include:

● galvanising
● focusing
● clarifying
● summarising
● gatekeeping
● mediating
● informing.

When working at the interface between local people and more formal and established organisations, the community worker also has to ensure that a number of other functions are carried out, which include broker, mediator, advocate, negotiator and bargainer. Again different people can perform these functions, but thought has to be given to what role will be played by which individuals. A balance has to be struck between the appropriate activity for the paid worker and the community members. The paid worker might act in some form of representative role for the group or community at, for example, town or city council meetings or interviews with local authority officers. Also when community members take lead roles, the paid worker might have a set of facilitative functions, which include observer/recorder, delegate or plenipotentiary. Finally, as in all work with people, it is important to recognise that power operates in all sorts of subtle ways, and that individuals might dominate in communities, but might not represent the views of the majority. The worker needs to ensure that as many people as possible feel included, and have their voices heard.

This notion of representative becomes more complex for a paid worker when he or she has to manage transactions about the group or community within her/his own employing agency. Henderson and Thomas identify two functions for the worker, but emphasise the need to establish guidelines between the community and the worker to clarify the worker's status and ensure effective communication. The functions are:

● Re-routing enquiries from the agency to the appropriate member of the local group.
● Opportunistic interventions by the worker on behalf of the group within the agency.

Many of the skills that have been referred to have resonance with those described in this text in other forms of intervention. Mayo sums these up as:

● engagement (with individuals, groups and organisations)
● assessment (including area profiles)
● research
● groupwork
● negotiation
● communication
● counselling
● management of resources
● resourcing (for example grant applications)
● recording and report writing (for a wide range of audiences)
● monitoring and evaluation.
  (Mayo, 2002, p. 16)

This serves to highlight that while community work might not necessarily be carried out by those employed in statutory social work agencies, workers undertaking community work draw on skills that are core to the social work profession. This is the complex relationship between social work and community work.

One of the main distinctions between the two has been said to be where the work actually takes place, that is, in a community rather than in a social work agency. However this raises questions about what we mean by 'community'.

'Community'

Many attempts have been made to define communities, most of which include notions of size and place. For example, a community is 'the smallest territorial group that can embrace all aspects of human life ... the smallest local group that can be, and often is, a complete society' (Davis, 1961). This might be a very large group indeed, and each term within the definition can be subject to interpretation. 'Locality' can include street, town or city boundaries, while societies can be regional, national and international, as reflected in the title of the European Community.

For these reasons, the notion of community is the most contested within sociological literature, and while there are often common elements in definitions (locality, attachment, shared interests) there is little agreement on the relative significance of any of these elements (Allan, 1991). For further discussion and a review of the literature see Henderson and Thomas (1981) and Orme (2001a).

At a very basic level there are two distinctions made which highlight the complexities of defining community:

Community as locality: sometimes called community of residence, where place is both synonymous with community and influences those who live in the community. The individual is expected to share things in common with others living in the same geographical area, and to feel some loyalty to that area and its inhabitants. Relationships develop (some positive, some antagonistic), and to some extent the lifestyle adopted by those living in the community will be influenced by the views of others in that locality. The individual will be part of many networks of relationships whose focus is on the local area. It is these local networks of formal and informal relationships together with their capacity to mobilise individual and collective responses that constitute a sense of community.

Community of interest: functional communities exist because individuals will also have a number of relationships with people and institutions outside a circumscribed geographical area. They might share a common interest based on leisure or work, and these networks of relationships might extend even beyond national boundaries. For example, international associations of social workers constitute a community with a shared interest in the profession of social work. Shared interests might also arise out of a particular social disadvantage, hence the Disability Rights Movement constitutes a community of interest which has a national context but also has links with groups experiencing similar disadvantage in other countries.

Over time, these distinctions have been challenged. The mobility of individuals and families due to economic changes has meant that networks are maintained in a variety of ways. Clubs and activities for people based on their place of origin, for example Ireland, Scotland or the West Indies, allowed for a celebration of character-istics related to place in a quite different geographic location. Advances in communication using different technologies have led to enormous increases in communities of interest. This might suggest that we either abandon the notion of community, or widen the definition.

For the purposes of working with communities, a useful defini-tion focuses on the conditions necessary for effective interventions for, and by, communities in order to bring about change or 'realise' the community. In this approach a community is:

● a unit large enough to be a political force and small enough to account for, and relate to, the individual person
● an optimal location to develop alternative models of social (and economic) organisation
● a point of mobilisation of people to effect social change that can be self-organised
● a unit of people that can command sufficient resources to establish alternative institutional arrangements
● a unit for analysis that will identify the forces and material conditions determining social relations.
(Provided by the Non-Violence Study Group and quoted in Thomas, 1983)

From this definition it is understandable that Thomas argues that it is the concept of 'neighbourhood' that has most influenced community work. He argues that, based on geographical areas, neighbourhoods may contain 'different intensities of networks that express people's support, care, trust, and responsibilities and obligations to one another. Neighbourhoods will vary in the presence or absence of these networks, and their function will vary in this respect over time and place' (Thomas, 1983, p. 173). While even this tentative notion of neighbourhood has been questioned, uses and understandings of 'networks' have become significant in the development of social work with communities. But this claim highlights another definitional conundrum, and that is the different approaches to work with communities within social work.

Community care

With the introduction of community care policies it might appear that emphasis on the working with communities has re-emerged in social work, but this is debatable. Separating discussion of community care from community work highlights that the policies of community care do not necessarily depend upon understandings of community work.

The philosophy of community care, focusing on individuals with need and meeting these needs with individualised packages of care, pays little heed to any of the various definitions that recognise the radical potential of communities. Also discussions about whether 'community care' is care *in* the community, or care *by* the community (Orme, 2001a) reflect a limited, liberal, top-down approach to communities. Community care policies require activities that ensure, not only that needs of people in the community are understood, but also that individuals, groups and organisations within communities are prepared, and able, to provide caring services and facilities (Orme and Glastonbury, 1993). Just as importantly, as was discussed in Chapter 3, those who require community care services have to be treated as full and active members of communities capable of both providing and receiving services.

Community work and social work

In a review of the role and tasks of social work, the Barclay Committee made a distinction between community work and social work. The committee claimed that community work embraced both direct work with community groups and work at the interorganisational and planning level, and was concerned to:

enable members collectively to overcome problems and enhance the common feeling, solidarity and competence in the community by direct working with groups and organisations within the community, or encouraging their formation. But community work also takes the form of involvement in planning and influencing policies. This work can be an element of social work, but it does not include the whole of social work, nor does social work embrace the whole of community work.

(Barclay, 1982, p. xiii)

This very positive statement counteracts perceptions of community work merely as activities that take place off the premises of statutory social work agencies; or as provided by voluntary agencies or volunteers – as opposed to professional workers (Jones, 1983). Such distinctions merely describe characteristics associated with community work, rather than analyse its purpose. All sorts of organisations and people undertake forms of community work, run clubs or organise community-based movements, such as residents associations, but this does not necessarily have to happen in a social work context.

Critiques of community work as a separate activity led, not to changes of attitudes within social work towards community workers, but to moves to embrace some of the principles and practices of community work. Policy developments that incorporated the language of community, if not a full appreciation of the work, began to inform activities of statutory social workers in the late 1970s and 1980s. These continued in initiatives for community care, albeit not in a way that many in social work would have hoped for. The focus was on service delivery and not communities. For example, the Barclay Committee defined community social work (as opposed to community work) as:

formal social work which, starting from the problems affecting an individual or group and the responsibilities and resources of social services departments and voluntary organisations, seeks to tap into, support, enable and underpin the local networks of formal and informal relationships which constitute our basic definition of community, and also the strengths of a client's communities of interest.

(Barclay, 1982, p. xvii)

An appendix to the main report (Appendix A) described a 'patch' approach that would enable workers to work with local resources to provide 'neighbourhood clusters' of formal and informal care. This would involve personal social services in:

● working in close collaboration with informal caring networks
● finding ways of developing partnerships between informal carers (including self-help groups), statutory services and voluntary agencies
● ensuring ready access of caring networks to statutory and voluntary services
● offering those who give and receive services opportunities to share decisions which affect their lives.
(Barclay, 1982, para. 13.13)

Here was a very instrumental approach to communities, with the emphasis not on community but on sources of care provision. Allan (1983) expressed doubts that informal networks existed, and argues that Barclay's recommendations seemed to be based on a particular, rather romantic, reading of the traditional urban community studies of the 1950s and early 1960s. He points out that those who brought problems to social services are either not connected to their communities, or the nature of their problems might actually lead to exclusion from communities.

Despite these, and other criticisms, the principles of Barclay, that there was an infrastructure for informal care in the community, formed the basis of policy initiatives which culminated in the National Health Service and Community Care Act 1990. However the move towards a mixed economy of welfare meant that communities were seen as replacements for state providers, not sources of innovation and challenge.

Community social work

Smale *et al.* (1988) offer a different critique. They see the approach represented by Barclay and Appendix A as reflecting the development of community social work as localisation. Other models, they argue, emphasise indirect service and local participation (Beresford and Croft, 1986). Smale *et al.* suggest that a shift in thinking is required, away from identified clients to a focus on the relationships between people, and the patterns of these relationships. They take the notion of partnership and involvement outlined in Barclay, and argue that through managing change and innovation in the practice of social workers, community social work involves a process of working out aims and objectives through a review of needs and resources with a wide range of people. This is dependent upon the *processes* the workers engage in and the *relationships* they make and how these are maintained and changed (Smale *et al.*, 1988, p. 23).

In focusing on processes and relationships Smale *et al.* do not prescribe specific sets of skills, or methods that could or should be utilised in 'doing' community social work. The whole emphasis of the 'approach' is that methods, skills and actions will evolve from the focus of the team of social workers identifying both what resources they have available within themselves and the 'community' and what is required. However they do list areas where more emphasis might be required in training social workers and other social work staff, either at basic level or as part of staff development activities. These include:

- Working across agency boundaries.
- Working on the margins of complex systems.
- Working in teams of peers and others.
- Working in ways open to public accountability.
- Working with devolved responsibilities and budgets.
- Working in networks of partnership.
- Working to understand sequences of behaviour that perpetuate problems and intervening to change these patterns.
  (Smale *et al.*, 1988)

It is apparent that there are some recurring themes in this chapter that relate to both community work and community social work. We have already said that many of the skills identified are those that social workers might use in work with individuals and groups. However another recurring theme is that social workers will need to work with networks: they will have to identify them, consult with them and, cynics might say, they will have to create them. It is therefore important that we give some attention to the skills involved in working with networks.

Networking

All of the literature on community work assumes that communities are based on 'a network, or networks of informal relationships between people connected with each other by kinship, common interests, geographical proximity, friendship, occupation, or the giving and receiving of services – or various combinations of these' (Barclay, 1982, p. 199). Work within the community is necessary to stimulate networks either to be part of collective action or to provide informal care services for community care. Three separate networking strategies from the literature include:

1. *Network therapy*: A therapeutic approach where network assemblies, using techniques drawn from large groupwork, help families in crisis by bringing together their network to act as the change agents; the case example is of a network assembly (see Rueveni, 1979).
2. *Problem-solving network meetings*. These bring together formal and informal carers; they are useful when unravelling non-complementary professional networks in order to sort out who is doing what (see Dimmock and Dungworth, 1985).
3. *Network construction*. This method aims to sustain, change and build new networks. Used originally to help those with chronic schizophrenia whose institutionalisation had led to the loss of their networks, network building can be used, for example, to provide community care services for older people (Challis *et al.*, 1990) and to engage supporters for those with learning disabilities (Atkinson, 1986).

A network construction

In Chapter 9 we saw how Hill (2002) developed the use of networks to help understand the dynamics of families. In community work the principles are similar but the scope and the focus is slightly different. This involves the social worker coaching someone in how to sustain, build or change her/his network. First, the person is helped to draw a network or ecomap (see Figure 12.1); a sheet with many circles is used to represent the household itself, neighbours, general practitioner, school, clubs, shop, work and so on. The network map is filled in using the same colour to connect who knows whom: relationships between the client and others that are strong, weak or stressful are depicted by different symbols.

Second, the person is helped to assess from this the sources of interference and intimacy and, if appropriate, asked if he or she wishes to lessen or strengthen these bonds.

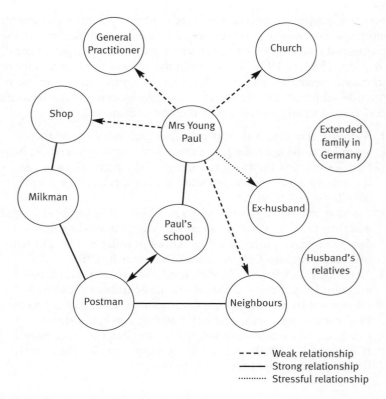

Figure 12.1 Network map

Third, overlooked sources of help are examined, with the client and worker planning how these could be developed.

Network strategies can provide exciting solutions in community care schemes to sustain and nurture helpers. On the other hand, undoing the original support network, encouraging friends and relatives to withdraw when they are under severe stress, has been important too (Challis *et al.*, 1990). So-called 'toxic' networks, for example those of people involved in criminal activities, similarly may need to be loosened. These practices provide 'people muscle', unite and reunite networks, and give back the chance to show concern for others in a non-bureaucratic way.

Case example

Mrs Young was a 35-year-old woman with one son, Paul, aged 12. She had recently divorced her husband, who had access to his son at weekends. Mrs Young had come to the UK from Germany 15 years previously, and although living on a busy council estate knew very few people. She applied to a large voluntary society to become a foster parent to an older child.

The worker from the placement team helped Mrs Young to map her network; as you can see from Figure 12.1 (and comparing it possibly with your own), the client had a small and not very active network to which she could turn for support. Some members had strong ties, but the client agreed that she was isolated and had wanted a companion for Paul.

Mrs Young had stopped writing to her own family in Germany: the worker encouraged her to rebuild these links, which she did, eventually being visited by them. Paul's school taught evening classes in German where, in time, Mrs Young began to help students. She withdrew her application to foster.

However all of these approaches could be seen to be within Mayo's (2002) description of liberal approaches to community. This is not surprising when the focus is on the provision of services to those in communities who were identified as having problems. Radical approaches to working with communities have been associated with community *development*, but that is not to say that these do not have a role in community care.

Community development

Although the funded Community Development Projects (CDP) were abandoned in 1970s the principles have continued, supported mainly by the left-wing Fabian tradition of trying to achieve change through rational discourse, fostering collective values and moral persuasion (Popple, 1995, p. 41). These principles have been translated into radical approaches to community work, where the aim is to change the balance and structure of social relations, informed by the causes of oppression, rather than merely change the mode of service delivery. Importantly community development is not exclusive to social work, but nor is social work excluded from it:

Community development is an approach that strengthens local democracy and the capacity and voice of communities to participate actively in determining the processes and outcomes of social and economic change. A range of professionals and agencies can adopt this approach.

(Scottish Community Education Council quoted in Barr, Drysdale *et al.*, 1998)

Significantly, Popple (1995) highlighted that the original CDP suffered from short-term funding and tokenism. The projects were set up to work in 12 'deprived areas' identified by policy-makers from a number of social and economic indicators. The resurgence of community development, linked as it is to plans for urban regeneration and measures to counteract social exclusion, could be seen to be equally short-term, tokenistic and palliative – designed to quell civil unrest and dissatisfaction with services. However there exist strong traditions in certain parts of the UK that are working to ensure that community development is more effective than this, and will harness social movements and other empowering initiatives to bring about changes in social structures.

Community development and social work

Community development is the process of establishing or re-establishing structures of human community within which new ways of relating, organising social life and meeting human needs become possible (Ife, 2002). That might suggest the end of social work as we know it, but more positively it has stimulated changes related to user participation and empowerment that emphasise a different relationship between those in need of services, and agencies that exist to meet those needs. As Ife (2002) emphasises, the principles of community development are that change comes from below, and the processes are just as important as the outcomes. It is not enough to secure user participation in service delivery – that participation has to come about because members of the particular community or group desire it, and in ways that they have identified. Clarke (2000, p. 12) argues that the principles of community development are uncompromising: the community identifies the need to change and organisation is through full, voluntary and cooperative efforts of the 'client' population. Hence Ife argues that the outcomes should not be driven or imposed by policy-makers or elected members (politicians) but should reflect what the community wants and needs. To achieve this there has to be attention to:

- process and outcomes
- integrity of the process
- participatory democracy
- decentralisation
- accountability
- education
- obligation.
  (Ife, 2002, p. 119)

This is to be achieved by dialogue with and within communities (Popple, 1995). But the challenge comes from those individuals and groups who are not necessarily part of, or welcome in, wider communities. Social justice, inclusiveness, anti-discrimination and equal opportunities are said to be core to community development (Barr *et al.*, 1998). But certain groups with community care needs might challenge communities, either because of how they are perceived, stereotyped and stigmatised, or because the community does not perceive itself as having the capacity to provide the neces- sary care for individuals and groups. Barr *et al.* (1998) argue that the capacity of service users to define their own needs and seek solutions to their problems is no different from other communities (or others in communities). What is required is for myths to be exploded, individuals and communities to be educated and for community capacity to be harnessed. The outcome might be, not that the community has to provide resources, but that service users organise themselves to demand different services or different allocation of resources to ensure that needs are met.

Case example

The Positive Mental Attitudes Project at Greater Easterhouse, Glasgow seeks to address the stigma experienced by people with mental ill health and promote positive attitudes in Greater Easterhouse. It developed from a meeting of Greater Easterhouse Mental Health Forum. The Forum itself came about as a result of threatened closure of services for people with mental health problems. It is a properly constituted organisation led by represen- tatives of mental health users. Local organisations, voluntary and statutory, can be members of the forum, and staff from Health and Social Services are invited to be advisers to the Forum. At a meeting in 2001, attended by 80 people, many of whom had mental health problems, stigma was identified as the main problem that needed to be addressed.

In response to the meeting a study was set up to assess knowledge and awareness towards mental health attitudes, and identify what training was available. It surveyed employers, service providers, pupils and students at schools and colleges. The study identified, among other things, lack of awareness of mental health issues, little effort to promote mental health in the work place and lack of training/guidelines on mental health issues.

The Project was launched in March 2002, funded by Greater Glasgow Health Board and Greater Easterhouse Pathfinder, which aims to encourage and innovate projects in partnership with the local community. Its activities are user-led and have included:

- the provision of information, training and stress management resources to local employers
- activities to raise awareness of mental health issues in local schools
- training for public sector workers (including social work students)
- a visual arts project developed by a group of mental health service users
- a video project (STIGMA) developed by a local mental health project has been completed and is available to buy
- a marketing campaign
- the development of an Internet site: http://www.positivemental attitudes.org.uk/
- a creative writing group.

The Project is user led and user controlled (see Chapter 3), and utilises a community development approach to ascertain the experiences of those who might otherwise be deemed to be service recipients. A centralised top-down approach might have identified the need for day centres or domiciliary care. The identification of stigma as the greatest barrier to those with mental health problems was significant in a number of ways. It meant activities and resources could be targeted to make a difference and, just as importantly, those resources could draw on the capacities of those who were experiencing the problems.

The Project also illustrates that a community development approach facilitates different ways of organising to involve all citizens in community profiling and community care planning (Barr et al., 1998).

Conclusion

This chapter has attempted to give an overview of different approaches to working with communities, and the relationship of this to social work practice. By acknowledging different definitions it has highlighted that policies for working with communities can involve top-down approaches that seek to placate and pacify individuals and groups. Alternative, radical approaches seek to mobilise and motivate. There is a danger that community care policies merely require communities to replace other statutory resources for meeting need. However a community development approach seeks to engage with communities to ensure that needs are identified and that resources are demanded. Also communities can operate creatively to advocate for resources, or to meet needs in ways that are meaningful to those in the community. Such approaches complement the social work processes associated with advocacy and user empowerment identified in the first section of this book. As such they represent an important context for social work practice.

---

putting it into practice

A useful way of trying to understand meanings of community is to try to develop a profile of one.

1. Identify what you think of as a community. It might be the neighbourhood in which you live, or one in which you work, or it might be the university where you are studying.
2. Develop a profile of this community. That is, try to describe it and get information about the community. Do this by:
   - walking round the area and observing (for example, age of buildings, characteristics of residents)
   - gathering data (for example, statistics on population) from websites and official documents
   - talking to people in the community
   - logging what resources there are (shops, meeting facilities, social services offices)
   - noting such things as how accessible the area is for those with limited mobility
   - reading local literature to find out what the issues are.

3. On the basis of what you observe/identify/collect/learn, identify what you think are the needs of this community. What do you think the strengths are that would enable the community to meet those needs?
4. If you do not think you can do this last task, how might you find out these things about the community?

Further reading

Popple, K. (1995) *Analysing Community Work: its theory and practice*. Buckingham: Open University Press. A useful text that gives a history of community work and an analysis of the political and practice dimensions.

Stepney, P. and Evans, D. (2000) 'Community social work: towards an integrative model of practice,'. In P. Stepney and D. Ford (eds) *Social Work Models, Methods and Theories*. Lyme Regis: Russell House. This chapter explores the links between community work and social work, using case examples and useful diagrams.

13 | Endings

All social work efforts have to come to an end some time. In fact as we noted in the introduction there are many endings in social work. Each time we end our contact with users, be it at the end of an interview, home visit or group or community session, important principles of preparing ourselves and the other person for the parting or ending have to be kept in mind. Also social work can be episodic. We can undertake an assessment as social worker, care manager or court officer, and then another worker may be involved. Although the contact with the agency might not end, the particular relationship between the worker and the user does. Final termination or transfers of work may be planned or unplanned, initiated by service user or worker, mutually agreed or unilaterally decided.

Increased managerialism, with its focus on targets, response times and throughput, means that there is a greater expectation that cases will be closed or passed on to other agencies. Care management and other changes in service delivery mean that more workers will be involved in cases and that contact might be transitory. Despite this there is little in the literature on the process of closing cases and ending relationships.

Ending social work intervention

Reasons for closure or transfer to another worker or agency are diverse. They include:

- agreed goals being achieved within a pre-set time
- clients deciding they have been helped enough
- workers leaving or clients moving from the district
- the end of statutory requirements
- agency policy on time limits

- workload management and priority systems
- resource limitations
- lack of time and pressure of work
- advice from supervisor
- influence of other agencies
- death of the client.

We saw in the chapters on crisis intervention, task-centred practice and behavioural approaches how these models were developed to allow for built-in termination. It was viewed as a positive step, a way of motivating people by focusing efforts at specified goals. Equally, family and marital therapists tell us that we should recognise when enough is enough (Carpenter and Treacher, 1989), letting families and couples get on with their lives without us. In groupwork it is recommended that workers take the process of termination seriously, learning to anticipate possible reactions of denial, backsliding into earlier difficulties, reminiscing and reviewing the worth of the experience. Although not all methods of helping or settings for practice lend themselves to a rational model that sets goals, assesses progress and then smoothly starts the process of withdrawing, there are models of good practice.

Increasingly in arrangements for community care, decisions about closure of establishments or rationalising provision can lead to service users being relocated geographically. This often has implications for relationships with a number of people involved in providing care and support. In the case of one establishment for people with mental health problems, workers were able to anticipate the closure and relocation of residents by setting up regular meetings to discuss both their fears and their hopes. While this did not totally alleviate the concerns and the disappointments, it did give people, both workers and service users, permission to express their feelings.

Though written some time ago, a couple of articles by Bywaters (1975) help us to understand why so many of our contacts end, not with a sense of achievement and neatness, but with feelings of loss, work not completed or not even begun. His research into social services revealed bureaucratic, theoretical and psychological drawbacks for clients and workers which affected both the decision to close or transfer and the process of achieving this. Coupled with the organisational reasons for closing cases, he found that workers often felt they could not control endings and neither were clients consulted about the decision. Social workers tended not to use the time-limited approaches; many were aiming for more extensive goals than clients were aware of, using open-ended casework methods. Practitioners often felt that they could do more, or that cases should be left open until a resource such as housing became available. Moreover, feelings of guilt, uncertainty and loss affected the process of handling endings. Thus, staff felt guilty knowing that time spent with one person was time not spent with another. They felt uncertainty about their effectiveness, and in addition the client's ability to cope in the future impeded a positive approach to endings. Feeling lost and resentful after putting in a lot of work were other reactions. More recently these feelings were identified by respondents to Postle's research (2001), and made clearer the claim that the 'social work side is disappearing'.

Clients and workers may experience transfer or termination of work as a type of crisis (even if the attachment has been short-term) if both have invested a part of themselves. Students on placement report feelings of sadness and anxiety at 'abandoning' clients; the death of a client is especially distressing, and might call for reassurance that shedding tears is not unprofessional. Clients and workers may be reminded of earlier losses by the experience of closure. And yet, much in the same way that crisis prevention is possible with 'worry work' and preparation, clients and workers can anticipate endings in advance, enhancing their growth-promoting opportunities.

A good model of ending could incorporate the following:

1. A discussion in the first meeting that help will not go on forever. Feelings and perceptions of this are important and need to be handled sensitively. For instance, those in crisis might ask, 'How long will this take?' and, for some, it might be reassuring to know that help will not suddenly be withdrawn. For others, it may be a relief to know that a social worker will not always need to visit.
2. Using the experience of termination or transfer as an opportunity for learning rather than a painful, separating experience. In groupwork it was noted that transitions are eased when people are helped to be weaned from the experience – outside relationships and activities are rewarded. Confirming the

individual's self-confidence and self-reliance underlines what he/she has gained and how he/she has dealt with the experience of help coming to an end.

3. Where possible employing a fixed time limit purposefully, using time itself as a therapeutic agent.
4. Deciding on certain objectives to achieve in the ending phase.
5. Beforehand, exploring a person's feelings about the end of the relationship. (Anticipate possible setbacks, which provide opportunity for worry work.) Gradual withdrawal helps, such as reducing the frequency of meetings, arranging for semi-independent living accommodation, progressively leaving longer time with future carers and so on.
6. Introduce the new worker if there is to be one, and talk in the meeting about feelings about the changes. After one social worker did this, the client vented much resentment but then was free to build a fresh relationship with the incoming practitioner.
7. Help the person construct a helping network in the community, mobilising practical resources if need be. Then do a follow-up visit.
8. Explore your own feelings; demonstrate that you will remember the person; have confidence in his or her ability to manage without you but express the goodwill of the agency, whose door is left open should he or she need to return for further help.
9. In some contexts a ritual or ceremonial ending with photographs, a party and a small farewell gift could mark the occasion.
10. Write a closing record, together, if appropriate.

Finally, it is important to remind ourselves that developments are not always linear. As has been discussed throughout the book, social workers need to reflect on, and to return to, situations that have gone before in order to make sense of them with new information and new insights. Only by reflecting on how we have applied our learning can we ever be sure that we have understood. To this end this book marks merely a beginning to learning, which can be enhanced by further reading and exploration. More particularly, reflecting on every situation and every social work interaction teaches us that in social work learning never ends.

References

Abrams, P. (1980) 'Social change, social networks and neighbourhood care', *Social Work Service*, February, **22**, pp. 12–23.

Adams, R. (1996) *Social Work and Empowerment*. Basingstoke: BASW/Macmillan.

Adams, R., Dominelli, L. and Payne, M. (2002) *Social Work: themes, issues and critical debates*. Basingstoke: Palgrave.

Ahmad, A. (1990) *Practice with Care*. London: Race Equality Unit/ National Institute for Social Work.

Ahmad, B. (1990) *Black Perspectives in Social Work*. Birmingham: Venture Press.

Ahmad, W. I. and Atkins, K. (eds) (1996) *'Race' and Community Care*. Buckingham: Open University Press.

Allan, G. (1983) 'Informal networks of care: issues raised by Barclay', *British Journal of Social Work*, **13**, pp. 417–33.

Allan, G. (1991) 'Social work, community care, and informal networks'. In M. Davies (ed.) *Sociological Perspectives on Social Work*. London: Routledge.

Allan, G. (2002) 'The family'. In M. Davies (ed.) *The Blackwell Companion to Social Work*. Oxford: Blackwell.

Allan, G. and Crow, G. (2001) *Families, Households and Society*. Basingstoke: Palgrave.

Aros-Atolagbe, J. (1990) 'Soapbox', *Social Work Today*, 21(35), p.36.

Atkinson, D. (1986) 'Engaging competent others: a study of the support networks of people with mental handicap', *British Journal of Social Work*, **16**, supplement, pp. 83–101.

Audit Report Commission (1994) *Seen But Not Heard*. London: HMSO.

Avison, D., Forbes, I., Glastonbury, B., Orme, J. and Waldman, J. (1995) *Havant and Petersfield Information System: a model for consulting pre-users of community care services for older people*. Research report. Southampton University (unpublished).

Bacon, R. (1988) 'Counter-transference in a case conference:

resistance and rejection in work with abusing families and their children'. In G. Pearson, J. Treseder and M. Yelloly (eds) *Social Work and the Legacy of Freud: psychoanalysis and its uses*. Basingstoke: Macmillan.

Bailey, R. and Brake, M. (eds) (1975) *Radical Social Work*. London: Edward Arnold.

Baker, P., Hussain, Z. and Saunders, J. (1991) *Interpreters in Public Services*. Birmingham: Venture Press.

Baldock, J. and Ungerson, C. (1994) *Becoming Consumers of Community Care: households within the mixed economy of welfare*. York: Joseph Rowntree Foundation.

Baldock, P. (1974) *Community Work and Social Work*. London: Routledge & Kegan Paul.

Ballard, R. and Rosser, P. (1979) 'Social network assembly'. In D. Brandon and B. Jordan (eds) *Creative Social Work*. Oxford: Blackwell.

Bandura, A. (1977) *Social Learning Theory*. Englewood Cliffs, NJ: Prentice-Hall.

Bar-On, A. A. (1990) 'Organisational resource mobilisation: a hidden face of social work practice', *British Journal of Social Work*, 20(2), pp. 133–49.

Barclay, P. (1982) *Social Workers: their role and tasks*. London: Bedford Square Press.

Barr, A., Drysdale, J. *et al.* (1998) 'Raising the potential of community care – the role of community development', *Issues in Social Work Education*, 18(1), pp. 26–46.

Barton, R. (2002) 'The carer's perspective'. In M. Davies (ed.) *The Blackwell Companion to Social Work*. Oxford: Blackwell.

Batten, T. R. (1967) *The Non-Directive Approach in Group and Community Work*. London: Oxford University Press.

Bayley, M, Parker, P., Seyd, R. and Tennant, A. (1987) *Practising Community Care: developing locally-based practice*. University of Sheffield: Joint Unit for Social Services Research.

Beck, A. T. (1989) *Cognitive Therapy and the Emotional Disorders*. Harmondsworth: Penguin.

Beecher, S. (1986) 'A gender critique of family therapy'. In H. Marchant and B. Wearing, *Gender Reclaimed: women and social work*. Sydney: Hale and Iremonger.

Bell, M. and Wilson, K. (2002) *Practitioner's Guide to Working with Families*. Basingstoke: Palgrave.

Benn, C. (1981) *Attacking Poverty through Participation: a community approach.* Sydney: Pit Publishing.

Beresford, P. (2000) 'Users' knowledges and social work theory: conflict or collaboration?' *British Journal of Social Work*, 30(4), pp. 489–504.

Beresford, P. and Croft, S. (1986) *Whose Welfare? – Private Care or Public Services.* Brighton: Lewis Cohen Centre for Urban Studies at Brighton Polytechnic.

Berger, P. and Luckman, T. (1967) *The Social Construction of Reality: a treatise in the sociology of knowledge.* New York: Doubleday.

Berne, E. (1961) *Transactional Analysis in Psychotherapy.* New York: Grove.

Berne, E. (1968) *Games People Play.* Harmondsworth: Penguin.

Bettelheim, B. (1988) *The Uses of Enchantment: the meaning and importance of fairy tales.* Harmondsworth: Penguin.

Bhaduri, R. (1990) 'Counselling with karma', *Social Work Today*, 21(33), p. 16.

Biehal, N. (1993) 'Changing practice: participation, rights and community care', *British Journal of Social Work*, 23, pp. 443–58.

Black, D. (1979) 'Early help for the bereaved child avoids later problems', *Modern Medicine*, 17 May, pp. 49–52.

Bornat, J., Pereira, C., Pilgrim, D. and Williams, F. (eds) (1993) *Community Care: a reader.* Buckingham: Open University Press.

Bottoms, A. and Stelman, A. (1988) *Social Inquiry Reports.* Aldershot: Wildwood House.

Bowen, M. (1978) *Family Therapy in Clinical Practice.* New York: Jason Aronson.

Box, S., Copley, B., Magagna, J. and Moustaki, E. (eds) (1981) *Psychotherapy with Families: analytical approach.* London: Routledge & Kegan Paul.

Boyce, L. and Anderson, S. (1990) 'A common bond', *Social Work Today*, 21(34), p.38.

Brady, J. and Johnston, V. (1995) 'Consultation – talk about meeting needs', *Research, Policy and Planning*, 13(1 and 2), pp. 19–24.

Brandon, M., Schofield, G. and Trinder, L. (1998) *Social Work with Children.* Basingstoke: Palgrave.

Braye, S. and Preston-Shoot, M. (1995) *Empowering Practice in Social Care.* Buckingham: Open University Press.

Brewster, B. (1988) *Supervision and Management in Social Work.*

London: Central Council for Education and Training in Social Work (CCETSW).

British Association of Counselling (BACP) (1990) *Membership Notes*. Rugby: BACP.

Brook, E. and Davis, A. (eds) (1985) *Women, The Family and Social Work*. London: Tavistock.

Brown, A. (1992) *Groupwork*. London: Heinemann Educational.

Brown, A. (2002) 'Groupwork'. In M. Davies (ed.) *Blackwell Companion to Social Work*. Oxford: Blackwell.

Brown, R., Bute, S. and Ford, P. (1986) *Social Workers at Risk: the prevention and management of violence*. Basingstoke: BASW/Macmillan.

Browne, K. and Saqi, S. (1988) 'Approaches to screening for child abuse and neglect'. In K. Browne, C. Davies and P. Stratton (eds) *Early Prediction and Prevention of Child Abuse*. Chichester: Wiley.

Bryer, M. (1989) *Planning in Child Care: a guide for team leaders and their teams*. London: British Agencies for Adoption and Fostering.

Buchanan, A. (ed.) (1994) *Partnership in Practice: The Children Act 1989*. Aldershot: Avebury (in association with CEDR).

Buckle, J. (1981) *Intake Teams*. London: Tavistock.

Burnham, J. B. (1986) *Family Therapy: first steps towards a systematic approach*. London: Tavistock.

Butler, I. and Roberts, G. (2004) *Social Work with Children and Families*. London: Jessica Kingsley.

Butler, J., Bow, I. and Gibbons, J. (1978) 'Task-centred casework with marital problems', *British Journal of Social Work*, 8(4), pp. 393–409.

Butler, K. and Forrest, M. (1990) 'Citizen advocacy for people with learning disabilities'. In L. Winn (ed.) *Power to the People: the key to responsive services in health and social care*. London: King's Fund.

Byng-Hall, J. and Campbell, D. (1981) 'Resolving conflicts in family distance regulation: an integrative approach', *Journal of Marital and Family Therapy*, 7(3), pp. 321–30.

Bywaters, P. (1975) 'Ending casework relationships', *Social Work Today*, 6(10), pp. 301–4 and 6(11), pp. 336–8.

Calouste Gulbenkian Foundation (1968) *Community Work and Social Change: a report on training*. London: Longman.

Caplan, G. (1964) *Principles of Preventive Psychiatry*. London: Tavistock.

Carpenter, J. and Schneider, J. (2004) 'Integration and targeting of community care for people with severe and enduring mental health problems: users' experiences of the care programme approach and care management,' *British Journal of Social Work*, 34(3), pp. 313–14.

Carpenter, J. and Treacher, A. (1989) *Problems and Solutions in Marital and Family Therapy*. Oxford: Blackwell.

Cavanagh, K. and Cree, V. E. (eds) (1996) *Working With Men: feminism and social work*. London: Routledge.

CCETSW (1989a) *Rules and Requirements for the Diploma in Social Work*. London: Central Council for Education and Training in Social Work.

CCETSW/IAMHW (1989b) *Multidisciplinary Teamwork: models of good practice*. London: Central Council for Education and Training in Social Work.

Challis, D. and Chesterman, J. (1985) 'A system of monitoring social work activity with the frail elderly', *British Journal of Social Work*, 15(2), pp. 115–32.

Challis, D., Chessum, R., Chesterman, J., Luckett, R. and Traske, K. (1990) *Case Management in Social and Health Care*. Canterbury: Personal Social Services Research Unit.

Challis, D. and Davies, B. (1989) *Case Management in Community Care*. Aldershot: Gower.

Chamberlin, J. (1988) *On Our Own*. London: MIND.

Chaplin, J. (1988) *Feminist Counselling in Action*. London: Sage.

Chapman, T. and Hough, M. (1998) *Evidence Based Practice: a guide to effective practice*. London: Home Office.

Christie, A. (2001) *Men and Social Work: theories and practices*. Basingstoke: Palgrave.

Clark, H. and Spafford, J. (2002) 'Adapting to a culture of user control', *Social Work Education*, 21(2), pp. 247–57.

Clarke, S. (2000) *Social Work as Community Development*. Aldershot: Ashgate.

Clulow, C. and Mattinson, J. (1989) *Marriage Inside Out*. Harmondsworth: Penguin.

Cohen, M. and Mullender, A. (eds) (2003) *Gender and Group-work*. London: Routledge.

Colton, M., Sanders, B. and Williams, C. (2001) *An Introduction to Working with Children*. Basingstoke: Palgrave.

Commission for Racial Equality (CRE) (1989) *Racial Equality in*

Social Services Departments: a survey of equal opportunities policies. London: CRE.

Cooper, J. (1989) 'From casework to community care: "The end is where we start from"', *British Journal of Social Work*, **19**, pp. 177–201.

Coote, A. (ed.) (1992) *The Welfare of Citizens*. London: Institute for Public Policy Research/Rivers Oram Press.

Corby, B. (1982) 'Theory and practice in long-term social work: a case study of practice with social service department clients', *British Journal of Social Work*, **12**(6), pp. 619–38.

Corby, B. (1996) 'Risk assessment in child protection work'. In H. Kemshall and J. Pritchard (eds) *Good Practice in Risk Assessment and Risk Management*. London: Jessica Kingsley.

Corey, G. (1986) *Manual for Theory and Practice of Counselling and Psychotherapy* (3rd edn). Monterey: Brooks/Cole.

Corey, G., Corey, M. S., Callanan, P. J. and Russell, J. M. (1982) *Group Techniques*. California: Brooks/Cole.

Cornish, P. M. (1983) *Activities for the Frail-Aged*. Bicester: Winslow Press.

Corrigan, P. and Leonard, P. (1978) *Social Work Practice Under Capitalism: a Marxist approach*, Basingstoke: Macmillan.

Coulshed, V. (1991) *Social Work Practice: an introduction*. Basingstoke: BASW/Macmillan.

Coulshed, V. and Abdullah-Zadeh, J. (1985) 'The side effects of intervention', *British Journal of Social Work*, **15**(5), pp. 479–86.

Coulshed, V. and Mullender, A. (1999) *Management in Social Work*. Basingstoke: Macmillan (now Palgrave).

Cox, A. and Bentovim, A. (2000) *The Family Pack of Questionnaires and Scales*. London: Department of Health.

Crisp, B., Anderson, M., Orme, J. and Green, P. (2003) *Knowledge Review 1: Learning and teaching in social work education: assessment*. London: Scie.

Croft, S. and Beresford, P. (1990) *From Paternalism to Participation: involving people in social services*. London: Open Services Project.

Currer, C. (2002) 'Dying and bereavement'. In R. Adams, L. Dominelli and M. Payne (eds) *Critical Practice in Social Work*. Basingstoke: Palgrave.

Dale, P., Davies, M., Morrison, T. and Waters, J. (1986) *Dangerous Families: assessment and treatment of child abuse*. London: Tavistock.

Dalrymple, J. and Burke, B. (1995) *Anti-Oppressive Practice: social care and the law.* Buckingham: Open University Press.

Dana, M. and Lawrence, M. (1988) 'Understanding bulimia: a feminist, psychoanalytic account of women's eating problems'. In G. Pearson, J. Treseder and M. Yelloly (eds) *Social Work and the Legacy of Freud: psychoanalysis and its uses.* Basingstoke: Macmillan.

Dant, T. and Gearing, B. (1993) 'Key workers for elderly people in the community'. In J. Bornat, C. Pereira, D. Pilgrim and F. Williams (eds) *Community Care: a reader.* Basingstoke: Macmillan/Open University.

Davies, B. and Knapp, M. (eds) (1988) 'The production of welfare approach: evidence and argument from the PSSRU', *British Journal of Social Work*, **18**, supplement.

Davies, M. (1985) *The Essential Social Worker: a guide to positive practice.* Aldershot: Wildwood House.

Davis, K. (1961) *Human Society.* New York: Macmillan.

de Shazer, S. (1988) *Clues: investigating solutions in brief therapy.* New York and London: Norton.

Department for Education and Skills (DfES) (2003) *Every Child Matters.* London: HMSO.

Department of Health (1988) *Protecting Children: a guide for social workers undertaking a comprehensive assessment.* London: HMSO.

Department of Health, Cmnd.849 (1989a) *Caring for People: community care in the next decade and beyond.* London: HMSO.

Department of Health/Social Services Inspectorate (SSI) (1989b) *Homes are for Living In.* London: HMSO.

Department of Health/SSI (1990) *Caring for Quality: guidance on standards for residential homes for elderly people.* London: HMSO.

Department of Health Social Services/SSI and Scottish Office Social Work Services Group (1991) *Care Management and Assessment: practitioner's guide.* London: HMSO.

Department of Health (1994) *Implementing Caring for People: care management.* London: HMSO.

Department of Health (1995) *Child Protection: messages from research.* London: HMSO.

Department of Health (1996) *Refocusing Children's Services.* London: HMSO.

Department of Health (2000a) *A Practitioner's Guide to Carers'*

Assessments under the Carers and Disabled Children Act. London: DoH.

Department of Health (2000b) The NHS Plan: a plan for investment, a plan to reform. London: DoH.

Department of Health (2001) The National Service Framework for Older People. London: DoH.

Department of Health (2002) The Single Assessment Process: Guidance for Local Implementation. London: DoH.

Department of Health (2003) Requirements for the Social Work Degree. London: DoH.

Devore, W. and Schlesinger, E. C. (1981) Ethnic-Sensitive Social Work Practice. St Louis: CV Mosby.

Dillon, J. T. (1990) The Practice of Questioning. London: Routledge.

Dimmock, B. and Dungworth, D. (1985) 'Beyond the family: using network meetings with statutory child care cases', Journal of Family Therapy, 7(1), pp. 45–68.

Doel, M. (2002) 'Task centred practice'. In R. Adams, L. Dominelli and M. Payne (eds) Social Work: themes issues and critical debates. Basingstoke: Palgrave.

Doel, M. and Marsh, P. (1992) Task-centred Social Work. Aldershot: Ashgate.

Doel, M. and Sawdon, C. (1999) The Essential Groupwork: teaching and learning creative groupwork. London: Jessica Kingsley.

Doel, M. and Sawdon, C. (2001) 'What makes for successful groupwork? A survey of agencies in the UK', British Journal of Social Work, 31(3), pp. 437–63.

Dominelli, L. (1988) Anti-Racist Social Work. Basingstoke: Macmillan.

Dominelli, L. (2000) 'Empowerment: help or hindrance in professional relationships'. In P. Stepney and D. Ford (eds) Social Work Models Methods and Theories: a framework for practice. Lyme Regis: Russell House Publishing.

Dominelli, L. and McLeod, E. (1989) Feminist Social Work. Basingstoke: Macmillan.

Downes, C. (1988) 'A psychodynamic approach to the work of an area team'. In G. Pearson, J. Treseder and M. Yelloly (eds) Social Work and the Legacy of Freud: psychoanalysis and its uses. Basingstoke: Macmillan.

Doyal, L. (1993) 'Human need and the moral right to optimal community care'. In J. Bornat, J. Johnson, C. Pereira, D. Pilgrim and F. Williams (eds) Community Care: a reader. Buckingham: Open University/Macmillan.

Doyal, L. and Gough, I. (1991) *A Theory of Human Need.* Basingstoke: Macmillan.

Dryden, W. (ed.) (1984) *Individual Therapy in Britain.* London: Harper & Row.

Egan, G. (1981) *The Skilled Helper: a model for systematic helping and interpersonal relating.* California: Brooks/Cole.

Eichenbaum, L. and Orbach, S. (1983) *Understanding Women.* Harmondsworth: Penguin.

Ellis, A. (1962) *Reason and Emotion in Psychotherapy.* New York: Lyle Stuart.

England, H. (1986) *Social Work as Art: making sense for good practice.* London: Allen and Unwin.

Epstein, L. (1980) *Helping People: the task-centred approach.* St Louis: CV Mosby.

Erikson, E. (1965) *Childhood and Society.* Harmondsworth: Penguin.

Evans, R. (1976) 'Some implications of an integrated model for social work theory and practice', *British Journal of Social Work,* 6(2).

Featherstone, B. (1997) '"I wouldn't do your job!" Women, social work and child abuse'. In W. Hollway and B. Featherstone (eds) *Mothering and Ambivalence.* London: Routledge.

Featherstone, B. (2004) *Family Life and Support: a feminist analysis.* Basingstoke: Palgrave.

Fischer, J. (1976) *The Effectiveness of Social Casework.* New York: Charles C. Thomas.

Fisher, M. (1997) 'Older male carers and community care'. In J. Bornat, J. Johnson, C. Pereira, D. Pilgrim and F. Williams (eds) *Community Care: a reader.* Buckingham: Open University/ Macmillan.

Fook, J. (2002) *Social Work Critical Theory and Practice.* London: Routledge.

Ford, D. and Ford, P. (2000) *Theorising Social Work Assessment.* Unpublished paper.

Ford, P. and Hayes, P. (eds) (1996) *Educating for Social Work: arguments for optimism.* Aldershot: Avebury (in association with CEDR).

Ford, P. and Postle, K. (2001) 'Task-centred practice and care management'. In P. Stepney and D. Ford (eds) *Social Work Models, Methods and Theories.* Lyme Regis: Russell House.

Forder, A. (1974) *Concepts in Social Administration: a framework for analysis.* London: Routledge & Kegan Paul.

Foucault, M. (1980) 'Two lectures'. In C. Gordon (ed.) *Michel Foucault – Power/Knowledge: selected interviews and other writings 1972–1977*. Harlow: Prentice Hall.

Freed, A. O. (1988) 'Interviewing through an interpreter', *Social Work*, 33(4), pp. 315–19.

Freire, P. (1972) *Pedagogy of the Oppressed*. Harmondsworth: Penguin.

Frost, N., Jefferys, L. and Lloyd, A. (2003) *The RHP Companion to Family Support*. Lyme Regis: Russell House.

Garrett, A. (1972) *Interviewing: its principles and methods*. New York: Family Service Association of America.

Garrett, P. (2003) 'Swimming with the Dolphins: the new assessment framework, New Labour and new tools for social work with children and families', *British Journal of Social Work*, 33(4), pp. 441–64.

Garrison, J. E. and Howe, J. (1976) 'Community intervention with the elderly: a social network approach', *Journal of the American Geriatric Society*, 24, pp. 329–33.

Gibbons, J. S., Bow, I., Butler, J. and Powell, J. (1979) 'Clients' reaction to task-centred casework: a follow-up study', *British Journal of Social Work*, 9(2), pp. 203–15.

Giddens, A. (1991) *Modernity and Self-Identity: self and society in the late modern age*. Cambridge: Polity.

Golan, N. (1978) *Treatment in Crisis Situations*. New York: Free Press.

Goldberg, E. M., Gibbons, J. and Sinclair, I. (1985) *Problems, Tasks and Outcomes: the evaluation of task-centred casework in three settings*. London: George Allen and Unwin.

Goldberg, E. M., Walker, D. and Robinson, J. (1977) 'Exploring the task-centred casework method', *Social Work Today*, 9(2), pp. 9–14.

Goldstein, H. (1973) *Social Work Practice: a unitary approach*. Columbia, SC: University of South Carolina Press.

Golembiewski, R. T. and Blumberg, A. (eds) (1970) *Sensitivity Training and the Laboratory Approach*. Itasca, Ill.: Peacock.

Gorrell Barnes, G. (1984) *Working with Families*. London: Macmillan.

Gorman, H. and Postle, K. (2003) *Transforming Community Care: a distorted vision?* Birmingham: Venture Press.

Gottman, J., Notarius, C., Gonso, J. and Markman, H. (1977) *A Couple's Guide to Communication: skills teaching for couples*. New York: Research Press.

Hadley, R., Cooper, M., Dale, P. and Stacy, G. (1987) *A Community Social Worker's Handbook*. London: Tavistock.

Hadley, R. and McGrath, M. (1984) *When Services Are Local – the Normanton experience*. London: George Allen and Unwin.

Haley, J. (1976) *Problem-Solving Therapy*. San Francisco: Jossey-Bass.

Hall, E. (1987) 'The gender of the therapist: its relevance to practice and training'. In G. Horobin (ed.) *Sex, Gender and Care Work*. London: Jessica Kingsley.

Hanmer, J. and Statham, D. (1988) *Women and Social Work: towards a woman-centred practice*. Basingstoke: Macmillan.

Hardiker, P. and Barker, F. M. (eds) (1981) *Theories of Practice in Social Work*. London: Academic Press.

Hawkins, P. and Shohet, R. (1989) *Supervision in the Helping Professions*. Milton Keynes: Open University Press.

Heap, K. (1985) *The Practice of Social Work with Groups: a systematic approach*. London: George Allen and Unwin.

Henderson, P. and Thomas, D. N. (1981) *Skills in Neighbourhood Work*. London: George Allen and Unwin.

Hester, M. and Radford, J. (1996) 'Contradictions and compromises: the impact of the Children Act on women and children's safety'. In M. Hester, L. Kelley and J. Radford (eds) *Women, Violence and Male Power*. Buckingham: Open University Press.

Hill, M. (1999) *Effective Ways of Working with Children and their Families*. London: Jessica Kingsley.

Hill, M. (2002) 'Network assessments and diagrams: a flexible friend in social work and education', *Journal of Social Work*, 2(2), pp. 233–54.

Hirayama, H. and Cetingok, M. (1988) 'Empowerment: a social work approach for Asian immigrants', *Social Casework*, 69(1), pp. 41–7.

Hodgkinson, P. and Stewart, M. (1991) *Coping with Catastrophe: a professional handbook for post-disaster aftercare*. London: Routledge.

Hollis, F. (1964) *Casework: a psychosocial therapy*. New York: Random House.

Hollis, F. (1970) 'The psychosocial approach to the practice of casework'. In R. W. Roberts and R. H. Nee (eds) *Theories of Social Casework*. Chicago: University of Chicago Press.

Holman, B. (1998) 'From children's departments to family departments', *Child and Family Social Work*, 3, pp. 205–11.

Home Office (1992) *National Standards for the Supervision of Offenders in the Community*. London: HMSO.

Home Office (1999) 'What works/effective practice initiative: the core curriculum', *Probation Circular 64/1999*. London: Home Office.

Hong Chui, W. and D. Ford (2000) 'Crisis intervention as common practice'. In P. Stepney and D. Ford (eds) *Social Work Models Methods and Theories: a framework for practice*. Lyme Regis: Russell House.

Horder, W. (2002) 'Care management'. In M. Davies (ed.) *The Blackwell Companion to Social Work*. Oxford: Blackwell.

Howe, D. (1987) *An Introduction to Social Work Theory*. Aldershot: Community Care Practice Handbooks.

Howe, D. (1992) *An Introduction to Social Work Theory: making sense in practice* (3rd edn). Aldershot: Wildwood House.

Howe, D. (1994) 'Modernity, postmodernity and social work', *British Journal of Social Work*, 24(5), pp. 513–32.

Howe, D. (1995) *Attachment Theory for Social Work Practice*. London: Macmillan.

Howe, D. (1997) 'Psychosocial relationship-based theories for child and family social work: political philosophy, psychology and welfare practice', *Child and Family Social Work*, 2(3), pp. 161–9.

Howe, D. (2000) 'Relating theory to practice'. In M. Davies (ed.) *Blackwell Companion to Social Work*, Oxford: Blackwell.

Hoyes, L., and Lart, L. (1992) 'Taking care', *Community Care*, 20 August, pp. 14–15.

Hudson, B. L. (1975) 'An inadequate personality', *Social Work Today*, 6(16), pp. 506–8.

Hudson, B. L. and Macdonald, G. M. (1986) *Behavioural Social Work: an introduction*. London: Macmillan.

Hughes, B. (1995) *Older People and Community Care*. Buckingham: Open University Press.

Ife, J. (2002) *Community Development: Community based alternatives in an age of globalisation*. Frenchs Forest NSW: Longmans.

IFSW/IASSW (2000). *Definition of Social Work*. http://www.ifsw.org/Publications/4.6e.pub.html.

Jack, G. and Jack, D. (2000) 'Ecological social work: the application of a systems model of development in context'. In P. Stepney and D. Ford (eds) *Social Work Models, Methods and Theories*. Lyme Regis: Russell House.

Jacobs, M. (1985) *Swift to Hear: facilitating skills in listening and responding*. London: SPCK.

Jacobs, M. (1986) *The Presenting Past: an introduction to Practical Psychodynamic Counselling*. London: Harper & Row.

James, A. L. and Wilson, K. (1986) *Couples, Conflict and Change*. London: Tavistock.

Jehu, F. (1967) *Learning Theory and Social Work*. London: Routledge & Kegan Paul.

Jervis, M. (1990) 'Family Fortunes', *Social Work Today*, 21(47), pp. 16–17.

Jones, C. (1983) *State Social Work and the Working Class*. London: Macmillan.

Jones, C. (1996) 'Anti-intellectualism and the peculiarities of British social work education'. In N. Parton (ed.) *Social Theory, Social Change and Social Work*. London: Routledge.

Jordan, B. (1972) *The Social Worker in Family Situations*. London: Routledge & Kegan Paul.

Jordan, B. (1987) 'Fallen idol', *Community Care*, 12 February, pp. 24–5.

Kadushin, A. (1972) *The Social Work Interview*. New York: Columbia University Press.

Kaufman, P. (1966) 'Helping people who cannot manage their lives', *Children*, 13(3).

Keating, F. (2000) 'Anti-racist perspectives. What are the gains?' *Social Work Education*, 19(1), pp. 76–87.

Kell, B. L. and Mueller, W. J. (1966) *Impact and Change: a study of counselling relationships*. New York: Meredith.

Kelly, G. A. (1955) *The Psychology of Personal Constructs*. New York: Norton.

Kemshall, H. and Littlechild, R. (eds) (2000) *User Involvement and Participation in Social Care: research informing practice*. London: Jessica Kingsley.

Kemshall, H. and Pritchard, J. (eds) (1996) *Good Practice in Risk Assessment and Risk Management*. London: Jessica Kingsley.

Kenny, L. and Kenny, B. (2000) 'Psychodynamic theory in social work: a view from practice'. In P. Stepney and D. Ford (eds) *Social Work Models, Methods and Theories*. Lyme Regis, Russell House.

Laming, Lord (2003) *The Victoria Climbié Inquiry: a report of an inquiry*. London: HMSO.

Langrish, S. V. (1981) 'Assertiveness training'. In C. Cooper (ed.) *Improving Skills in Interpersonal Relations*. Aldershot: Gower.

Lau, A. (1984) 'Transcultural issues in family therapy', *Journal of Family Therapy*, 6(2), pp. 91–112.

Leadbetter, M. (2002) 'Empowerment and advocacy'. In R. Adams, L. Dominelli and M. Payne (eds) *Social Work Themes: issues and critical debates*. Basingstoke: Palgrave.

Lindemann, E. (1965) 'Symptomatology and management of acute grief'. In H. J. Parad (ed.) *Crisis Interventions: selected readings*. New York: Family Service Association of America.

Lindon, V. and Morris, J. (1995) *Service User Involvement: synthesis of findings and experience in the field of community care*. York: Joseph Rowntree Foundation.

Lishman, J. (1995) *Communication in Social Work*. Basingstoke: BASW/Macmillan.

Liverpool, V. (1986) When Backgrounds Clash, *Community Care*, 2 October, pp. 19–21.

Lloyd, M. (2000) 'Where has all the care management gone? The challenge of Parkinson's disease to the health and social care interface', *British Journal of Social Work*, 30(6), pp. 737–54.

Loney, M. (1983) *Community Against Government*. London: Heinemann.

Luft, J. (1963) *Group Processes Palo Alto*. California: National Press.

Lupton, C. (1998) 'User empowerment or family self-reliance? The family group conference model', *British Journal of Social Work*, 28(1), pp. 107–28.

Lupton, C. and Gillespie, T. (eds) (1994) *Working With Violence*. Basingstoke: BASW/Macmillan.

Lyons, J. (1977) *Chomsky*. London: Fontana/Collins.

Macrae, R. and Andrews, M. (2000) 'Work with men who abuse women partners', *Probation Journal*, 47(1), pp. 30–8.

Magee, B. (1982) *Men of Ideas*. Oxford: Oxford University Press.

Mahrer, A. R. (1989) *The Integration of Psychotherapies*. New York: Human Sciences Press.

Mainprice, J. (1974) *Marital Interaction and some Illness in Children*. London: Institute of Marital Studies, Tavistock Institute of Human Relations.

Marris, P. (1986) *Loss and Change*. London: Routledge.

Marsh, P. (2002) 'Task centred work'. In M. Davies (ed.) *Blackwell Companion to Social Work*. Oxford: Blackwell.

Marsh, P. and Fisher, M. (1992) *Good Intentions: partnership in social services*. York: Joseph Rowntree Foundation.

Marsh, P. and Triseliotis, J. (1996) *Ready to Practice? Social Workers and Probation Officers: their training and first year in work*. Aldershot: Avebury.

Marshall, M. (ed.) (1990) *Working with Dementia: guidelines for professionals*. Birmingham: Venture Press.

Marziali, E. (1988) 'The first session: an interpersonal encounter', *Social Casework*, **69**(1), pp. 23–7.

Mattinson, J. (1975) *The Reflection Process in Casework Supervision*. London: Institute of Marital Studies, Tavistock Institute of Human Relations.

Mattinson, J. and Sinclair, I. (1979) *Mate and Stalemate: working with marital problems in a social services department*. Oxford: Blackwell.

Maximé, J. E. (1986) 'Some psychological models of black self-concept'. In S. Ahmed, J. Cheetham and J. Small (eds) *Social Work with Black Children and their Families*. London: BT Batsford/British Agencies for Adoption and Fostering.

Mayer, J. E. and Timms, N. (1970) *The Client Speaks: working class impressions of casework*. London: Routledge & Kegan Paul.

Mayo, M. (2002) 'Community work'. In R. Adams, L. Dominelli and M. Payne (eds) *Social Work: themes, issues and critical debates*. Basingstoke: Palgrave.

McGuire, J. (ed.) (1995) *What Works: reducing re-offending*. Chichester: Wiley.

McNay, M. (1989) 'Social work and power relations'. In M. Langan and L. Day (eds) *Women, Oppression and Social Work*. London: Routledge.

Means, R. and Smith, R. (1994) *Community Care: Policy and Practice*. Basingstoke: Macmillan.

Means, R. and Smith, R. (1998) *Community Care: policy and practice* (2nd edn). Basingstoke: Macmillan.

Meichenbaum, D. (1978) *Cognitive Behaviour Modification: an integrative approach*. New York, Plenum Press.

Merry, T. (1990) 'Client-centred therapy: some trends and some troubles', *Counselling*, **1**(1), pp. 17–18.

Milner, J. (2001) *Women and Social Work: narrative approaches*. Basingstoke: Palgrave.

Milner, J. and O'Byrne, P. (2002) *Assessment in Social Work*. Basingstoke: Palgrave.

Minuchin, S. (1974) *Families and Family Therapy*. London: Tavistock.

Mitchell, J. (1984) *Women: the Longest Revolution: essays in feminism literature and psychoanalysis*. London: Virago.

Monach, J. and Spriggs, L. (1994) 'The consumer role'. In N. Malin (ed.) *Implementing Community Care*. Buckingham: Open University Press.

Morgan, S. (1986) 'Practice in a community nursery for black children'. In S. Ahmed, J. Cheetham and J. Small (eds) *Social Work with Black Children and their Families*. London: BT Batsford/British Agencies for Adoption and Fostering.

Morris, J. (1993) 'Feminism and disability', *Feminist Review*, 43, pp. 57–70.

Moyes, B. (1988) 'The psychodynamic method in social work: some indications and contra-indications', *Practice*, 2(3), pp. 236–42.

Mullender, A. (1996) *Rethinking Domestic Violence: the social work and probation response*. London: Routledge.

Mullender, A. and Morley, R. (eds) (1994) *Children Living with Domestic Violence: putting men's abuse of women on the child care agenda*. London: Whiting & Birch.

Mullender, A. and Ward, D. (1991) *Self-Directed Groupwork: users take action for empowerment*. London: Whiting and Birch.

NAPO (1995) *Good Practice Guide*. London: National Association of Probation Officers.

Neill, J. (1989) *Assessing Elderly People for Residential Care: a practical guide*. London: Institute for Social Work.

Nelson-Jones, R. (1983) *Practical Counselling Skills*. New York: Holt, Rinehart and Winston.

Neville, D. and Beak, D. (1990) 'Solving the care history mystery', *Social Work Today*, 21(42), pp. 16–17.

Newburn, T. (ed.) (1996) *Working with Disaster: social welfare interventions during and after tragedy*. Harlow: Longman.

Noonan, E. (1983) *Counselling Young People*. London: Methuen.

Northen, H. (1969) *Social Work with Groups*. New York: Colombia University Press.

Northen, H. (1982) *Clinical Social Work*. New York: Colombia University Press.

O'Brian, C. (1990) 'Family therapy with black families', *Journal of Family Therapy*, 12(1), pp. 3–16.

O'Connor, G. G. (1988) 'Case management: system and practice', *Social Casework*, 69(2), pp. 97–106.

O'Hagan, K. (1986) *Crisis Intervention in Social Services*. London: Macmillan.

Oliver, M. (1996) *Understanding Disability: from theory to practice*. Basingstoke: Macmillan (now Palgrave).

Orten, J. D. and Rich, L. L. (1988) 'A model for assessment of incestuous families', *Social Casework*, 69(10), pp. 611–19.

Orme, J. (1994) 'Violent women'. In C. Lupton and T. Gillespie (eds) *Working with Violence: feminist practice*. Basingstoke: BASW/Macmillan.

Orme, J. (1995) *Workloads: measurement and management*. Aldershot: Avebury (in association with CEDR).

Orme, J. (1996) 'Participation or patronage: changes in social work practice brought about by community care policies in Britain'. In *Participating in Change – Social Work Profession in Social Development Proceedings of the Joint World Congress of IFSW/IASSW*. Hong Kong, pp. 250–2.

Orme, J. (1998) 'Feminist social work'. In R. Adams, L. Dominelli and M. Payne (eds) *Social Work Themes, Issues and Critical Debates*. Basingstoke: Macmillan.

Orme, J. (2000a) 'Social work: "The appliance of social science" – a cautionary tale', *Journal of Social Work Education*, 19(4), pp. 323–34.

Orme, J. (2000b) 'Interactive social sciences: patronage or partnership', *Science and Public Policy*, 27(3), pp. 211–19.

Orme, J. (2001a) *Gender and Community Care: social work and social care perspectives*. Basingstoke: Palgrave.

Orme, J. (2001b) 'Regulation or fragmentation? Directions for social work under New Labour', *British Journal of Social Work*, 31, pp. 611–24.

Orme, J. (2002) 'Social work: gender, care and justice', *British Journal of Social Work*, 32(6), pp. 799–814.

Orme, J. (2003) '"It's feminist because I say so!": feminism, social work and critical practice in the UK', *Qualitative Social Work*, 2(2), pp. 131–54

Orme, J., Dominelli, L. and Mullender, A. (2000) 'Working with violent men from a feminist perspective', *International Social Work*, 43(1), pp. 89–108.

Orme, J. and Glastonbury, B. (1993) *Care Management*. Basingstoke: BASW/Macmillan.

Papell, C. P. and Rothman, B. (1966) 'Social groupwork models: possession and heritage', *Journal of Education for Social Work*, 2(2), pp. 66–77.

Parad, H. J. and Caplan, G. (1965) 'A framework for studying families in crisis'. In H. J. Parad (ed.) *Crisis Intervention: selected readings*. New York: Family Service Association of America.

Parker, J. and Bradley, G. (2003) *Social Work Practice: assessment, planning, intervention and review*. Exeter: Learning Matters.

Parkes, C. M. (1986) *Bereavement: studies of grief in adult life*. London: Tavistock.

Parry, G. (1990) *Coping with Crises*. Leicester: British Psychological Society/Routledge.

Parton, N. (1998) 'Risk, advanced liberalism and child welfare: the need to rediscover uncertainty and ambiguity', *British Journal of Social Work*, 28(1), pp. 5–27.

Parton, N. (2000) 'Some thoughts on the relationship between theory and practice in and for social work', *British Journal of Social Work*, 30, pp. 449–63.

Parton, N. and O'Byrne, P. (2000) *Constructive Social Work: towards a new practice*. Basingstoke: Palgrave.

Payne, M. (1986) *Social Care in the Community*. Basingstoke: Macmillan.

Payne, M. (1991) *Modern Social Work Theory: a critical introduction*. Basingstoke: Macmillan.

Payne, M. (1995) *Social Work and Community Care*. Basingstoke: Macmillan.

Payne, M. (1997) *Modern Social Work Theory: a critical introduction*. Basingstoke: Macmillan.

Payne, M. (1998) 'Social work theories and critical practice'. In R. Adams, L. Dominelli and M. Payne (eds) *Social Work: themes, issues and critical debates*. Basingstoke: Palgrave.

Payne, M. (2000) *Narrative Therapy: an introduction for counsellors*. London: Sage.

Payne, S., Horn, S. and Relf, M. (1999) *Loss and Bereavement*. Buckingham: Open University Press.

Pearson, G., Treseder, J. and Yelloly, M. (eds) (1988) *Social Work and the Legacy of Freud: psychoanalysis and its uses*. Basingstoke: Macmillan.

Pease, B. and Fook, J. (eds) (1999) *Transforming Social Work Practice: postmodern critical perspectives*. London: Routledge.

Penn, P. (1982) 'Circular questioning', *Family Process*, 21(3), pp. 267–79.

Perelberg, R. G. and Miller, A. C. (eds) (1990) *Gender and Power in Families*. London: Tavistock/Routledge.

Perlman, H. H. (1957) *Social Casework: a problem-solving process*. Chicago: University of Chicago Press.

Perls, F. (1973) *The Gestalt Approach and Eye Witness to Therapy*. Ben Lomond, Cal.: Science and Behaviour Books.

Perrott, S. (1994) 'Working with men who abuse women and children'. In C. Lupton and T. Gillespie (eds) *Working With Violence*. Basingstoke: BASW/Macmillan.

Petch, A. (2002) 'Work with adult service users'. In M. Davies (ed.) *Blackwell Companion to Social Work*. Oxford: Blackwell.

Pilalis, J. (1986) 'The integration of theory and practice: a re-examination of a paradoxical expectation', *British Journal of Social Work*, 16(1), pp. 79–96.

Pilalis, J. and Anderton, J. (1986) 'Feminism and family therapy: a possible meeting point', *Journal of Family Therapy*, 8(2), pp. 99–114.

Pincus, A. and Minahan, A. (1973) *Social Work Practice: model and method*. Itasca, Ill.: Peacock.

Pincus, L. (1976) *Death and the Family*. London: Faber & Faber.

Popple, K. (1995) *Analysing Community Work: its theory and practice*. Buckingham: Open University Press.

Popple, K. (2002) 'Community work'. In R. Adams, L. Dominelli and M. Payne (eds) *Critical Practice in Social Work*. Basingstoke: Palgrave.

Postle, K. (2001) 'The social work side is disappearing. It started with us being called care managers', *Practice*, 13(1), pp. 13–26.

Preston-Shoot, M. (1987) *Effective Groupwork*. London: Macmillan.

Prevatt Goldstein, B. (2002) 'Black perspectives'. In M. Davies (ed.) *Blackwell Companion to Social Work*. Oxford: Blackwell.

Prochaska, J. O. and DiClemente, C. (1984) *The Transtheoretical Approach: crossing the traditional boundaries of therapy*. Homewood, Ill.: Dow Jones/Irwin.

QAA (1998) *Benchmarking Statement for Social Work Degrees*. London: Quality Assurance Agency.

Randall, P. (1990) 'Too old to learn new tricks?' *Community Care*, 1 March, pp. 20–1.

Raphael, B. (1984) *The Anatomy of Bereavement: a handbook for the caring professions*. London: Unwin Hyman.

Raphael, B. (1986) *When Disaster Strikes: a handbook for the caring professions*. London: Hutchinson.

Rapoport, L. (1970) 'Crisis intervention as a brief mode of treatment'. In R. W. Roberts and R. H. Nee (eds) *Theories of Social Casework*. Chicago: University of Chicago Press.

Redgrave, K. (1987) *Child's Play: 'direct' work with the deprived child*. Cheadle: Boys' and Girls' Welfare Society.

Redl, F. (1951) 'Art of group composition'. In S. Schultze (ed.) *Creative Living in a Children's Institution*. New York: Association Press.

Reed, B. G. and Garvin, C. D. (eds) (1983) *Groupwork with Women, Groupwork with Men: an overview of gender issues in social groupwork practice*. New York: Haworth Press.

Rees, S. (1991) *Achieving Power: practice and policy in social welfare*. Sydney: Allen and Unwin.

Reid, W. J. (1978) *The Task-Centred System*. New York: Colombia University Press.

Reid, W. J. and Epstein, L. (1972) *Task-Centred Casework*. New York: Colombia University Press.

Reid, W. J. and Epstein, L. (eds) (1977) *Task-Centred Practice*. New York: Colombia University Press.

Reid, W. J. and Hanrahan, P. (1981) 'The effectiveness of social work: recent evidence'. In E. M. Goldberg and N. Connolly (eds) *Evaluative Research in Social Care*. London: Heinemann.

Reid, W. J. and Shyne, A. W. (1969) *Brief and Extended Casework*. New York: Colombia University Press.

Remington, B. and Barron, C. (1991) 'Working with problem drinkers: a cognitive behavioural approach', *Probation Journal*, 38(1) pp. 15–19.

Renshaw, J. (1988) 'Care in the community: individual care planning and case management', *British Journal of Social Work*, 18, pp. 79–105.

Rich, J. (1968) *Interviewing Children and Adolescents*. London: Macmillan.

Richards, S. (2000) 'Bridging the divide: elders and the assessment process', *British Journal of Social Work*, 30(1), pp. 37–50.

Richmond, M. (1922) *What is Social Case Work?* New York: Russell Sage.

Robinson, L. (1998) *Race: communication and the caring professions*. Buckingham: Open University Press.

Robson, P., Begum, N. *et al.* (2003) *Increasing User Involvement in Voluntary Organisations*. York: Joseph Rowntree Foundation.

Rogers, C. (1980) *A Way of Being*. Boston, Mass.: Houghton Mifflin.

Rojek, C. (1986) 'The "subject" in social work', *British Journal of Social Work*, 16(1), pp. 65–77.

Rojek, C., Peacock, G. and Collins, S. (1988) *Social Work and Received Ideas*. London: Routledge.

Rothman, J. (1968) 'Three models of community organization practice their mixing and phasing'. In F. M. Cox *et al.* (eds) *Strategies for Community Organization* (3rd edn). Itasca, Ill.: Peacock.

Rueveni, U. (1979) *Networking Families in Crisis*. New York: Human Sciences Press.

Runciman, P. (1989) 'Health assessment of the elderly: a multi-disciplinary perspective'. In R. Taylor and J. Ford (eds) *Social Work and Health Care*. London: Jessica Kingsley.

Sainsbury, E. (1970) *Social Diagnosis in Casework*. London: Routledge & Kegan Paul.

Sainsbury, E. (1986) 'The contribution of client studies to social work practice'. In P. Wedge (ed.) *Social Work – Research into Practice*. Birmingham: British Association of Social Workers.

Schless, A. P., Teichman, A., Mendels, J. and Di Giacomo, J. N. (1977) 'The role of stress as a precipitating factor of psychiatric illness', *British Journal of Psychiatry*, **130**, pp. 19–22.

Schon, D. A. (1987) *Education and the Reflective Practitioner: toward a new design for teaching and learning in the professions*. California: Jossey-Bass.

Schutz, W. C. (1966) *FIRO: the interpersonal underworld*. New York: Science and Behaviour Books.

SCIE (2004) *Teaching and Learning Communication Skills in Social Work Education*. London: Social Care Institute for Excellence.

Scott, M. (1983) *Group Parent-Training Programme*. Liverpool: Liverpool Personal Service Society.

Scott, M. (1989) *A Cognitive Behavioural Approach to Clients' Problems*. London: Routledge.

Scott, M. J. and Stradling, S. G. (1990) 'Group cognitive therapy for depression produces clinically significant reliable change in community-based settings', *Behavioural Psychotherapy*, **18**, pp. 1–19.

Scottish Executive (2000) *Community Care: a joint future, Report of the Joint Future Group*. Edinburgh: Scottish Executive.

Scottish Executive (2001) *Guidance on Single Shared Assessment of Community Care Needs*. Edinburgh: Scottish Executive.

Scourfield, J. and Coffey, A. (2002) 'Understanding gendered practice in child protection', *Qualitative Social Work*, **1**(3), pp. 319–40

Scrutton, S. (1989) *Counselling Older People: a creative response to ageing*. London: Edward Arnold.

Seden, J. (1999) *Counselling Skills in Social Work Practice*. Buckingham: Open University Press.

Sharkey, P. (1989) 'Social networks and social service workers', *British Journal of Social Work*, 19(5), pp. 387–405.

Sharkey, P. (2000) *Essentials of Community Care*. Basingstoke: Palgrave.

Sheik, S. (1986) 'An Asian mothers' self-help group'. In S. Ahmed, J. Cheetham and J. Small (eds) *Social Work with Black Children and their Families*. London: BT Batsford/British Agencies for Adoption and Fostering.

Sheldon, B. (1983) 'The use of single-case experimental designs in the evaluation of social work', *British Journal of Social Work*, 13(5), pp. 477–500.

Sheldon, B. (1984) 'Behavioural approaches with psychiatric patients'. In M. R. Olsen (ed.) *Social Work and Mental Health*. London: Tavistock.

Sheldon, B. (1995) *Cognitive Behavioural Therapy: research, practice and philosophy*. London: Routledge.

Sheldon, B. (2000) 'Cognitive behavioural methods in social care: a look at the evidence'. In P. Stepney and D. Ford (eds) *Social Work Models, Methods and Theories*. Lyme Regis: Russell House.

Sheldon, F. (1997) *Psychosocial Palliative Care*. Cheltenham: Stanley Thornes.

Shulman, L. (1979) *The Skills of Helping: individuals and groups*. Itasca, Ill.: Peacock.

Simmonds, J. (1988) 'Thinking about feelings in group care'. In G. Pearson, J. Treseder and M. Yelloly (eds) *Social Work and the Legacy of Freud: psychoanalysis and its uses*. London: Macmillan.

Siporin, M. (1975) *Introduction to Social Work Practice*. New York: Macmillan.

Skinner, B. F. (1938) *The Behaviour of Organisms*. New York: Appleton.

Smale, G., Tuson, G., Cooper, M., Wardle, M. and Crosbie, D. (1988) *Community Social Work: a paradigm for change*. London: NISW.

Smale, G., Tuson, G., Biehal, N. and Marsh, P. (1993) *Empowerment, Assessment, Care Management and the Skilled*

Worker, National Institute for Social Work Practice and Development Exchange. London: HMSO.

Smith, P. B. (1980) *Group Processes and Personal Change*. London and Cambridge (Mass.): Harper & Row.

Social Information Systems (SIS) (1990) *Social Services and Quality Assurance*. Manchester: SIS.

Social Services Inspectorate (SSI)/SWG (1991) *Care Management and Assessment: practitioners guide*. London: HMSO.

Social Services Inspectorate (SSI) (1999) 'Modern social services: a commitment to improve' in *Eighth Annual Report of the Chief Inspector of Social Services*. London: Department of Health.

Solomon, B. (1976) *Black Empowerment: social work with oppressed communities*. New York: Colombia University Press.

Specht, H. and Vickery, A. (eds) (1977) *Integrating Social Work Methods*. London: Allen and Unwin.

Speck, R. V. (1967) 'Psychotherapy of the social network of a schizophrenic family', *Family Process*, 7, pp. 208–14.

Spurling, L. (1988) 'Casework as dialogue: a story of incest'. In G. Pearson, J. Treseder and M. Yelloly (eds) *Social Work and the Legacy of Freud: psychoanalysis and its uses*. Basingstoke: Macmillan.

SSSC (2003) *Standards in Social Work Education*. Edinburgh: Scottish Executive.

Stanley, L. and Wise, S. (1990) *Feminist Praxis: research, theory and epistemology in feminist sociology*. London: Routledge.

Stepney, P. and Ford, D. (eds) (2000) *Social Work Models, Methods and Theories*. Lyme Regis: Russell House.

Stevenson, O. (1963) 'The understanding caseworker', *New Society*, 1 August, pp. 84–96.

Stevenson, O. and Parsloe, P. (1993) *Community Care and Empowerment*. York: Joseph Rowntree Foundation.

Stewart, I. (1989) *Transactional Analysis Counselling in Action*. London: Sage.

Stuart, O. (1996) '"Yes, we mean black disabled people too": thoughts on community care and disabled people from black and minority ethnic communities'. In W. U. I. Ahmad and K. Atkin (eds) *'Race' and Community Care*. Buckingham: Open University Press.

Thoburn, J. (1988) *Child Placement: principles and practice*. Aldershot: Wildwood House.

Thomas, D. (1983) *The Making of Community Work*. London: George Allen & Unwin.

Thompson, N. (1991) *Crisis Intervention Revisited.* Birmingham: PEPAR publications

Thompson, N. (1993) *Anti-Discriminatory Practice.* Basingstoke: Macmillan.

Thompson, N. (1995) 'Men and anti-sexism', *British Journal of Social Work,* 25, pp. 459–75.

Thompson, N. (2002) 'Social work with adults'. In R. Adams, L. Dominelli and M. Payne (eds) *Social Work Themes Issues and Critical Debates.* Basingstoke: Palgrave.

Thompson, N. (2003) *Communication and Language: a handbook of theory and practice.* Basingstoke: Palgrave.

Timms, N. and Timms, R. (1977) *Perspectives in Social Work.* London: Routledge.

Treacher, A. and Carpenter, J. (eds) (1984) *Using Family Therapy.* Oxford: Blackwell.

Trevithick, P. (2005) *Social Work Skills: a practice handbook.* Maidenhead: Open University Press.

Trotter, C. (1999) *Working with Involuntary Clients.* London: Sage.

Truax, C. B. and Carkhuff, R. (1967) *Towards Effective Counselling and Psychotherapy.* Chicago: Aldine.

Tsoi, M. and Yule, J. (1982) 'Building up new behaviours: shaping, prompting and fading'. In W. Yule and J. Carr (eds) *Behaviour Modification for the Mentally Handicapped.* London: Croom Helm.

Tuckman, B. W. and Jensen, M. A. C. (1977) 'Stages of small group development revisited', *Group and Organisation Studies,* 2(4), pp. 419–27.

Tully, J. B. (1976) 'Personal construct theory and psychological changes related to social work training', *British Journal of Social Work,* 6(4), pp. 481–99.

Tuson, G. (1996) 'Writing postmodern social work'. In P. Ford and P. Hayes (eds) *Education for Social Work: Arguments for Optimism.* Aldershot: Avebury (in association with CEDR).

Twelvetrees, A. (1991) *Community Work* (2nd edn). London: Macmillan.

Ungerson, C. (1987) *Policy is Personal: sex gender and informal care.* London: Tavistock.

Van der Velden, H. E. M., Halevy-Martinin, J., Ruhf, L. and Schoenfield, P. (1984) 'Conceptual issues in network therapy', *International Journal of Family Therapy,* 6(2), pp. 68–81.

Vernon, S., Harris, R. and Ball, C. (1990) *Towards Social Work*

Law: legally competent professional practice, Paper 4.2. London: CCETSW.

Vetere, A. (1999) 'Family therapy'. In M. Hill (ed.) *Effective Ways of Working with Children and their Families*. London: Jessica Kingsley.

Vickery, A. (1976) 'A unitary approach to social work with the mentally disordered'. In M. R. Olsen (ed.) *Differential Approaches in Social Work with the Mentally Disordered*. Birmingham: British Association of Social Workers.

Walker, L. (1978) 'Work with a parents' group'. In N. McCaughan (ed.) *Group Work: learning and practice*. London: George Allen and Unwin.

Walrond-Skinner, S. (ed.) (1979) *Family and Marital Psychotherapy: a critical approach*. London: Routledge & Kegan Paul.

Ward, D. (2002) 'Where has all the groupwork gone?' In R. Adams, L. Dominelli and M. Payne (eds) *Social Work Themes, Issues and Critical Debates*. Basingstoke: Palgrave.

Ward, H. (ed.) (1995) *Looking After Children: research into practice. Second Report to the Department of Health on Assessing Outcomes in Child Care*. London: HMSO.

Ward, H. (2000) *The Development Needs of Children: implications for assessment*. London: Department of Health.

Waterhouse, L. and McGhee, J. (2002) 'Social work with children and families'. In R. Adams, L. Dominelli and M. Payne (eds) *Social Work Themes, Issues and Critical Debates*. Basingstoke: Palgrave.

Webb, S. A. and McBeath, G. B. (1990) 'Political critique of Kantian ethics: a reply to Professor R. S. Downie', *British Journal of Social Work*, 20(1), pp. 65–71.

Weinberg, A., Williamson, J., Challis, D. and Hughes, J. (2003) 'What do care managers do? A study of working practice in older peoples' services', *British Journal of Social Work*, 33(7), pp. 901–19.

Whan, M. (1983) 'Tricks of the trade: questionable theory and practice in family therapy', *British Journal of Social Work*, 13(3), pp. 321–38.

Whitaker, D. S. (1975) 'Some conditions of effective work with groups', *British Journal of Social Work*, 5(4), pp. 423–40.

Whitaker, D. S. (1985) *Using Groups to Help People*. London: Routledge & Kegan Paul.

White, J. (2002) 'Family therapy'. In M. Davies (ed.) *The Blackwell Companion to Social Work*. Oxford: Blackwell.

White, M. and Epston, D. (1990) *Narrative Means to Therapeutic Ends*. New York: Norton.

Winnicott, D. W. (1957) *The Capacity to Be Alone*, paper read at a meeting of the British Psychoanalytical Society, 24 July.

Wise, S. (1990) 'Becoming a feminist social worker'. In L. Stanley and S. Wise, *Becoming a Feminist Social Worker*. London: Routledge.

Wittenberg, I. S. (1970) *Psychoanalytic Insight and Relationships: a Kleinian approach*. London: Routledge & Kegan Paul.

Wolfensberger, W. (1983) 'Social role valorisation: a proposed new term for the principle of normalisation', *Mental Retardation*, 21(6), pp. 234–9.

Wootton, B. F. (1959) *Social Science and Social Pathology*. London: George Allen and Unwin.

Yalom, I. D. (1970) *The Theory and Practice of Group Psychotherapy*. New York: Basic Books.

Yelloly, M. A. (1980) *Social Work Theory and Psychoanalysis*. Wokingham: Van Nostrand Reinhold.

York, A. (1984) 'Towards a conceptual model of community social work,' *British Journal of Social Work*, 14, pp. 241–55.

Zastrow, C. (1985) *Social Work with Groups*. Chicago: Nelson-Hall.

Index